GCSE

Business and Communication Systems

Complete Revision and Practice

Contents

Section One — Business Essentials

Why Businesses Exist 1
Enterprise 2
Business Ownership Structures 3
Practice Questions 4
Customers 6
Stakeholders 7
Measuring Business Success 8
Starting a New Business 9
Succeeding as a New Start-Up 10
Businesses and the Law 11
Practice Questions 12
Revision Summary for Section One 14

Section Two — Marketing and Finance

Marketing and Market Research 15
Analysing the Market 16
Prices, Revenue, Costs and Profit 17
Finance and Cash Flow 18
The Economic Environment 19
Practice Questions 20
Revision Summary for Section Two 22

Section Three — Organisation and Administration

Organisational Structure 23
Administration in Business 24
Routine & Non-Routine Tasks 25
Practice Questions 26
Planning 28
Efficient Use of Resources 29
Office Layout 30
Practice Questions 31
Revision Summary for Section Three 33

Section Four — Human Resources

Patterns of Work 34
Recruitment — Job Analysis 35
Recruitment — The Selection Process 36
Employment Law 37
Practice Questions 38
Staff Training 40
Financial Rewards 41
Modern Working Practices 43
Health and Safety at Work 44
Practice Questions 45
Revision Summary for Section Four 47

Section Five — Businesses and Data

Data Processing Systems 48
Computers and Input Devices 49
More Input Devices 50
Data Storage 51
Data Storage and Back-Up 52
Practice Questions 53
Output Devices — Printers 55
More Output Devices 56
Keeping Data Secure 57
Data Protection and the Law 58
Practice Questions 59
Revision Summary for Section Five 61

Section Six — Communication

Purposes of Communication 62
Internal and External Communication 63
Barriers to Communication 64
Practice Questions 65
Written Communication — Letters 67
Internal Written Communication 68
More Written Communication 69
Electronic Communication 70
Practice Questions 72
Face-to-Face Meetings 74
Other Oral Communication 75
Visual Communication 76
Changing a Communication System 77
Practice Questions 78
Revision Summary for Section Six 80

Section Seven — Businesses and the Web

How Businesses Use the Internet 81
Business Websites — Benefits and Costs 82
Domain Names and Hosting 83
Websites and the Law 84
Success of Business Websites 85
Creating a Website 86
Practice Questions 87
Revision Summary for Section Seven 89

Contents

Section Eight — Business Applications

Software Applications ... 90
Word Processors: Text Formatting ... 91
Word Processors: Text and Graphics ... 92
Word Processors: Business Letters ... 94
Word Processors: Mail Merge ... 95
Practice Questions ... 96
Spreadsheets ... 98
Spreadsheets: Using Formulas ... 99
Spreadsheets: Using Functions ... 100
Spreadsheets: Graphs and Charts ... 101
Practice Questions ... 103
Databases ... 105
Databases: Data Input Forms ... 106
Databases: Simple Queries and Sorting ... 107
Databases: Producing Reports ... 108
Practice Questions ... 109
Graphics: Creating Images ... 111
Graphics: Manipulating Images ... 112
Presentation Software ... 113
Presentations ... 114
Web-Authoring Software ... 115
Other Software Applications ... 116
Evaluating Software ... 117
Practice Questions ... 118
Revision Summary for Section Eight ... 120

Assessment Tips

Assessment ... 121
Controlled Assessment ... 122
Written Exams ... 123
Computer-Based Assessment ... 124

Practice Assessment

Practice Controlled Assessment ... 125
Practice Written Papers ... 129
Practice Computer-Based Assessment ... 137

Answers ... 141
Index ... 153

You'll see this symbol scattered throughout Section 8.

It means there's an animated tutorial to help walk you through an important practical skill. See the next page of this book for more info.

You Won't Need To Learn All The Pages In This Book

This is the book you need if you're studying the following subjects:

- **AQA: Business and Communication Systems**
- **OCR: Business and Communication Systems**
- **Edexcel: Business Communications**

But whichever of these you're studying, you won't need to learn every page in the book.

- ***AQA***: Business and Communication Systems
  You won't be directly tested on pages 3, 10, 17, 18 and 19.
- ***OCR***: Business and Communication Systems
  You won't be directly tested on pages 34, 35, 36, 40, 41 and 42.
- ***Edexcel***: Business Communications
  You won't be directly tested on pages 25, 28 and 30.

See page 121 for more information about pages you can safely ignore.

Check Out Our Animated Tutorials

- If you're doing Business and Communication Systems with either AQA or OCR, then part of your exam will be a computer-based assessment.
- This book will help you understand the practical skills you'll be tested on. But it can't always show you exactly what buttons to press in your software.

That's why our tutorials are so handy

- These tutorials will walk you through some of the trickier skills step by step. They'll show you exactly what buttons to press, and why.

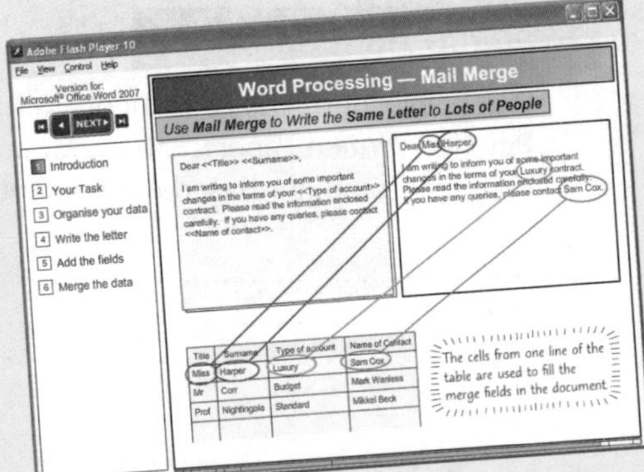

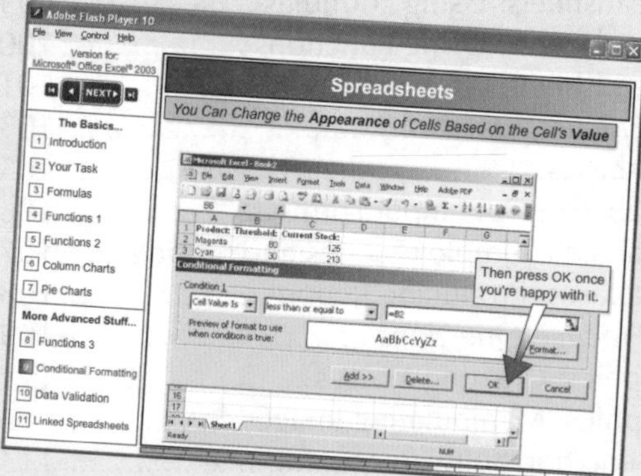

- They cover some of the most popular software packages around.
- Wherever you see this symbol, there's a tutorial about that page's content. 

See the CD at the back of the book...

- You'll find all the tutorials on the CD.
- You'll also find all the files we used in the tutorials. This means you can practise, and check that you get the same results we did.
- The CD also includes the files for all the computer-based questions in the book.

Published by Coordination Group Publications Ltd.

Editors:
Helena Hayes, Murray Hamilton, Andy Park, Dave Ryan

Contributors:
Colin Harber Stuart, Neil Burrell, Cassandra Mettleton, David Morris, Ali Palin, Katherine Reed, Michael Southorn

With thanks to Simon Little and Victoria Skelton for the proofreading.

Screenshots from *Cumbria Vision* website (www.cumbriavision.co.uk) published with kind permission of Cumbria Vision Ltd.
Screenshots from *GoLakes* website (www.golakes.co.uk) published with kind permission of Cumbria Tourism.
Microsoft® and Windows® are either registered trademarks or trademarks of Microsoft Corporation in the United States and/or other countries
Microsoft product screenshots reprinted with permission from Microsoft Corporation.

ISBN: 978 1 84762 434 5
Website: www.cgpbooks.co.uk
Clipart source: CorelDRAW® and VECTOR
Printed by Elanders Hindson Ltd, Newcastle upon Tyne.

Based on the classic CGP style created by Richard Parsons.

Text, design, layout and original illustrations © Coordination Group Publications Ltd. 2010
All rights reserved.

Why Businesses Exist

This is the Complete Revision & Practice book for Business and Communication Systems (for AQA and OCR) and Business Communications (for Edexcel). And already there's some good news — whichever of these you're studying, you won't need to learn all the pages. See page 121 for more information. Right then, away we go...

Most Businesses Have the Same Main Objective...

1) Businesses exist to provide goods or services to customers. Most businesses are started when somebody decides that they can make goods or provide a service that they can sell to people who are willing to pay.
2) It's a good idea for businesses to set themselves objectives. (An objective is anything that someone wants to achieve — for example, your objective in using this book is to get a better GCSE grade.) For a business, one objective is more important than any other...

1) The most important objective (or aim) is to make a profit in order to survive. If a business does not make a profit it will go bankrupt and have to close down.

Businesses will usually have other objectives too. For example...

2) Some will try to be the biggest in their market.
3) Others will try to provide the highest quality product possible.
4) Some might aim to maximise sales or wealth creation.
5) Others might be more concerned with stability — maintaining their market share or a reasonable income.
6) Other possible objectives include being independent, satisfying customers, or trying to limit the environmental damage caused.

Usually firms will only pursue these other objectives if it will help make a profit in the longer term — although firms with genuinely public-spirited owners might give up some profit for other objectives.

...But Some Businesses Have Different Priorities

1) For some businesses, profit is not their main objective.
2) This is either because it's a 'not-for-profit' organisation (e.g. a charity) or it's in the public sector (which means it's owned by the government — like most schools and hospitals).
3) Not-for-profit organisations and public-sector businesses need to earn enough income to cover their costs. Any surplus is then put back into the business.
4) Some profit-seeking businesses exist to achieve social objectives such as providing help for the homeless, or farmers in poorer countries. They're called social enterprises or 'more than profit' organisations. This is because their main aim is to use the profit that they make for the benefit of society.

Different People Start Businesses for Different Reasons

Here are some possible reasons why people might want to start a business...

1) Lots of entrepreneurs (p2) have financial objectives — e.g. to earn a huge fortune or a steady income.
2) There might also be non-financial reasons, like the freedom of being your own boss.
3) For many people, running a business is a challenge that they enjoy.
4) Some people start a business because they want to benefit others. This could be done by starting a charity, or by having social objectives for their business.

Your first objective should be to get this page learnt...

Well that's an easy enough page to start with. Make sure you know why businesses exist and why people start them up. You should also know what the main objectives of the different types of businesses are. Cover up the page, scribble down everything you can remember, then check that you didn't forget anything. Champion.

Enterprise

Enterprise can mean either a business or organisation, or the personal qualities that mean you can see and take advantage of new business opportunities (e.g. "That boy will go far — he's got enterprise.")

Entrepreneurs **Take Advantage** of Business **Opportunities**

1) Enterprise involves identifying new business opportunities, and then taking advantage of them. There's always a risk of failure, but the reward for a successful enterprise activity is profit.
2) Enterprise can involve starting up a new business, or helping an existing one to expand by coming up with new ideas.
3) A good business idea is usually a product/service that no other business is already providing, but which customers will be willing to pay for — i.e. there's a gap in the market.
4) A market niche (or niche market) is a similar idea. A market niche is a small part of the overall market, and is made up of customers with a particular need. Big companies often don't bother trying to make products for niche markets, so they're great opportunities for small companies.

An entrepreneur is someone who takes on the risks of enterprise activity.

Enterprise Means **Taking Risks**

Enterprises always involve balancing risks against possible rewards.

1) An entrepreneur needs to gather together all the resources needed to start or expand a business. The key resource is money, which is needed to buy equipment and pay workers.
2) Very often an entrepreneur will use their own money, but they'll probably need to raise more from banks or other investors as well.
3) An entrepreneur will hope that the business will make enough profit to pay back any money that's been borrowed. If not, the business will fail and the entrepreneur will lose all the money that's been invested in the company.
4) A good entrepreneur will take a calculated risk — they'll do research, plan the business carefully to make sure it has a good chance of success, and weigh up the consequences of failure. If the risk is worth taking, the entrepreneur will go ahead with the new business venture.

Entrepreneurs Need Particular **Qualities**

A successful entrepreneur is likely to have most of the following qualities:

- **the ability to think ahead** — to identify opportunities for the future
- **initiative** — to seek out or seize business opportunities
- **drive and determination** — to turn ideas into practice
- **decisiveness** — so they don't shy away from making tough decisions
- **networking skills** — to identify people who can provide money or other resources
- **leadership skills and powers of persuasion** — to motivate other people to support their ideas
- **a willingness to take calculated risks** — and to profit from their enterprise activities
- **an ability to plan carefully** — to minimise the risk of failure
- **an ability to learn from mistakes** — and to see mistakes as "part of learning to succeed"

Enterprise — think Dragons' Den...

Bit of a funny page this one, all about concepts and personal qualities. It's still got to be learnt though — so cover up the page and jot down a list of the personal qualities you'd expect to find in a successful entrepreneur. Check your list against the one on the page and repeat until you've got them all. Got them all? Quality.

Business Ownership Structures

Businesses have different legal structures — and you need to know about a couple of different types. One of the main differences is whether they have unlimited liability or limited liability.

Unlimited Liability — Sole Traders and Partnerships

1) Some businesses don't have a separate legal identity of their own — they're unincorporated.
2) Sole traders are examples of unincorporated businesses. To set up as a sole trader, you don't need to do anything except start trading. Common examples include plumbers, newsagents and fishmongers.
3) But because the business is not legally separate from its owner, if the business goes bust owing £10 million, then it's the owner personally who can be sued. They may have to sell everything they own to pay the debts.
4) A lot of partnerships are also unincorporated — partnerships are a bit like multi-person sole traders really. In partnerships, partners have an equal say in decisions and an equal share of the profits (unless they have an agreement called a deed of partnership that says different).

Partnerships aren't all that common — but you get them a lot in jobs like accountancy and solicitors.

Limited Liability Firms — Private (Ltd) and Public (plc)

There are two types of limited company — private and public. But both kinds have these five important differences compared to sole traders and partnerships.

1) The business is incorporated — it has a separate legal identity from the owner.
2) It has limited liability, so the owners only risk losing the money they have invested in the business — no matter how big its debts are.
3) It must have a Memorandum of Association and an Article of Association. These tell the world who the business is, where it's based, and how it'll be run.
4) There's more paperwork involved in setting up a limited liability business, making it more expensive to do. And these companies are also legally obliged to publish their accounts every year. But because it has an identity of its own, a limited liability company can continue trading after the owners die.
5) A limited liability business is owned by shareholders. The more shares you own, the more control you get.

- In a private limited company, shares can only be sold if all the shareholders agree.
- The shareholders often belong to the same family.
- Private limited companies have Ltd. after their name.

- In a public limited company, shares in the company can be bought and sold by anyone — on a stock exchange.
- Public limited companies have 'plc' after their name.
- Firms generally become PLCs when they want to expand.

You also Have to Know About Franchises and Cooperatives

1) A franchise is the right to sell another firm's products (or use their trademarks). For example, most car manufacturers sell their cars through dealer franchises. And most of the big firms in the fast-food industry sell their products through franchise outlets.
   Although a franchise is technically a separate company, it looks a lot like it's part of a much bigger business. The franchisor (the company that makes the products or owns the trademarks) will be paid either a flat fee or a percentage of the franchisee's profits. It's less risky, but you also get less control.
2) Co-operatives work a bit like limited-liability partnerships. Producer co-operatives are owned and controlled by their workforce. Retail co-operatives are owned and controlled by their customers (though usually a board of directors makes the day-to-day business decisions).

Franchises are different from the legal structures above, since a franchise is an arrangement between two separate firms.

Make sure you have more than a limited knowledge of this...

The really important point on this page is that bit about limited liability and separate legal identity. It's a slightly weird concept, but a massively important one to get your head round. So cover up the page and scribble a mini-essay on what limited liability means and the difference between private and public limited liability firms.

Warm-up and Worked Exam Questions

Warm-up Questions

1) Give four reasons why someone might want to start their own company.
2) What is the most important objective for most businesses?
3) Give two benefits of being a sole trader.
4) What is a co-operative?
5) Name the two types of limited company.

Worked Exam Question

It's really important to get the key business terms clear in your mind before going on to the rest of the section. Have a look at this worked exam question, then have a go at the questions on the next page.

1 Read **Item A** and then answer the questions that follow.

> **Item A**
>
> Edwina runs a successful limited-liability business. Initially, she ran the company as a sole trader, but she later decided to change the legal status of the firm, and so she set up Anyfirm Ltd. She now wants to expand the business, and is considering whether to change the status of her company to a public limited company (plc). However, Edwina is worried that this might lead to her losing control of the company.

a) Explain what is meant by the term "limited liability".

Limited liability means the owners of the business are not personally liable for the debts of the business. ✔ [1 mark] *The owners only risk losing the money they have invested in the business.* ✔ [1 mark]

There are 2 marks available for this question, so you should aim to give at least two pieces of information in your explanation.

(2 marks)

b) A sole trader is unincorporated. Explain what this means.

This means that the business does not have a legal identity of its own. ✔ [1 mark]

The owner is personally responsible for everything the business does. ✔ [1 mark]

(2 marks)

c) Explain why Edwina could lose control of the company if it became a public limited company.

Shares in PLCs are traded openly on the stock exchange. ✔ [1 mark] *This means anyone can become a shareholder.* ✔ [1 mark] *Someone who bought a lot of shares could end up with a big say in how the company should be run,* ✔ [1 mark] *meaning that Edwina has less control overall.* ✔ [1 mark]

(4 marks)

Exam Questions

1 Anna Conda runs a franchise selling industrial cleaning products to public-sector organisations.

a) What is meant by the term "public-sector organisation"?

....

....

(1 mark)

b) What is a franchise?

....

....

(2 marks)

c) Explain one advantage and one disadvantage for Anna of operating as a franchisee.

....

....

....

....

(4 marks)

2 David is a successful entrepreneur who runs a company selling toothbrushes.

a) Identify and explain **two** qualities that are needed by an entrepreneur.

1. ....

....

2. ....

....

(4 marks)

b) David believes that business success is all about planning, and then taking calculated risks.

Explain what is meant by a calculated risk, and why planning is important when assessing whether a risk is worth taking.

....

....

....

....

....

(5 marks)

Customers

There are lots of things that a business has to remember... and one of the most important things must always be its customers. A firm's potential customers are important even before the firm has made anything...

Finding Out **What Customers Need** is Essential

1) Without customers, a business can't survive — it's as simple as that.
2) So to succeed, a business has to make a product or provide a service that customers will be willing to pay for. There are a couple of different ways to approach this...

   Market-driven firms will find out what people want, then make it.
   This usually means the product is useful — like an MP3 player with a built-in radio.

   Product-driven firms will design or invent a new product and then try to sell it.
   This often means they make something nobody really wants
   — like an MP3 player with a built-in toaster.

3) With few exceptions, market-driven firms do best.
   This probably isn't all that surprising, since they start out with the customers' actual needs in mind.

A Business Should **Never** Forget its Customers

Worrying about customer needs or wants starts way before any product is actually made, and carries on way after they've bought something. (In theory, anyway.)

Before customers make a purchase

- Market research is the process of asking customers what they want or need. It also involves finding out what products competitors provide, and at what price.

  There's more about this on page 15.
- Products must be designed and manufactured to be reliable and fit for purpose (p11) — customers don't want to have to keep phoning a helpline because their vacuum cleaner explodes every two weeks.

When customers make a purchase

Customer orders should be fulfilled accurately and on time. If a customer orders a ham and cheese pizza, don't send them a meat and potato pie. If you've promised next-day delivery, deliver the next day — don't turn up three weeks later saying you overslept.

Customers make two types of purchase:

- Product trials (when customers buy a product for the first time to try it out),
- Repeat purchases (when customers come back and buy the product again and again).

All businesses want customers to make repeat purchases.

After customers make a purchase

Many businesses have a customer service department — others train all staff to provide a good level of customer service. Some businesses do both. There's lots to think about...

- After-sales support and warranties — sometimes things go wrong, leading to customer questions and complaints — businesses need to put the problem right. Some products (e.g. cars and computers) might need to be serviced and updated throughout their life.
- Like the product itself, customer service needs to be reliable — e.g. you'd expect to have your call answered and the problem resolved every time you phone a helpline.
- Company websites can also provide customer services. Some companies let customers access services on the web (e.g. banks let their customers pay bills online). (There's more about how companies can use their websites on page 81.)

In business, the customer really is the King (or Queen)...

Customer service is so important that companies often use secret shoppers to evaluate how they're doing. These are people who pretend to be customers, but who then report back on how they were treated. Customer service should be important to you too, so cover up the page and scribble down a list of its main points.

Stakeholders

Everyone who is affected by a business is called a stakeholder, and different stakeholders often want different things from the business. There are two main types: internal stakeholders and external stakeholders.

Internal Stakeholders are *Inside* the Firm

1) The most important stakeholders are the owners, who make a profit if the firm's successful, and can decide what the firm does. A limited company's owners are its shareholders.
2) Shareholders delegate responsibility for running the business (including deciding on its general direction, or strategy) to the board of directors. The directors are interested in making sure the company is successful so the shareholders make a profit.
3) Employees (including managers) are stakeholders — they're interested in their job security and promotion prospects, as well as wanting decent wages and pleasant working conditions. Directors and employees may become unemployed if the company does badly.

External Stakeholders are *Outside* the Firm

A business has lots of external stakeholders — many of them wanting different things.

1) Customers are very important stakeholders — they want high quality products at low prices.
2) Suppliers are who the firm buys raw materials from, so the firm provides them with their income. They may face cash-flow problems if they do not get paid quickly enough, and will also lose work if the firm has to close.
3) The local community where the business is based will suffer if the firm causes noise and pollution (which might also interest environmental groups). The local community may benefit if the firm provides good jobs and sponsors local activities. Firms may also provide facilities which the local community can use.
4) The government will receive taxes from the firm and its employees.
5) Trade unions will want good pay and working conditions for their members employed by the firm.
6) Pressure groups put pressure on firms to behave in particular ways. They might organise demonstrations, or draw attention to behaviour they don't approve of.

Some people say that competitors are stakeholders too — since they're affected if they start to lose some of their customers to the firm.

The Most Important Stakeholders are the *Shareholders*

A business probably won't be able to satisfy all its stakeholders — it'll usually have to compromise.

1) No business can ignore its customers. If it can't sell its products it will go bust.
2) And if a business doesn't keep its workers happy it may become unproductive.
3) But a company may not mind being unpopular in the local community — if it sells most of its products somewhere else.
4) The one group no business can ignore for long is its shareholders. Their interests lie at the heart of the business — if they're unhappy they can sack the directors or sell the business to someone else.

Limited liability companies have to produce an annual written report to tell shareholders about the company's activities and their future financial prospects (traditionally this has always been a paper document, but nowadays companies sometimes supply them over the internet). And there's often an annual general meeting (AGM), where the shareholders can ask the directors questions.

More or less anyone affected by a firm's actions is a stakeholder...

Two key points... 1) there are various groups of stakeholders, and 2) shareholders usually get their way — after all, it's their business. A firm can't annoy its other stakeholders though — it's all about compromise.

Measuring Business Success

Examiners want you to tell them that there's more to being a successful business than just making a big profit. This page tells you about a few other ways to think about success.

A Firm and its Stakeholders may have Different Objectives

1) For a business to be successful it has to meet its objectives (see p1). The business will set itself targets to measure whether or not it has met these objectives.
2) The way that a business coordinates the activities of its various departments in order to try and achieve its objectives is called its strategy (this is decided by the directors — see p7).
3) But other stakeholders will have different opinions about what success is. Some of these might be in conflict with the objectives the firm sets itself.

Success for a Business Can Mean Different Things

Most stakeholders will define success using one or more of these ideas...

1) **Survival** is the main short-term objective of any business. Over two-thirds of new businesses close within five years of starting. Unless a business survives, it can't achieve its other objectives.
2) **Profitability** is important for many stakeholders, especially a business's owners. Profitable firms are an important source of wealth creation for the economy.
3) **Growth** can be measured in different ways — e.g. number of employees, number of products sold, or income from sales.
4) **Market share** is found by dividing the sales of the firm's products by the total sales of the market (and multiplying by 100%). The bigger a firm's market share, the greater its ability to control the market.
5) **Customer satisfaction** measures how happy consumers are with the products and service provided by the firm. The firm can measure this by carrying out customer opinion surveys, a type of market research.
6) **Ethical considerations** are about whether the company acts in a way that society believes is morally right (e.g. many consumers think that it's wrong to test cosmetics on animals).
7) **Environmental sustainability** is about minimising the impact of the firm's activities on the environment.

You need to know how the different stakeholders will have different ideas of success based on their interests. Here are four examples — learn them.

"I am an activist in a pressure group. I think most firms are too big and powerful. They pollute the environment and treat animals badly. I know they create a lot of jobs but I think we'd be better off with a lower income and a healthier planet."

"I'm a shareholder. I want the firm to be as profitable as possible so I can earn a large dividend when the profit gets shared out. I don't care too much how the business achieves this, but I don't want the firm upsetting the other stakeholders too much — otherwise profitability might suffer."

"I'm in the government. I want the business to create wealth and jobs for the economy — that way the voters will think I'm doing a good job and vote for me again at the next election."

"I'm a consumer. I want the firm to make good quality products at a low price — but I worry that some firms are too powerful and charge too much. I am also concerned about the environment but I can't always afford to buy environmentally friendly products."

Different stakeholders will have different ideas of success...

The basic idea is that success can be measured — but different people will measure different things. Make a list of objectives that you think different stakeholders might have (see p7 for more about stakeholders). Then for each stakeholder find one or two objectives that might conflict with the interests of others.

Starting a New Business

Some of the biggest businesses you can think of started as just one person and a bloomin' good idea. But what makes an idea good, I hear you ask. Well... there are a few pointers on this page.

Successful New Businesses are ***Innovative*** not ***Inventive***

Invention and innovation sound a bit similar, and mean similar things. But there is a slight difference in meaning when you're talking about business.

1) If a new business is going to succeed it must provide something that other competitors do not.
2) An invention is a new idea — a new product or a new method of doing something, e.g. a new way to dry hair or make chocolate.
3) An innovation is a successful introduction of a new idea.
4) Creating a toaster that contains a radio would be an invention, but it would only be innovative if the idea was successful and people wanted to buy it.

Businesses Have to ***Add Value***

Adding value means making a product that customers will pay more for than it cost the business to produce. It's all about making a product or service seem more desirable to a customer. Here are six ways a business can add value to a product:

1. **USP** The secret is to have a unique selling point (USP) — something that makes your product different from your competitors' products. As long as customers value the USP they will pay more for your product.

This is the key to increasing sales — offering something that your competitors don't (or can't).

2. **DESIGN** Having a good design is important — e.g. clothes with attractive, distinctive designs are often more desirable. This means customers may be prepared to pay more for them.

These other ways of adding value are really just types of USP.

3. **QUALITY** People are often prepared to pay more for a high quality product. Some brands of car are better built than others, and the manufacturers charge more to reflect this.
4. **BRANDING** Having a strong brand image is important. Some brands of portable MP3 player are more expensive than others, but people are happy to pay more because they have a well-known and trusted name. Brands that are seen as fashionable or 'cool' also tend to be able to charge more for their products.
5. **CONVENIENCE** The product could be made more convenient — e.g. ready-grated cheese tends to cost more than blocks of cheese.
6. **SPEED** Customers may pay more to have a product delivered quickly — e.g. some firms charge more to deliver products the next day.

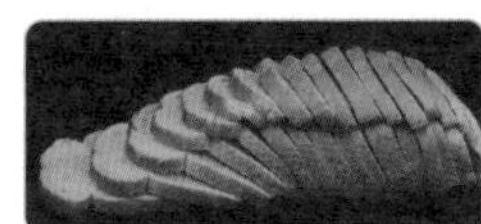

A commonly used benchmark of added value.

I can't stress enough the value of learning this page...

Learn the six main ways successful businesses add value to their products. The trickiest bit here is the difference between invention and innovation — remember that innovation means bringing a new idea successfully to the market (you could remember that mArket and innovAte both contain the letter 'a' — yeah, that's pretty good).

Succeeding as a New Start-Up

If you're going to start a new business, you need to be clear about what you're going to do, how you're going to do it, how much you're going to charge for doing it, and so on and so on (this is all information that you'd need to put in a business plan). Part of your business plan will also be to follow these 3 simple steps...

*Pick the **Right Location**...*

You need to decide where you're going to locate your business — usually a compromise between where it's cheapest to produce stuff and where your income will be biggest. These factors are usually pretty vital...

Labour Supply

Ideally, your location will have a local labour force with suitable skills for the business. Or be somewhere people are happy to relocate to. Governments may give subsidies or tax breaks to firms locating in areas of high unemployment.

Transport and Communication Links

Depending on your product, you might need sea ports, road and rail links, or an airport. Good telephone, internet and postal services will most likely also be important.

Location of Raw Materials versus the location of the Market

If you're going to need a lot of big and bulky raw materials (e.g. if you're a power station) then you'll probably be best off locating somewhere near those. But if your finished product is harder to transport than your raw materials (e.g. if you're a brewery), then it might be better to locate near your customers. The same goes if your customers need to get to you (e.g. if you're a dentist or barber).

*...**Protect** the **Secrets** of Your Success...*

You'll need to prevent competitors copying your ideas. There are various ways to do this, including:

- Using your rights as a copyright holder. If you write or record something original, then you own the copyright to it. Other people and businesses must seek permission (and possibly pay you) if they want to use your copyrighted material. Registering original work can be a useful thing to do — this way, you can prove when you made it if someone else claims they did it first.
- Taking out a patent. If you have a patent for your product or your method for producing it, no one else can copy it unless you give them a licence — and you can charge for the licence. Patents only apply to products or methods that are new and inventive in some way.

*...And Keep Your **Fingers Crossed***

There are lots of risks and uncertainties involved in operating a business. These include:

1) The health of the economy. The UK entered a sharp recession in 2009 that very few people predicted. Many businesses closed as a result.
2) The actions of competitors. Few businesses know exactly what their competitors are planning. Businesses can try to avoid being caught out by new threats by regularly carrying out market and competitor research.
3) Changes in the market. A lot of airlines were hit hard after the terrorist attacks of September 11 2001, since far fewer people wanted to fly. There wasn't really anything the airlines could have done to predict or get ready for that.

Plan your work, and work your plan...

There's a lot to think about when you're starting a new business — where to locate, how to protect your business ideas, and what risks there are, for example. You need to think about these things — so cover up the page and scribble a mini-essay covering the main points of each. Make sure you've got 'em all.

Businesses and the Law

Like everybody else, businesses need to stay within the law. And there are plenty of laws to think about...

Laws About **Staff, Customers** and the **Environment**

1) Health and Safety legislation means risks to people at work must be properly controlled. Businesses will benefit if staff take fewer days off due to sickness or injury.

See p44 for more info.

2) Employment laws aim to prevent employees (and potential employees) from being treated unfairly.

   - When recruiting, employers can't discriminate against candidates unfairly.
   - Staff must be paid at least the national minimum wage.
   - Staff can only be dismissed if they're incompetent, or break the firm's rules in a serious way.

See p37 for more info.

3) Consumer protection laws mean that anything sold must:
   - be fit for its purpose (do the job it was designed for),
   - match its description (in terms of materials, size, properties...),
   - be of satisfactory quality (not fall apart really quickly).

Consumer protection laws include: Sale of Goods Act (1979), Supply of Goods and Services Act (1982), and Sale and Supply of Goods Act (1994).

4) The Waste Electrical and Electronic Equipment (WEEE) Regulations were designed to reduce the amount of electronic equipment being thrown away, and to get people to recycle it or upgrade it instead. Firms that make or sell electrical goods must now collect and dispose of (or recycle) old products at the end of their lifespans.

See p29 for more about the environment.

Some Laws Relate to **Information** and **Electronic Data**

Nearly all businesses now use ICT to handle data, produce documents, and send messages.
The laws below regulate the use of electronic information — both for businesses and their customers.

The Data Protection Act 1998 describes how data about people can be stored and processed. The data must be accurate and relevant, and only used for the purpose specified by the business. The Act also allows people to see the personal data about them that organisations hold.

See p58 for more info.

The **Privacy and Electronic Communications Regulations** regulate firms that want to use the phone, emails or faxes to advertise their products. Everyone has the right not to receive these types of message — and companies can get into trouble if they contact people against their wishes.

The **Freedom of Information Act 2000** gave people access to data held by public sector organisations (e.g. local and national government). This could affect businesses if they need to find reasons for, say, refused planning permission. There's plenty of data that you can't ask for, though (e.g. if it would affect national security or police investigations).

The **Copyright, Design and Patents Act 1988** makes it illegal to copy a file without permission from the owner or copyright holder. This includes using software without a proper licence, using text or images from the internet without the copyright holder's permission, and copying software at work to use at home without permission.

The **Computer Misuse Act 1990** was introduced to cope with threats from hackers and viruses. It made it illegal to gain unauthorised access to electronic material (e.g. by hacking).

Complying with laws takes time and costs money. But firms can be fined if they break these laws. Breaking some of them can land people in prison.

Haven't learned this yet? Get your Acts together...

Some of the laws on this page were designed to protect people's rights and privacy, whilst still giving them access to public information. It can be a difficult balance, but it's one businesses have to get right.

Warm-up and Worked Exam Questions

Warm-up Questions

1) Explain the difference in approach between a market-driven firm and a product-driven firm.
2) What's the difference between a "product trial" and a "repeat purchase"? Why are repeat purchases so important for a business?
3) Name two different types of internal stakeholders. And five different types of external stakeholders.
4) Give seven different measures of success a business might use.
5) In business, what's the difference between an invention and an innovation?
6) What do the WEEE Regulations say?

Worked Exam Question

Here's a typical exam question. Try covering up the answers and working through the question on your own. Then you can compare your answers with the answers in blue.

1 Different groups of stakeholders in Affirm plc have different ideas about what the company should be trying to achieve. The directors have set the objective of increasing market share.

a) What is meant here by the term "stakeholders"?

Stakeholders are people who are affected in some way by the actions of the company. ✔[1 mark]

(1 mark)

b) Explain how a firm's market share is calculated.

The firm's total annual sales in a particular market ✔[1 mark] *is divided by* ✔[1 mark] *the total annual sales for that whole market,* ✔[1 mark] *and then multiplied by 100% (market share is usually expressed as a percentage).* ✔[1 mark]

(4 marks)

c) An employee suggests that Affirm should set itself an objective of improving its environmental sustainability rather than increasing market share.

Explain why the aims of different stakeholders in a firm often conflict.

Firms have many different types of stakeholders, such as shareholders, customers and employees. ✔[1 mark] *Different stakeholders will have different interests and priorities,* ✔[1 mark] *and so will also often have different aims for the firm.* ✔[1 mark] *For example, this employee is thinking about the environment, while shareholders may think profits are most important, and a customer may prefer a firm to invest in its product range or customer service.* ✔[1 mark]

✔[There is also 1 mark available for an answer that is well structured and well written.]

(5 marks)

Exam Questions

1 Karen wants to open a new shop selling sports equipment.

a) Consumer protection laws set minimum standards for goods being sold.
State **three** requirements of these laws.

1. ....

2. ....

3. ....

(3 marks)

b) Karen is looking for a good location for her shop. Explain **two** factors she should consider.

1. ....

....

2. ....

....

(4 marks)

c) Karen is making a poster to put into the window of her shop when it opens.
She finds a picture on the Internet that she would like to use in her poster.

Explain the precautions she should take before using that image on her poster.

....

....

(2 marks)

d) Karen's shop will be competing against other shops selling sports equipment. Describe how Karen could try to make buying from her shop as attractive as possible to customers.

....

....

....

....

(Continue your answer on a separate piece of paper) *(9 marks)*

e) Explain why even careful planning cannot prevent some businesses failing.

....

....

....

....

(4 marks)

Revision Summary for Section One

Okay, so that's the first section over with — now it's time to find out how much you remember. Have a bash at these questions. If you can do them all, pat yourself on the back and feel smug. If you can't, then go back and look at the section again and keep plugging away until you can answer them all. Yes, I know it's a pain but life's like that — and after all, it's the only way you're going to get ready for the exam.

1) What's the main objective for most businesses?
2) Describe objectives other than profit that a business might pursue.
3) Do charities aim to make a profit?
4) What is a social enterprise?
5) Give four reasons why people start their own businesses.
6) What is meant by a calculated risk?
7) List five qualities that an entrepreneur is likely to have.
8) What is the difference between a sole trader and a partnership?
9) What information might be contained in a deed of partnership?
10) If you own part of a business and the business goes bankrupt, would you rather have limited or unlimited liability? Why?
11) Describe the main difference between a private limited company (Ltd) and a public limited company (plc).
12) What is a franchisor?
13) Are market-driven firms or product-driven firms usually more successful?
14) What kind of information would market research aim to find out?
15) What kind of things can a business do to take care of customers once they've made a purchase?
16) Name six groups of stakeholders and say which are internal.
17) What role do the directors carry out in an organisation?
18) Who are the most important stakeholders and why?
19) Explain why the shareholders of a business and consumers might have different opinions about how successful the business is.
20) Explain what is meant by 'adding value' to a product.
21) Explain what is meant in business by a "unique selling point".
22) Describe six ways that a business can add value to their products.
23) Describe three things a new business might want to think about before choosing where to locate.
24) Why might a firm locate in an area of high unemployment?
25) Describe two ways entrepreneurs can protect their ideas.
26) Give three examples of things businesses have to do to comply with employment laws.
27) What does WEEE stand for? And who's responsible for disposing of it?
28) Give five examples of laws that relate to electronic information. Describe the main purpose of each law.

Marketing and Market Research

Marketing is all the things a business does to separate people from their money — from designing a product people want, through to telling them where to buy it, and everything in between.

Learn the **Four Ps of Marketing**

The four Ps are the key to understanding what marketing is all about.
If a firm gets them right it should be easy to sell its product. If it gets even one of them wrong, it's in trouble.

Together the four Ps are called the marketing mix.

1. PRODUCT — the firm must come up with a product that people will want to buy. It must fulfil some of the customer's needs or wants.

2. PRICE — the price must be one that the customer thinks is good value for money. This is not the same as being cheap.

3. PROMOTION — the product must be promoted so that potential customers are aware that it exists.

4. PLACE — the product must be available for sale in a place that the customer will find convenient.

1) Depending on the situation, some of the Ps might be more important than others. For example, if customers really want the product, they may be prepared to pay a higher price.
2) Customers' needs and wants usually change over time — a business should adapt its marketing mix to meet these changing needs.

Market Research Can Help a Firm Choose a **Marketing Mix**

There are two main types of market research a business can use:

1) **PRIMARY RESEARCH** is when a business does its own questionnaires and surveys.
   Primary research can be expensive and time-consuming, but contacting potential customers directly is the best way to find out about their preferences.

2) **SECONDARY RESEARCH** involves looking at data that's been published by other people.
   It might include things like specialist market research reports, government publications, and articles in newspapers, magazines and on the internet.
   Secondary research is cheap and instantly available. This can save time and money, but it may not be completely relevant to what the business wants to find out.

Data Can be **Quantitative** or **Qualitative**

The information that's found from market research is called data. Again, there are two basic types:

1) QUANTITATIVE DATA is anything you can measure or reduce to a number. If you're researching the pizza market, asking "How many chocolate pizzas will you buy each week?" will give a quantitative answer.

2) QUALITATIVE DATA can't be expressed in numbers. Market researchers often ask for feelings and opinions — e.g. asking "What do you think of chocolate pizzas?" will give a qualitative answer.

Qualitative data is tricky to analyse because it's hard to compare lots of people's opinions and draw strong conclusions. Good market research will use both types of information.

Make sure you know your Four Ps from your Qs...

Customers are absolutely crucial to marketing. Market research can help firms to collect solid data about what their customers want. Interpreting this data can then help them to plan their marketing mix.

Analysing the Market

Businesses can't succeed without understanding their market — market analysis helps firms to find out who their customers are, what they want, and whether their needs are being met by the competition.

Businesses **Map the Market** to Find Market **Gaps**

A market map can help a new business to understand the key features of the market it's operating in. The kinds of information usually shown in a market map include...

1) The number of customers in the market — and how much they spend.
2) Which market segments the customers belong to. A market segment is a group of customers who all have something in common (e.g. they're in the same age group, the same location, or the same social class).
3) The products that are popular and unpopular.
4) Competitors selling similar products — and where they sell them.

1) Sometimes a market map will show up a group of customers with a need that isn't being met. This is called a gap in the market.
2) Businesses need to move quickly to fill the gap — before their competitors do. This usually means launching a new product or service that will meet the group's identified need.
3) A gap in the market can be a great opportunity for a business. If it gets the marketing mix right, a gap can expand to become a large market.

Businesses Need to Analyse Their **Competitors**

Businesses need to think about:

1) **The strengths and weaknesses of competitors** — most new businesses won't try to compete with the strongest aspects of other firms. It's usually much better to find an area where competitors are weak, and try to do those things better (e.g. if competitors are using out-of-date equipment, a new firm may be able to offer lower prices by using modern, more efficient equipment).
2) **How their own products compare to others** — looking closely at what competing products offer (and what they don't) may allow firms to spot new opportunities that they hadn't seen before.

Customer Preferences Don't Stay the Same Forever

Market research and market analysis can tell firms what customers want at a particular time. But customers' views and habits can change over time.

EXAMPLE

These pie charts show the results of Crazy Juice Ltd's recent research into why people buy their juice, as well as the results from similar research carried out in 1992.

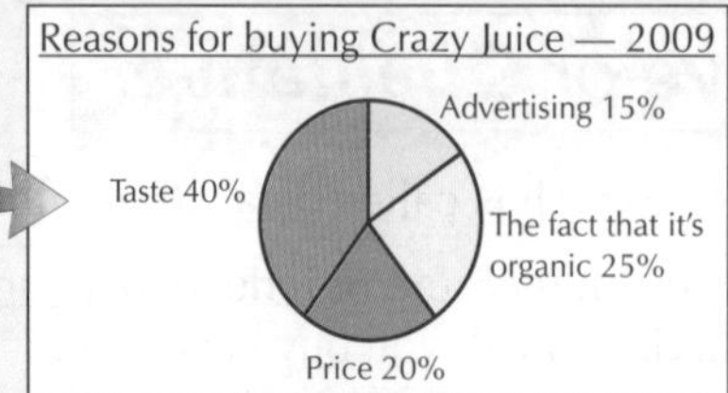

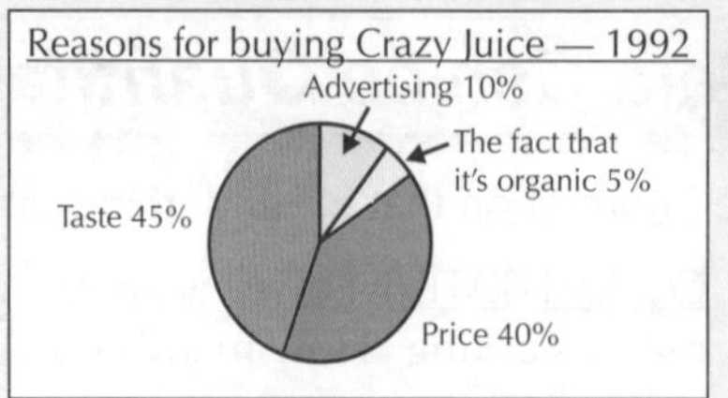

An analysis of the charts would include points like...

'Taste is still the most important factor,'
'The biggest increase is in the fact that it's organic,'
or *'Price is less important now than in 1992.'*

This analysis could lead to a new marketing mix based on the quality and environmental friendliness of the product.

Analyse this page to make sure there's no gaps in your knowledge...

All new firms need to analyse their market before they start doing business — if they don't, they run the risk of making a product customers don't want. But remember that customer preferences also change over time.

Prices, Revenue, Costs and Profit

Markets through the ages have traditionally involved a bit of haggling between buyers and sellers before they agree on the final price of something. The same kind of thing goes on in modern markets. Let me explain...

Prices May be Affected by Supply and Demand

1) Demand is the quantity of a product that consumers are willing and able to buy. The law of demand is that as the price increases the quantity demanded will fall — and vice versa.
2) Supply is the quantity of a product producers are willing and able to make for sale. The law of supply is that as the price increases, the quantity supplied increases — and vice versa.
3) So consumers want to buy at a low price, while producers want to sell at a high price. This is where the marketplace forces a clever compromise...

- If the price is too low there'll be a shortage of supply. Some consumers will be willing to pay more, so producers increase prices.
- If the price is too high, there'll be a surplus of supply. Producers will have to reduce prices to persuade people to buy unsold goods.
- Eventually producers and consumers agree on the price and quantity to be exchanged. The point where they agree is called equilibrium.

4) These laws of supply and demand are particularly powerful in commodity markets (a commodity is something that's essentially the same wherever you buy it — e.g. petrol, gas, water).
5) In a market where competing products are different from one another, the laws of supply and demand might not hold quite as rigidly. Things like 'brand' and 'quality' affect demand, as well as price.

Profit Depends on Revenue and Costs

1) A business's revenue (or turnover, or income) is what it earns from selling its products. Revenue is calculated by multiplying the quantity sold by the selling price.
2) Costs are the expenses paid out by a business. Costs can be split into different categories...

revenue = quantity sold × price

Direct and Indirect Costs...

- Direct costs are expenses that can be attributed to making a particular product. Examples include costs of factory labour and raw materials.
- Indirect costs are the general expenses of running the business. Examples include management salaries, telephone bills and office rent.

total costs = direct costs + indirect costs

...or Fixed and Variable Costs

- Fixed costs do not vary with output. They're mostly indirect costs. They have to be paid even if the firm produces nothing.
- Variable costs are costs that will increase as the firm expands output. They're mostly direct costs.

total costs = fixed costs + variable costs

3) You calculate the profit over a period of time with this formula: **profit = revenue – costs**

Example

Britney's Spheres Ltd. sells 20,000 tennis balls in a month at £2 each.
Over the same month its total costs are £30,000.
Profit = Revenue – Costs = (20,000 × £2) – £30,000 = £40,000 – £30,000.
So the business makes £10,000 profit in the month.

A lot to take in — maybe you'd profit from a recap...

Prices are paid by customers, while costs are paid by producers. A firm's fixed costs are only fixed over a short time — they'll probably increase as the firm grows. Make sure you know how each type of cost is different.

Finance and Cash Flow

This page is about the money that flows in and out of businesses — where it comes from, and where it goes.

Firms Get **Finance** from **Different Sources** as They **Grow**

New firms need start-up finance. Some entrepreneurs may be able to finance their businesses with their personal savings — but most will have to borrow money to buy the assets (e.g. machinery) they need.

1) Long-term sources of finance are used if money's needed for more than a year. For example:

    LOANS — a small firm might borrow money from a bank, or from friends and family. Bank loans have to be repaid with interest.

    VENTURE CAPITAL is money lent by people or businesses who specialise in financing new or expanding small firms.

2) Short-term sources are used if the money's only needed for a short time (less than a year). For example:

    OVERDRAFTS let the firm take more money out of its bank account than there is in it — but the bank will charge interest or a fee.

    TRADE CREDIT — when a business buys supplies, it's often given a credit period of one or two months after they've received the goods before they need to pay. (Trade credit is a form of short-term loan.)

3) As a firm grows, other sources of finance become available to keep the business running smoothly.

    RETAINED PROFITS are profits that the owners have decided to plough back into the business.

    ASSET SALES Businesses can raise cash by selling assets (e.g. buildings) that are no longer in use.

    SELLING SHARES If the business is a limited company (see p3), it can sell more shares. The money raised doesn't have to be repaid, but those people would now own a part of the company — this means less control for the existing owners.

4) All these sources of finance can be split into two types...
    - Internal sources provide money from inside the business (e.g. retained profits).
    - External sources are located outside the business (e.g. bank loans, venture capital).

Cash Flow is a Firm's **Everyday** Flow of Money

1) When a firm sells its products, money flows in. When it buys materials or pays wages, money flows out. This is cash flow. All firms need to keep careful track of their cash flow.
2) Poor cash flow (when there's not enough money flowing in to pay the bills) can lead to business failure.

- Businesses make a cash-flow forecast by estimating future sales and spending. (These estimates are often based on figures from previous months or years.)
- The net cash flow for a given month is the difference between cash inflow and cash outflow.
- Cumulative cash flow is like a running total — it shows the overall cash flow over a longer period. To find this month's cumulative cash-flow figure, add this month's net cash flow to last month's cumulative cash flow.

CASH FLOW FORECAST — FOOTY MAGS LTD.

	April	May	June	July
Total receipts (cash inflow)	15,000	8000	7000	4000
Total spending (cash outflow)	12,000	9000	10,000	2000
Net cash flow (inflow – outflow)	3000	-1000	-3000	2000
Cumulative cash flow	3000	2000	-1000	1000

The predicted net cash flow is negative in both May and June — more money is spent than received. The predicted cumulative cash flow between April and July is positive — overall, more money flows in than out during this period.

As well as sales and spending, stock levels and credit terms can have an effect on a firm's cash flow.

1) Credit terms describe how long customers are given to pay for goods. Giving customers long credit periods is bad for cash flow. (But getting long credit periods from your suppliers is good.)
2) If a firm has plenty of unsold stock, it could stop production and simply sell this until stocks run out. By destocking, cash inflows will be the same — but spending on production costs will fall.

Cash flow — it's all money in and money out...

The tricky thing here is cumulative cash flow. Remember, it's not describing cash flow in a single month, but over a longer period — always ask yourself when that period started. (In the example above, it was April.)

The Economic Environment

Changes in the economy can have a huge impact on businesses. Firms have to adapt, or risk going bust.

Changes in *Economic Growth* Result in the *Business Cycle*

1) A country's gross domestic product (GDP) is the total value of all the goods and services it produces over a period of a year. GDP is often called "the size of a country's economy".
2) A country's economic growth is also shown by its GDP. If GDP increases from one year to the next, the economy is in a period of growth. If GDP decreases, it's called negative growth.

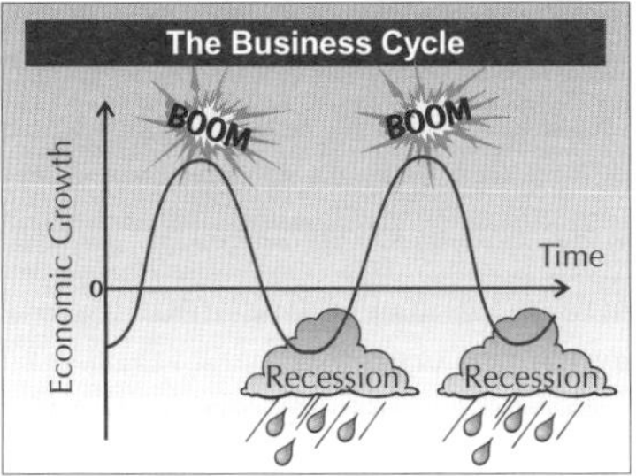

3) Economic growth seems to move in a regular pattern. It grows, then declines, then grows again. This pattern is called the business cycle.
4) Periods of high growth are called booms. Consumer demand is strong, so sales of products are high.
5) Times of negative growth are called recessions. During a recession, consumer demand is weak and firms often struggle to sell their products. Some firms will make losses and have to close down.

Changes in *Interest Rates* Affect *Loans* and *Savings*

Interest rates are affected by the state of a country's economy.

1) Interest is the extra money that you pay back on a loan, or earn on savings. The amount of interest you pay or earn depends on the interest rate.

An interest rate of 5% means that in one year, you'll pay interest of 5% of the amount you've borrowed.

2) When interest rates are low, it's cheaper to borrow money. This is often good news for businesses.
   - This is because firms with loans and overdrafts (see p18) will have less interest to repay.
   - It also means that consumers spend more, since credit cards are cheaper to use, and they'll be paying less on other loans such as mortgages. This increases demand for products.
3) High interest rates can make life difficult for firms. Repaying debt becomes more expensive, and consumers prefer to save rather than spend as their savings earn more interest — so product demand falls.

Changes in *Exchange Rates* Affect *Imports* and *Exports*

1) Exchange rates tell you how much one currency is worth compared to another. For example, exchange rates can tell you how many US dollars ($), or Euros (€) you can buy for one British pound (£).
2) You can work out prices in different currencies by multiplying or dividing by the exchange rate.
3) Exchange rates change over time — the pound can become weaker or stronger compared to other currencies.
4) When the pound is weak, one pound buys less of another currency (or the other currency buys more pounds). This means:
   - British exports become less expensive abroad — resulting in more sales for UK firms that export to other countries,
   - foreign goods become more expensive in the UK.
5) However, foreign raw materials also become more expensive — which can be bad news for UK firms.
6) A strong pound has the opposite effects to a weak pound.

- If £1 = $2, a British cricket ball that costs £5 will sell in the USA for 5 × 2 = $10. And a baseball that costs $6 in the USA can be sold for 6 ÷ 2 = £3 in the UK.
- If the value of the pound falls so that £1 = $1.50 the £5 cricket ball would sell in the USA for 5 × 1.50 = $7.50. The $6 baseball can now be sold in the UK for 6 ÷ 1.50 = £4.

Firms can be affected by changes in the economy...

Small businesses can be especially vulnerable in recessions — they often don't have enough money saved to help them through the hard times. Some of this stuff is quite tricky — try writing a mini-essay explaining how economic growth, interest rates and exchange rates might affect a firm's cash flow (p18).

Warm-up and Worked Exam Questions

Warm-up Questions

1) What's the difference between primary market research and secondary market research?
2) Is "Number of people buying Brand X" an example of qualitative data or quantitative data? Explain.
3) Explain the difference between fixed and variable costs.
4) What is a "credit period"?
5) What is "destocking"? How can this help improve cash flow?
6) What's a recession? Why are recessions bad for companies?

Worked Exam Question

It's one thing to know lots of facts — it's another thing to be able to apply that knowledge to get maximum marks in an exam. Read the answers below, and then try the questions on the next page yourself.

1 Read **Item A** and then answer the questions that follow.

> **Item A**
> Myfone Ltd is a mobile phone supplier. The marketing director of the company believes that the key to success is the "marketing mix". The marketing director is considering using an Internet promotional campaign. A different director is unsure whether this is a sensible strategy.

a) Promotion and place are two factors in the marketing mix. State the other two factors.

Product ✔[1 mark] *and price.* ✔[1 mark]

(2 marks)

b) Explain why promotion and place are such important factors for the success of a company.

Promotion is important because, unless customers know that a company exists ✔[1 mark] *and that the products it sells can fulfil one of their needs or wants,* ✔[1 mark] *they will not buy anything from that company.* ✔[1 mark] *Place is important because, if customers are persuaded to buy something from a company,* ✔[1 mark] *they must be able to do this as easily as possible.* ✔[1 mark] *If they can't, they may just turn to a different firm.* ✔[1 mark]

(6 marks)

c) Would you recommend that Myfone should use an Internet-based promotional campaign? Give reasons for your answer.

I think Myfone should use the Internet for a promotional campaign. ✔[1 mark] *Teenagers are probably a key group of customers* ✔[1 mark] *for Myfone, and they will probably be Internet users.* ✔[1 mark] *Also, an Internet campaign needn't be expensive, as web sites are cheap to set up.* ✔[1 mark]

(4 marks)

Exam Questions

1 Brit Smoothies Ltd. wants to launch a new product, made with British fruit, into the UK and the European smoothie markets. The marketing department has been instructed to carry out a market analysis for the product. Part of this analysis involves making a market map.

a) What is meant by the phrase "market map"?

....

(2 marks)

b) Explain why it is important to analyse the market before launching a new product.

....

....

(Continue your answer on a separate piece of paper) *(5 marks)*

c) Explain how changes in the exchange rate between the pound and the euro could affect the launch of the smoothies in Europe.

....

....

....

....

(5 marks)

2 Electronorum plc has just won a contract to supply computer services to the government. It is to be paid for its services every six months. The company's finance director is concerned about how this will affect cash flow, as the company already has large amounts of debt. For this reason, he is preparing a cash-flow forecast.

a) What is meant by the term "cash-flow forecast"?

....

....

(2 marks)

b) Explain why a business needs to manage its cash flow carefully.

....

....

....

(3 marks)

c) Interest rates are predicted to rise. Explain how this might affect Electronorum's cash flow.

....

....

....

(4 marks)

Revision Summary for Section Two

Well, that was an amazing section. Marketing, money and economics — what more could you want... The only thing that could possibly make your life any better at this point is a whole page full of questions to remind you of everything you've just read.

But what's this... surely not a whole page full of questions to remind you of everything you've just read? We're too good to you...

1) What are the 4 Ps in the marketing mix? Explain what each one means.
2) Give an example of a situation where one marketing P might be more important than another. (If you're feeling enthusiastic, think up more than one example.)
3) Why do businesses usually have to change a product's marketing mix over time?
4) Give one advantage and one disadvantage of both primary market research and secondary market research.
5) Explain the difference between quantitative and qualitative data.
6) Explain what a market segment is, and give three examples.
7) Give three things (apart from market segments) that might be included on a market map.
8) What is a gap in the market? How can a new business take advantage of a gap?
9) Explain why it's important for businesses to analyse their competitors.
10) State the laws of supply and demand. Give a quick explanation of why each law holds.
11) Why do the laws of supply and demand have a greater effect in commodity markets?
12) In March, ScribblyBits Ltd. sells 1200 pens, priced at £6 each. Calculate their revenue for March.
13) What's the difference between direct and indirect costs? Give one example of each type. Now repeat the question for fixed and variable costs.
14) ScribblyBits Ltd. has total costs of £4300 in March. Use your answer to question 12 to work out their profit for March.
15) Explain the difference between cost and price.
16) Describe two long-term sources and two short-term sources of start-up finance.
17) Describe three more sources of finance that become available to a firm as it grows.
18) The table shows a firm's receipts and spending for three months. Calculate:
    a) The firm's net cash flow in each month (June, July and August).
    b) The firm's cumulative cash flow between June and August.

	June	July	August
Total receipts (cash inflow)	13,000	15,000	10,000
Total spending (cash outflow)	11,000	12,000	11,000

19) Explain how stock levels and credit terms can affect a firm's cash flow.
20) What is GDP? How does it relate to economic growth?
21) Explain how changes in interest rates can have an effect on a firm's profits.
22) Suppose the exchange rate between pounds and Euros is £1 = €1.20. If a book costs €18 in France, what would its price be in the UK?
23) If the pound is strong against the US dollar, explain the effects on:
    a) UK firms that export products to the USA
    b) UK firms that import materials from the USA

12. £7200
14. £2900
18. a) June: £2000
July: £3000
Aug: –£1000
b) £4000
22. £15

Organisational Structure

A large business could employ hundreds of people, all with different skills and levels of experience.
The structure of the business describes how all the different people are organised.

Staff Work at Different Levels Within a Business

There are four basic levels of job that staff can have.

1) DIRECTORS are responsible for the business's strategy (its overall direction). The directors decide on strategy and targets at regular board meetings.

2) MANAGERS organise the carrying out of the directors' strategy. A large firm may have senior, middle and junior managers.

3) SUPERVISORS are ranked below managers. They usually look after specific projects or small teams of operatives.

4) OPERATIVES are workers who aren't responsible for other staff. They're often given specific tasks to perform by managers or supervisors.

Managers and supervisors are responsible for planning, organising and decision-making (see pages 25 and 28).

Organisation Charts Show the Structure of a Business

A firm's structure can be shown on an organisational chart. Here are some examples...

1) A **HIERARCHICAL** firm is structured in layers — the directors are on the top layer, and operatives on the lowest layer. The number of people on each layer increases as you go down the hierarchy.
In a firm with a 'tall' hierarchy, communication from the directors to the operatives can be difficult and slow because there are lots of layers to go through.

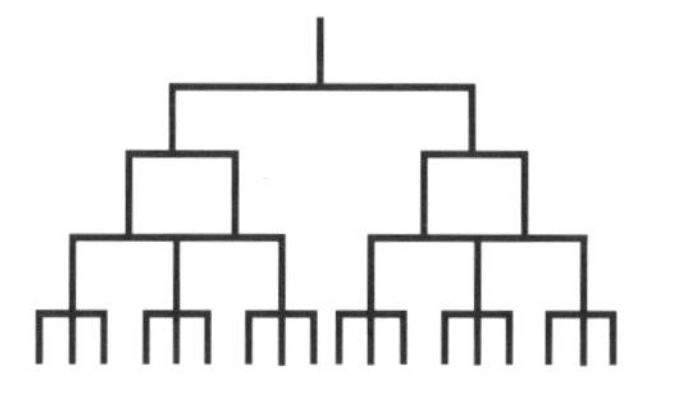

2) A **FLAT HIERARCHY** has fewer layers — this can make communication clearer and more efficient. But managers can get overwhelmed if they're in charge of too many people.

3) In a **MATRIX STRUCTURE**, groups of operatives work under two or more managers. In the diagram, the research operatives all work under the research manager. But each operative also works under one of the project managers, depending on which project they're involved in.
A matrix structure is designed to encourage flexibility — allowing operatives to move easily to different projects (and project managers). But there may be problems if the two managers give the same operatives conflicting tasks.

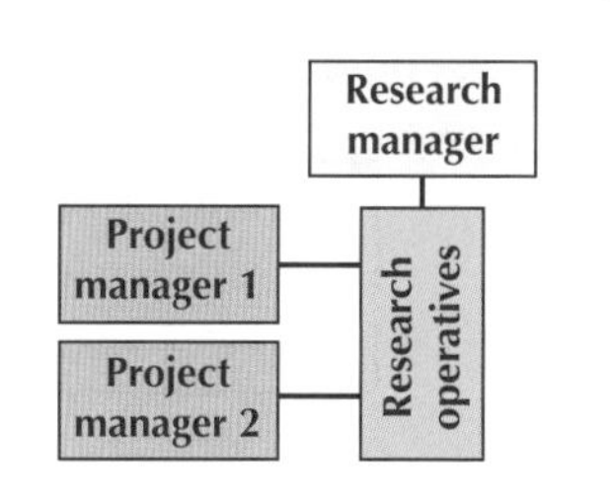

4) A **CIRCULAR CHART** arranges employees in circles. Directors and senior managers are at the centre of the circle, and operatives are on the outside. The idea behind circular charts is that no one's "at the bottom" (which can make people feel unimportant).
They're supposed to be good for making people feel like part of a team.

Time to get organised and learn this page...

Business structure is about decision-making and communication. Businesses can use these kinds of charts to spot potential problems with their structure — e.g. if a hierarchy has grown too tall over the years, then maybe decision-making will be too slow. These days, businesses use ICT to draw up this kind of chart.

Administration in Business

Businesses must have quick access to accurate information. This is why good administration is so important. It's not glamorous, but businesses can't do without it.

Administration Involves **Four** Main Activities

These are the four parts of "information administration" you need to know about. Learn them well...

1) STORING Information can be stored for future use in either electronic or paper-based filing systems.
2) PROCESSING Information can be processed to generate new information. For example, sales figures can be processed to help decide future production levels.
3) RETRIEVING Stored information often needs to be retrieved and used again. For example, last year's sales figures might be needed so they can be compared to this year's.
4) DISSEMINATING Information often needs to be disseminated (distributed) to other people and organisations. This could be done verbally, in writing, in graphs and charts...

ICT can make administration faster, more accurate and more flexible than paper-based filing — see p48 for more information.

Admin Helps **All Parts** of a Business to Operate **Efficiently**

See p29 for more about efficiency.

1) Administration is vital for all the departments in a business — human resources, finance, operations, sales and marketing, customer service, research and development...
2) For example, human resources will need information about how staff are performing so that they can provide appropriate support and training.
3) Good administration helps businesses operate efficiently, and compete effectively.
   - For example, having access to up-to-date and reliable information on competitors allows managers to make sensible, well-informed marketing decisions.
   - Administrative errors can lead to misleading information being given to customers — e.g. a customer might be sent a bill for products they haven't ordered.
   - If a company is struggling, it may need to reduce its costs. To do this effectively, it will need accurate records of how it currently spends its money before it can work out where to reduce spending in the future.

Good Admin is Vital for the **Tax** System

A business's accountant needs accurate information to look after a firm's finances. For example, financial records are important when it comes to paying business taxes.

VALUE ADDED TAX (VAT) — depends on the difference between the price a business charges for its products and the amount they cost to make. So businesses need accurate records of what's been paid to suppliers and received from customers.

INCOME TAX and NATIONAL INSURANCE — these depend on how much employees are paid, so a business needs accurate records of how much it pays its workers.

Employers have to deduct income tax and National Insurance from their employees' pay and give it to the government.

Employers also make an extra National Insurance payment for each person they employ.

CORPORATION TAX — depends on how much profit a business makes. Again, accurate sales figures and records of the firm's total spending are essential.

Business administration is all about handling information...

Accurate administration is vital if a business is to run effectively. I reckon it's time to write a life-enhancing mini-essay all about admin and its importance. Check that you've covered all the main points on this page.

Routine & Non-Routine Tasks

Business activities can be divided into routine tasks and non-routine tasks — you need to know the difference between them and who might be involved in carrying them out.

Routine Tasks Can be Done by Operatives

1) In most businesses, there are certain tasks that need to be carried out regularly and are basically the same each time. These are called routine tasks. Examples include:

- Storing documents in the correct place so that they can be easily retrieved (either paper documents in filing cabinets, or electronic ones on computers).
- Entering details of invoices into a financial database (or other data-inputting tasks).
- Re-stocking shelves in a shop or supermarket.

2) Routine tasks can usually be done by operatives — they tend not to involve much decision-making. This doesn't mean they're not important — if routine tasks weren't done, the business would soon suffer.
3) The growth of ICT has meant that many routine tasks are now done by computers rather than humans. For example, invoices can be created automatically by a computer using stored information, and files can be automatically backed-up using basic software.

Non-Routine Tasks Often Involve Managers and Teams

1) Non-routine tasks are less predictable — they often involve high-level decisions. *See below for more on decisions.*

- Product development — this requires creativity and technical expertise. Since a failed product could lead to huge losses, this needs the input of experienced staff.
- Recruiting new employees — managers will need to look through all the applications and decide which candidates are the best. Decisions about recruitment are very complicated and are best made by senior members of staff, since employing the wrong person can be expensive for the company (and unpleasant for the employee).
- Upgrading equipment — this involves researching and comparing the possible upgrade options. The firm then decides which will be best suited to its present and future needs, and its budget.

2) Non-routine tasks are often carried out by teams of operatives, with managers taking overall responsibility for the success or failure of the task.
3) Non-routine tasks can't usually be handled by computer software alone.

Decisions Can Also Be Routine or Non-Routine

Managers have more responsibility than operatives, and have to make tougher decisions. Like tasks, decisions come in two flavours — routine and non-routine.

1) **ROUTINE DECISIONS** Routine decisions involve day-to-day judgements. These decisions are usually made by operational managers (the people in charge of teams of operatives) or by operatives themselves.

   Some routine decisions can be taken by computers — for example, a warehouse may use a software package to order more of an item when stocks drop below a particular level.

2) **NON-ROUTINE DECISIONS** These are more important decisions that may have a major effect on the business — deciding on the design of a new product, for example. As a result, non-routine decisions are generally made by senior managers or directors.

Tasks and decisions can be either routine or non-routine...

Don't be fooled by the name — routine tasks don't change much, but they're crucial for keeping businesses running smoothly. Non-routine tasks involve more decisions — these are usually made by managers.

Warm-up and Worked Exam Questions

Warm-up Questions

1) Describe a matrix structure.
2) Describe the four different information-related tasks involved in administration.
3) Give three examples of taxes that need accurate financial records to be kept if the amounts owed are going to be calculated accurately.
4) Give an example of a routine task in a typical office.
5) Explain why non-routine tasks can't easily be automated.

Worked Exam Question

Remember... practising exam questions is a really good way to revise.
So have a look at these sample answers, then try the questions on the next page.

1 Read **Item A** and then answer the questions that follow.

> **Item A**
>
> Customers of CompTechneis Ltd have complained that the company is slow to take decisions if a non-routine fault is spotted during routine service calls. In an attempt to improve their service, the Board of Directors has decided that they need to make improvements in the organisational structure of the business and the administrative systems. The firm is currently structured as a tall hierarchy.

a) Explain the term "tall hierarchy".

A many layered structure, ✔[1 mark] *with the most senior people such as Directors at the top, managers in the middle, and the operatives on the lower layers.* ✔[1 mark]

(2 marks)

b) Explain why communication within a tall hierarchy can be inefficient.

Communication is usually passed up or down a hierarchy one layer at a time. ✔[1 mark] *In an organisation with many layers, this can take a long time,* ✔[1 mark] *and involve many people.* ✔[1 mark]

(3 marks)

c) A director suggests the company should be organised using a flat hierarchical structure. Discuss the possible effects on the company this could have.

A flatter hierarchy has fewer layers in its structure, ✔[1 mark] *and so communication can be more efficient,* ✔[1 mark] *since messages pass through fewer tiers of management.* ✔[1 mark] *However, a flat hierarchy can mean more operatives reporting to a single manager,* ✔[1 mark] *and this can lead to problems if those managers are unable to cope.* ✔[1 mark]

(5 marks)

Exam Questions

1 A company is in the process of calculating how much VAT it has to pay to the government.

a) Explain what information is needed by a company to calculate the VAT it must pay.

(2 marks)

b) The company's directors believe that good administration is vital to any company.
Explain how good administration can help firms improve their service and increase profits.

(Continue your answer on a separate piece of paper) *(7 marks)*

2 A supermarket chain has recently appointed a new manager in one of its stores.
Part of the manager's duties involves giving his staff tasks to perform.
Both routine and non-routine tasks need to be assigned to various members of staff.

a) Explain what is meant by the term "routine task".

(2 marks)

b) One of the manager's responsibilities is the recruitment of shop-floor staff.
This involves making a lot of non-routine decisions.
Why are recruitment decisions generally considered to be non-routine?

(3 marks)

c) Every week the prices of various products are reduced as a special offer. The manager can:

- **either** choose which products to put on special offer himself,
- **or** ask a more junior member of staff to choose.

Which of these options would you recommend to the manager. Explain your answer.

(Continue your answer on a separate piece of paper) *(6 marks)*

Planning

Planning is vital in business — firms need to have a clear idea of what they're going to do in the future, and how they're going to do it.

Planning is About Making Decisions for the Future

1) Planning means thinking about what the business is trying to achieve, and working out the best way to do it with the resources available.
2) Even for routine tasks, it's important to plan ahead — e.g. deciding where to store files. Planning meetings carefully is also important, so that time isn't wasted on irrelevant discussions.
3) Planning can help to prepare for potential problems — for example, a firm might make a plan for dealing with a breakdown in its computer systems.
4) Planning also involves prioritising — deciding which activities are most important. High priority tasks will be dealt with sooner, and may be given more resources.
5) Access to accurate information is essential while making plans. For example, information about past projects, current projects, prices, competitors, changes in the market... etc. can all help while planning.
6) Good planning increases efficiency. Bad planning can mean projects are completed late or over budget. It can also reduce quality — e.g. if deadlines are unrealistic and staff feel pressured into cutting corners.

Planning Involves Several Stages

1 Identify your objectives

This means knowing:
- what it is you want to achieve
- when you need to achieve it by

2 Break the project down into separate tasks

Work out the individual tasks involved in completing the project.
Prioritise the tasks — decide on the order these tasks will need to be performed in.
Which ones need to be started right now? Can any be left until later?

3 Estimate the time needed for each task

- If you know how long the individual tasks in a project take, you can work out how long you'll need to complete the whole project.
- Decide whether you can do the separate tasks one at a time, or whether you'll need to do some of them simultaneously.
- Set milestones — these show what tasks need to be completed by certain times during the project. (Milestones help to keep projects on schedule — if a milestone is missed, then the project is running late and might not be completed in time.)

Using data from previous projects is often the best way to do this.

Compare the total project time to the time limit in your objectives.

You can then try to catch up — more people might be needed, or people may need to work overtime.

4 Identify the resources needed

This includes estimating: a) materials, b) equipment, c) staff, d) money.

5 Think about how the project is affected by people outside the firm

For example, can suppliers provide what you need when you need it?

Don't just plan to learn this page — really do it...

Planning is about deciding on the targets that need to be met, and calculating the time, money and other resources that will be needed to meet them. Businesses aim for good plans based on sound admin. Cover up the page, jot down the main points and then check that you got them all. Repeat until you don't miss any out. Good job.

Efficient Use of Resources

Businesses don't like waste. Wasted space, wasted time, wasted money... they all reduce efficiency. Also, waste has to go somewhere — and very often it ends up causing pollution.

Efficiency Means Getting Big Results from Few Resources

1) Efficiency is all about achieving your aims using as few resources as possible. ('Resources' means things like raw materials, money, staff, fuel... and so on.)
2) An inefficient business may achieve its aims, but waste a lot of resources along the way.
3) A firm that uses few resources but fails to achieve what it was trying to do is also inefficient.

Work Areas and Equipment Should be Efficient

The buildings and equipment a firm uses can have a big impact on its efficiency...

1) If a building is too large for the firm's needs, it may waste money on rent, lighting and heating (especially if the rooms are badly insulated). On the other hand, a growing business needs premises it can "grow into". Premises that are too small may mean the firm will soon need to relocate (which can be expensive).
2) The design and layout of buildings and work areas can affect efficiency too. Employees need easy access to equipment they use often (e.g. printers).
3) But firms need to find a balance. For example, a firm could save its employees time if it bought them each a printer to put on their desk. But it'd need to be sure the time savings would be worth the expense.
4) Choosing equipment also involves a similar kind of balance. For instance, buying cheaper computers may save money in the short term. But if they can't cope with the needs of the business (e.g. if they're too slow), they'll be inefficient. This may cost the firm more in the long run.

Tasks Should Also be Designed Efficiently

1) Designing tasks efficiently means planning them so there's as little waste (of resources and people's time) as possible. See p28 for more information about planning.
2) Tasks should be done by staff with the right skills. This will mean fewer errors and higher quality. But getting highly skilled people to perform fairly simple tasks isn't the best idea — it'd be more efficient for them to be performing more difficult tasks.
3) And tasks should be timetabled so that staff don't waste time waiting for other tasks to be finished before they can start theirs.

The most efficient way to perform some routine tasks is to automate them using ICT.

Modern Businesses Need to Think About the Environment

1) Energy efficiency is important for the environment. Carbon emissions from fossil fuels like coal and gas are thought to contribute to global warming — firms are under pressure to reduce their use of these fuels.
2) Resource depletion is also a problem — the Earth's supplies of raw materials and fuels can't last forever. Firms need to use these resources efficiently, reduce waste and find sustainable alternatives for the future. Laws can help — e.g. the WEEE Regulations (p11) encourage the recycling of electronic equipment.
3) But laws aren't always necessary. For example, lots of firms now choose to use less packaging for their products, recycle more, and use recyclable materials more often. These actions can help to reduce costs, and even increase sales — many customers prefer to buy from ethical, environmentally-friendly firms.

Efficiency is all about using as few resources as possible....

Very often you can save one resource (e.g. time) by using more of another (e.g. money). In practice, it's finding the right balance of resources to use that's tricky. That's where good planning is important (see previous page).

Office Layout

The layout of an office can affect how well staff do their jobs.
If the layout doesn't suit the type of work the business does, it can lead to problems.

There are Two Main Types of Office Layout

Open-Plan Offices

1) An open-plan office is one large space containing many desks.
2) Open-plan offices can improve communication, since staff sit together. They also make it easier to supervise staff (managers often work in the same office).
3) But open-plan offices can be noisy, which affects concentration. It also means there's little privacy — everyone might be able to hear you on the phone.

Cellular Offices

1) Cellular offices are smaller rooms with solid walls. These rooms are used by a few workers or just one person.
2) Cellular offices give staff quiet and privacy to do their work. They can often be locked to protect valuables or confidential documents.
3) A disadvantage of a cellular office layout is that it can make supervision of junior staff more difficult. It can also result in less communication between staff.

- The nature of the tasks staff carry out affects the layout of the office.
- For example, open-plan offices are often used in call centres (though these are sometimes divided up using temporary partitions into separate cubicles). This is efficient because lots of operators can be fitted into the space.
- But if employees need privacy for confidential meetings (e.g. between lawyers and their clients), then cellular offices are more suitable.
- These two basic layouts can be combined. For example, some offices have a large open-plan space surrounded by cellular rooms. This is useful if only a few employees (e.g. managers) need the privacy of a private office.

Ergonomic Design Makes Staff More Comfortable

Businesses need to take care of their employees. Partly because there are laws that say they have to (p44). But partly because it's good business — people who are permanently uncomfortable won't be very efficient.

1) Office equipment (e.g. chairs, desks and keyboards) can be ergonomically designed — this means they're designed to be comfortable, and easy to use. For example, some office chairs can be adjusted to suit the needs of different users.
2) Poorly-designed equipment can lead to back pain, eye strain and repetitive strain injury. Health and Safety laws require businesses to minimise the risk of these injuries — using ergonomically-designed equipment can help them to do this.

This page has been designed to make revision more comfortable...

If you want people to work effectively for 40 hours a week, they'll need to be comfortable. Managers also need to get the right balance between supervising staff and trusting them to work. Cover the page and write a mini-essay about different office layouts and office equipment. Then check you didn't forget anything.

Warm-up and Worked Exam Questions

Warm-up Questions

1) What does "prioritising" a task mean?
2) "Efficiency doesn't just mean spending as little money as possible, or saving as much time as possible." Explain whether or not this is true.
3) Explain the link between efficiency and planning.
4) How is efficiency linked to the environment?
5) Would you recommend an open-plan office or cellular offices for the solicitors in a legal firm? Explain.

Worked Exam Question

For the second and last time in this section, read through the sample exam answers below, and then try the question on the next page yourself. You'll find the answers in the back of the book.

1 The directors of Negotia plc have decided that it is time to change their office layout from a cellular arrangement to an open-plan design.

a) What is meant by the term "open-plan office"?

An open-plan office is one large space that contains many desks. ✔ [1 mark]
There are no barriers separating people working in the office. ✔ [1 mark]

(2 marks)

b) Describe the advantages and disadvantages of an open-plan office layout.

In an open-plan office, communication can be easier ✔ [1 mark] *because of the lack of barriers between people.* ✔ [1 mark] *This also makes it easier for managers to supervise staff as they work in the same office.* ✔ [1 mark] *However, the office can be noisy,* ✔ [1 mark] *which can affect concentration* ✔ [1 mark] *and there is little privacy.* ✔ [1 mark]

(6 marks)

c) The directors believe Health and Safety laws may affect how they equip the office. They decide to seek advice from a specialist in ergonomic office design.

(i) What is meant by "ergonomically designed"?

Ergonomically designed equipment is designed to be comfortable ✔ [1 mark] *and easy for a person to use* ✔ [1 mark] *while performing a particular task.*

(2 marks)

(ii) Explain how ergonomically designed equipment can make a company's employees work more efficiently, and so increase profits for a company.

Employees who are uncomfortable or in pain ✔ [1 mark] *because of unsuitable equipment are unlikely to be efficient.* ✔ [1 mark] *Inefficient employees effectively cost a company money,* ✔ [1 mark] *since they take longer to perform tasks,* ✔ [1 mark] *so providing comfortable equipment can increase a company's profits.* ✔ [1 mark]

(5 marks)

Exam Questions

1 Read **Item A** and then answer the questions that follow.

Item A

Sue is a manager in a rapidly growing company. The director of the company feels the firm's current building is too large, and wants Sue to investigate the advantages and disadvantages of relocating to different premises. He has suggested a nearby office building that is much smaller than the firm's current premises. However, it is old and not very energy efficient.

a) Explain what is meant by the term "efficiency".

....

....

(2 marks)

b) Explain why a building that is too large for a firm's needs can be inefficient.

....

....

(2 marks)

c) Explain why Sue should plan her investigation carefully.

....

....

....

(3 marks)

d) Suggest the processes and stages Sue should go through when planning her investigation.

....

....

....

....

(Continue your answer on a separate piece of paper) *(8 marks)*

e) Would you recommend that Sue's company move to the building suggested by the director? Explain your answer.

....

....

....

....

....

(Continue your answer on a separate piece of paper) *(9 marks)*

Revision Summary for Section Three

Organisational structure, admin, planning, office layout... all things that businesses have to get right if they want to succeed and be as efficient as they can possibly be.

Reading about these things is all very well, but what you really need is some revision questions. Try the ones below — if you get any wrong, read up on the bits you didn't remember and try again.

1) Explain the role of each of the following types of staff in a business.
   a) Directors b) Managers c) Supervisors d) Operatives
2) Give one advantage that a flat hierarchy has over a tall hierarchy.
   Explain one possible disadvantage of a flat hierarchy.
3) Explain what a matrix structure is, and give one advantage and disadvantage of this structure.
4) Explain one advantage of using a circular chart to show a firm's structure.
5) Explain the four main activities involved in business administration.
6) How can good administration help businesses to be efficient?
7) What records would a business need in order to calculate each of these?
   a) Value Added Tax (VAT) b) Income Tax c) Corporation Tax
8) Give some examples of routine tasks in a business. Which type of staff usually does routine tasks?
9) Explain why non-routine tasks are usually performed by higher-ranking staff than routine tasks.
10) What's the difference between routine and non-routine decisions?
    Which type of staff are most likely to make each type of decision?
11) Give one reason why it's important to plan for a business meeting.
12) Explain three problems that can be caused by poor planning.
13) Describe five processes that may be involved in planning a business project.
14) What does it mean for a business to be efficient?
15) Explain how the size of business premises can affect a firm's efficiency.
16) Give two reasons why businesses are being encouraged to use fossil fuels more efficiently.
17) Give three ways that businesses can use materials more efficiently.
    Give two benefits that this can have for the business.
18) What's the difference between open-plan offices and cellular offices?
    Give one advantage and one disadvantage of each type.
19) What does it mean for office equipment to be ergonomically designed?
20) Why might a firm want to provide ergonomically-designed equipment to its staff?

Patterns of Work

You need to know about different types of contract of employment.
To be more specific, you need to know about permanent, temporary, part-time and full-time work.

Employment Can be **Full Time** or **Part Time**...

1) Working full time usually means around 35-40 hours a week.
   Part-time staff work 'less than a full working week' — usually between 10-30 hours per week.
2) Some people prefer to have a full-time job, or need to work full time for financial reasons.
   Other people choose to work part time, so they can spend more time with family or on other interests.
   Or they may only be able to work part time because of other commitments.
   Many businesses are now more flexible about letting staff work around their family lives (see p43).
3) There are pros and cons for businesses. Full-time staff are good if there's enough work for them to do.
   But employing staff part time can make sense if a business is only really busy at certain periods.

- In 1997, the law was changed to give part-time and full-time workers equal employment rights. (Before then, part-time workers weren't entitled to all the benefits that full-time workers were.)
- As a result, employees in the UK are now more willing to take on part-time positions.

...and **Permanent** or **Temporary**

1) A permanent contract of employment has no end date. The person stays at the firm unless:
   (i) they choose to leave, (ii) they're dismissed for misconduct, (iii) their job is made redundant.
2) A temporary contract is for a fixed period (e.g. six months, one year, or whatever).
   At the end of the period, the contract can be renewed, or the person can leave the company.
3) Temporary contracts can make it easier for the firm to employ people with particular skills for a particular period (without the commitment of a permanent contract). This can make it easier to adjust the number of staff employed according to the circumstances of the business.
4) The main problem for temporary workers is that they often have a less stable income.
   This can make it more difficult to get loans or a mortgage.

All Employees Have a **Contract of Employment**

All employees have a contract of employment — a legal agreement between the employee and the employer. This can be verbal or written. However, most employers must give employees the following information in writing within two months of starting work:

- the job title (or a brief job description)
- the starting date of the employment (and the end date for a temporary employee)
- the hours of work, the starting pay and the regular date of payment
- where the employee will be working
- the holiday the employee's entitled to
- details of sickness pay and any company pension scheme
- information about disciplinary procedures
- the length of notice the employee has to give if they want to leave

Different types of contract have their pros and cons...

All employees have a contract of employment — it doesn't matter if they're full-time, part-time, permanent, temporary, or whatever. Learn what these different terms mean, as well as their pros and cons for the business and the employees. Then learn all those bits of information that employers must give all new employees in writing.

Recruitment — Job Analysis

Recruitment is about appointing the best person to do the job. A business needs to understand what the job will involve so that it can decide what the right person will be like.

The *Job Description* Says What the Job Involves

1) The job description is a written description of what the job consists of. It includes the formal title of the job, its main purpose, its main duties and any occasional duties.
2) It also includes details of who the job holder will report to and whether they're responsible for managing other staff. It may include some performance targets.
3) Without a job description it would be impossible to write the person specification...

The Necks Directory Ltd. — Job Description
Job Title: Full-time Vampire Operative.
Reports to: Vampire Team Leader.
Responsible for: Trainee Vampire Operatives.
Main purpose of job: To climb through people's windows at night and suck their nourishing blood.
Duties and Responsibilities:
— to bite the necks of humans while they sleep;
— to wear a large black cape and cackle menacingly;
— to meet neck-biting targets set by Vampire Team Leader.

The *Person Specification* Describes the Ideal Person

Vampire Operative — Person Specification
Essential: 5 GCSEs including Business Studies, NVQ Anatomy Level 3.
Desirable: Two years of vampiring experience.
Skills: Ability to climb through windows, bite necks, turn into a bat etc. Good communication skills.
Attitudes: Fear of daylight, willingness to work unsocial hours, must enjoy meeting new people.

1) The person specification lists the qualifications, experience, skills and personal qualities needed for the job.
2) They are sometimes divided into:
   - essential criteria — things the candidate must have, and
   - desirable criteria — things the candidate would ideally have.

See next page for more about skills and attitudes.

The Job Can Be Advertised *Internally* or *Externally*

1) The purpose of a job advert is to get as many suitable people as possible to apply for the job.
2) The advert should describe the job and the skills required. It will often state what the pay is, and what training and other benefits are offered. It must also explain how the person should apply for the job.
3) The firm can decide to advertise the job internally or externally:

Internal Advertising

- When advertising internally, adverts are usually put up on noticeboards or sent round to staff.
- It's much cheaper, the post can be filled more quickly, and the candidates will already know a lot about the firm.
- On the downside, there will be no 'new blood' or ideas, and the promotion will leave a vacancy to fill.

External Advertising

- If the job is advertised externally, the advert will be seen by more people.
- Possible locations include local and national newspapers, job centres, trade journals and employment agencies.
- Advertising in the national press is expensive, so firms may only do that for specialist jobs.
- The firm may also advertise the job on their own website, or on the websites of agencies.

The aim of the job advert is to get the best people to apply...

Although it can sometimes be tricky to find that person, having a clear job description and person specification can help a firm find the best candidates. The firm also has to decide where to advertise the job — internally or externally. Cover the page, and write down the benefits and drawbacks of both. Check you got them all.

Recruitment — The Selection Process

The selection process happens after the job has been advertised. All the candidates' applications are looked at and employers create a short list of the people they want to interview in person. Here's how it's done...

Candidates Apply with a **Written Application**...

A written application helps firms to decide which candidates match the person specification.

1) A curriculum vitae (CV) (p69) is a summary of a person's personal details, skills, qualifications, experience and interests. It's designed to give the firm the basic facts. Almost all employers ask for a CV.
2) An application form is designed by the firm and filled in by the applicant. It gives the firm the information it wants — and nothing else. This makes it easier to compare applications.
3) Most businesses now accept electronic versions of written applications. Some even have online application forms.

Some firms also ask for a letter of application — these allow candidates to choose what they want to say. They're more personal, but harder to compare.

...Which Helps the Firm to Make a **Short List**

Candidates are usually short-listed in the following way:

1) Each candidate's application is read — sometimes by more than one person.
2) The application is compared to the job description and person specification. Any essential or desirable characteristics met by the candidate are recorded.
   - A good application will be to the point and refer to skills and qualities mentioned in the job description and person specification.
   - A bad application might be waffly, inaccurate, not contain enough information or be poorly written.
3) The employers also look for a balance of skills and attitudes:

SKILLS are things a person has learnt (such as being able to program a computer).
ATTITUDES are personal qualities a person has (such as being able to work in a team).

A highly skilled person should be good at technical tasks. But they may cause problems for other reasons — e.g. not cooperating with other staff or demanding higher pay.

A candidate with a good attitude may fit in better. But they might need extra skills training.

4) The candidates who seem to have the right qualities, skills and attitudes to do the job are included on a short list. These people are usually then invited to an interview.

Employers **Meet** Short-Listed Candidates in **Interviews**

1) Written applications are great for narrowing down a list of job candidates. But people can exaggerate in CVs and application forms, and they don't give much idea of what the candidate is like in person. That's why face-to-face interviews are really important when recruiting new staff.
2) Interviews are used to assess a candidate's confidence, their social and verbal skills, and whether they'll be compatible with existing workers. Businesses also want to find out about the candidate's general attitude.
3) Some people think that interviews are not a good way to select — people don't behave naturally in a formal interview. The skills needed to be good at interview are often different from the skills needed to do the job.

Have the right attitude and apply yourself to revising this page...

In your exam, you might be asked to read some applications and judge how suitable each candidate would be for a job. Don't panic — just remember to keep the job description and person specification in mind.

Employment Law

This page is crammed full of facts about the law. Make sure you know what each law says, and understand the impact it has on employers.

1 Contracts of Employment and the Minimum Wage

1) Within two months of starting work, most employees must be told in writing information about pay, hours they're expected to work, holidays, pension schemes, and so on (see p34 for more information).
   This is covered by the Employment Rights Act 1996.
2) All staff should also have a copy of the firm's discipline procedure. This explains which offences would lead to a warning, and which would lead to dismissal.
   This is covered by the Employment Act 2002.
3) The Government sets a national minimum wage for all workers, depending on their age. This means businesses can't cut costs on their wage bills by paying workers less than the legal minimum.

2 Anti-Discrimination Laws

1) Employers must not discriminate against employees or candidates for employment on the basis of:
   - gender,
   - ethnicity,
   - disabilities,
   - age,
   - sexual orientation,
   - religion.

Covered by: **gender**: Sex Discrimination Act 1975,
ethnicity: Race Relations Act 1976,
disabilities: Disability Discrimination Act 2005,
age, **sexual orientation** and **religion**: Employment Equality Regulations.

2) For example, employers might need to adapt the workplace for people with disabilities (e.g. install adapted toilets). And women must be paid the same as men doing the same job for the same employer.

3 Leaving Employment

1) Employees are also protected against unfair dismissal. This means that firms need a good reason for dismissing staff.
   This is covered by the Employment Act 2002.
2) This could be because they're incompetent, or are guilty of gross misconduct.
3) Employees can only be made redundant if the job they're employed to do no longer exists (e.g. if machines can now do the same job). The firm cannot re-advertise a redundant job.
4) Employees who think they have been unfairly dismissed or made redundant can usually appeal to an employment tribunal. The tribunal can award compensation or reinstate the employee.

All These Laws Aim to Give Employees a **Fair Deal**

1) All the laws on this page are designed to make sure that staff are treated fairly.
2) These laws can cause problems for businesses. For example, it can be expensive and time consuming to keep up to date with new legislation. And firms may also have to go through costly court cases to prove that they've behaved legally (and be fined if they haven't).
3) But treating staff fairly means they'll be happier and better motivated. They'll also be more likely to stay with the firm for longer (which saves money on recruiting and training new staff).

Don't discriminate — learn about all these laws...

Staying within the law is expensive — keeping up to date with new laws costs money and creates a lot of paperwork. Businesses have to do it though — if they don't, they can be fined or the owners sent to prison.

Warm-up and Worked Exam Questions

Warm-up Questions

1) Describe what's meant by "part-time" work.
2) What *exactly* is meant by a contract of employment being "permanent"?
3) Describe the advantages of advertising a job externally. And the disadvantages.
4) Describe one of the disadvantages of getting job applicants to write a letter of application.
5) Give two grounds that a firm can legally use to dismiss an employee.
6) What can an employee who feels they've been unfairly dismissed do? What can this achieve?

Worked Exam Questions

You know the drill by now. Work through these examples, then try the questions on page 39.

1 When Securepath Stores Ltd was taken over by Buy-Right Supermarkets plc, all Securepath employees were invited to apply for jobs in the new Buy-Right stores. Jobs were also advertised in the local press.

a) Before writing the job advertisement, the Human Resources Manager created a person specification.
Describe what is meant by the term "person specification".

A person specification describes the ideal person ✔[1 mark] for a job. It describes the qualifications, experience and personal qualities a candidate should have. ✔[1 mark]

(2 marks)

b) Suggest the information that should be included in the local press advertisements.

Adverts should describe the jobs available, ✔[1 mark] as well as the skills, qualifications and personal qualities required. ✔[1 mark] Also essential is how and where to apply for the jobs. ✔[1 mark] Rates of pay, training and other benefits offered could also be included. ✔[1 mark]

(4 marks)

c) State **two** advantages for Buy-Right of recruiting old Securepath employees.

Recruiting would be cheaper ✔[1 mark] and the workers would already know the job, ✔[1 mark] so training could be done more quickly.

(2 marks)

d) It is illegal to use certain personal characteristics to discriminate between applicants.
State **three** factors that Buy-Right **must not** consider when assessing applications.

1. *gender* ✔[1 mark]
2. *ethnicity* ✔[1 mark]
3. *age* ✔[1 mark]

You could also put "disabilities", "sexual orientation" or "religion".

(3 marks)

Exam Questions

1 Read **Item B** and then answer the questions that follow.

Item B

Riveted is an engineering firm. They are currently recruiting new operatives to their manufacturing department. Applicants must first send in a copy of their CV.
The department manager then makes a shortlist of people to interview. Depending on their skills and attitudes, she may then decide to offer the job to one of the candidates.

a) What is meant by the term "CV"?

....

....

....

(3 marks)

b) Describe the difference between a "skill" and an "attitude".

....

....

(2 marks)

c) Explain the advantages of using interviews during the recruitment process.

....

....

....

(3 marks)

d) Describe two disadvantages of relying on interviews when assessing a candidate for a job.

....

....

(2 marks)

e) Evaluate the relative importance of skills and attitudes when deciding who is most suitable for a particular job.

....

....

....

....

....

(6 marks)

Staff Training

Training is the main way that a firm invests in its employees. This page covers three basic types of training. You need to be able to judge which type would be most suitable in a given situation.

① *Induction Training is for New Staff*

1) Induction training introduces the new employee to their workplace, and should help to make the new employee feel welcome.
2) It includes introducing them to their fellow workers and advising them of company rules — including health and safety rules. They should also be given a tour of the site so they don't get lost. It may also include initial training on how to do their new job.

② *On-the-Job Training is Learning by Doing*

1) This is the most common form of training. The employee learns to do their job better by being shown how to do it, and then practising. It's also sometimes called internal training (as it's handled within the business).
2) It's cost-effective for the employer because the employee works and learns at the same time.
3) A problem is that the training is often given by colleagues — so bad working practices can be passed on.

③ *Off-the-Job Training Can be Internal or External*

1) Off-the-job training happens when staff learn away from their workplace.
2) If the firm has its own training department, it can still be done internally. Training given by other organisations (e.g. college courses) is called external training.
3) It's more expensive than on-the-job training, and sometimes not as directly related to the actual job. But it's often higher quality because it's taught by people who are better qualified to train others.
4) It's best used when introducing new skills or training people for promotion.

Training Benefits Both the Employer and the Employee

Benefits of training to employers

1) Trained staff should be better at their jobs, which should mean they're more efficient and productive.
2) Training can give staff the skills to do new jobs within the company. This may save time and money on advertising the jobs externally.
3) Training can help staff stay up to date with changes in the business.
4) Staff may feel like they're progressing in the firm, which might make them stay with the firm for longer (which will save on recruitment costs).

Benefits of training to employees

1) Employees with up-to-date knowledge and skills should be able to do their jobs better with fewer problems — which often increases job satisfaction and motivation.
2) Over time, gaining new skills may mean that they can be promoted to jobs with better pay and more responsibility.
3) They may also be able to get better jobs with other businesses. Staff can take advantage of training to help them meet their career ambitions.

Get on with the job of revising this page about training...

The different types of training on this page are all used for slightly different purposes. But the end result should be the same for them all — well trained staff who are more motivated and productive.

Financial Rewards

Most businesses pay their employees for their work. But these financial rewards can be worked out in different ways. You might need to do some pay calculations in the exam, but they won't be too bad, honest.

If People Do **More Work** Their **Wages Increase...**

Wages are paid weekly or monthly — usually to manual workers. Wages are calculated in one of two ways:

TIME RATE pays workers by the hour.

- If a painter is paid £6 per hour and works 40 hours in a week, their week's wage will be £6 × 40 = £240.
- Time rate encourages people to work long hours — the problem is they also have an incentive to work slowly.
- Time rate is best for jobs where measuring a worker's output is difficult — e.g. a bus driver.

PIECE RATE is often used if a worker's output can be measured.

- Say a worker who sews sleeves onto shirts is paid a piece rate of 10p per sleeve. If they sew 2000 sleeves per week, their weekly wage will be £0.10 × 2000 = £200.
- Piece rate encourages people to work quickly — this may be a problem if they work so fast that quality starts to suffer.

Here's the formula for calculating total wages using time rate and piece rate:

Total wage = rate x amount of work done

...But a **Salary** Stays the **Same**

1) A salary is a fixed amount paid every month. Salaries are usually paid to office staff and management who don't directly help to make the product. A salary of £24,000 per year means you're paid £24,000 ÷ 12 months = £2000 per month.
2) The advantage of a salary is that the business and workers both know exactly how much the pay will be.
3) A disadvantage is that it doesn't link pay directly to performance, so it doesn't encourage employees to work harder to earn more money.

Employers Can Give Staff **Extra** Payments

1) Some employers pay staff an overtime rate if they work extra hours on top of their normal working week. E.g. a painter who's normally paid £6 an hour might be paid £9 an hour to work at the weekend.
2) With performance-related pay the amount employees earn depends on how well they work.
    - Commission is paid to sales staff. They earn a small basic salary and then earn more money for every item they sell.
    - A bonus is a lump sum added to pay, usually once a year. It's paid if the worker has met their performance targets.
3) Some businesses make payments into a pension scheme for employees. Others offer a profit sharing scheme — where a percentage of the company's profits is divided up between employees, for example.

Different methods of payment give workers different incentives...

The way workers are paid affects their incentives — that's really important. So time-rates "encourage" (i.e. provide an incentive for) slow work, piece-rates encourage fast work, and so on. Work out what kind of incentives are provided by commission, and what kinds of jobs commission is suitable/unsuitable for. Do the same for overtime payments. What are the pros and cons of each? Incentives... they're really important — don't forget that.

Financial Rewards

Rates of pay can <u>change</u>. Also, money is usually <u>deducted</u> (taken away) from people's pay before they're paid. You might need to do some pay calculations in your exam — so read this page very carefully.

Changes in Pay are Sometimes Worked Out as Percentages

1) <u>Gross pay</u> is the amount of money an employee is paid — their wage or salary. The amount that an employee gets to <u>keep</u> after <u>deductions</u> (e.g. taxes and pension contributions) is called <u>net pay</u>.
2) Rates of pay can change over time. People may be given <u>pay rises</u>, or paid extra to work <u>overtime</u>. Some deductions and changes in pay are calculated as <u>percentages</u> of gross pay.

Example 1

An employee earns a gross salary of £1600 per month. She pays 3% of her gross salary into a pension fund. How much does she pay into her pension each month?

You need to work out 3% of £1600.

$$1\% \text{ of } £1600 = \frac{£1600}{100} = £16$$

So 3% of £1600 = £16 x 3 = <u>£48 per month</u>

Example 2

A worker earns a time-rate wage of £8 per hour. If he is given a 5% pay rise, calculate his new hourly wage.

Here, you need to <u>add</u> 5% to the old wage.

$$5\% \text{ of } £8 = \frac{£8}{100} \times 5 = £0.40$$

So the new hourly wage is £8 + £0.40 = <u>£8.40 per hour</u>

Fringe Benefits are Extra Perks Given to Employees

<u>Fringe benefits</u> are sometimes given to staff <u>in addition</u> to their pay. For example...

Staff Discounts Many businesses offer their staff <u>money off</u> their own products. This <u>saves money</u> for the staff, and <u>discourages</u> them from buying from <u>competing companies</u>.

Employee Pensions The firm pays a fixed amount into the employee's <u>pension account</u> each month. This money is <u>saved up</u> over the years, ready to be used when the employee <u>retires</u>.

Private Medical Insurance The firm pays for medical <u>insurance policies</u> for its staff. This means that employees can <u>claim back money</u> if they need to pay for private medical treatment.

Life Insurance This provides <u>financial payments</u> to an employee's family if he or she <u>dies</u> while working for the firm. Again, the company <u>pays</u> for the insurance policy.

Gym Membership Or free use of other <u>leisure facilities</u>.

Daily Meal Allowance This could mean the employee is <u>compensated</u> for food they've bought while travelling, say. Or it could be free food in a <u>staff canteen</u>.

Praise Most staff like it when their boss says something <u>nice</u> about them. And it's <u>free</u>.

The reward for revision — better exam marks...

In your exam, you might get asked to work out some changes in pay. If you know how the calculations work, then these are <u>easy marks</u>. So make sure you understand the two examples at the top of the page.

Modern Working Practices

Flexible working has become quite widespread in recent years. 'Flexible' means any pattern of work that doesn't follow the normal '35-hours-a-week in an office' kind of thing.

Flexitime *Means Employees Can* ***Vary*** *Their Hours*

1) Employers are sometimes flexible about when employees work.
2) Some employers require their staff to work during core hours each week. But outside these core hours, they can work the rest of their weekly hours when they choose. This is known as flexitime working.
3) This can be good for employees as it gives them a greater sense of control over their working week.
4) But employers have to monitor work more closely to make sure that staff are still producing the required quantity and quality of work.
5) Part-time work (see p34) is also a form of flexible working.

Work in Different Places — ***Teleworking*** *and* ***Hot-Desking***

Employers are sometimes flexible about where their employees work (as well as when they work).

1) Teleworking is when people work away from their normal workplace — usually from home. Internet technology makes it possible for employees to transfer files and communicate easily from anywhere in the world. The advantage is that people don't have to travel into an office every day.
2) Hot-desking is when employees don't have their own special desks in an office. Instead, they sit at any free desk in an office — sometimes in a work centre used by more than one organisation.
3) Teleworking and hot-desking reduce the amount of office space needed by an employer, reducing costs. But it can make it harder to keep information secret, since data is regularly transferred away from a firm's own network into the 'outside world' (where it's harder to maintain security).
4) Teleworking means employees spend less time commuting and can fit their work more easily around home life. But it can be lonely, as there is less personal contact with colleagues. Hot-desking can also be stressful — never knowing where you're going to be working next.

Teleconferencing *Links People in* ***Different Places***

1) Teleconferencing uses ICT to connect people in different locations using sound and/or video.
2) Locations are connected by a telecommunications system (e.g. a phone line, an internet connection, or a satellite link) so that several people can communicate. Examples of teleconferencing include:
   - Audio conferencing — this is a bit like having a telephone conversation, only with more people. Everyone can hear what the others are saying, but they can't see each other.
   - Video conferencing — this provides a video feed between the locations. Everyone can see and hear the others on monitors.
3) Teleconferencing saves time and money on travelling to a meeting place — people can hold meetings without leaving their offices.

There's more about teleconferencing on p75.

Flexible working has become much more common in recent years...

A lot of office workers still work 9 till 5 every day, but modern ICT makes it possible to do things differently. Staff may enjoy having more flexibility, but it doesn't necessarily suit everyone. As usual, learn it all.

Health and Safety at Work

There are laws to help ensure people don't get ill or injured at work.
The laws make health and safety the responsibility of both the employer and employees.

Employers Need to Follow **Health and Safety Legislation**

The Health and Safety at Work Act 1974 means everyone is responsible for health and safety.

Businesses have to:

- assess the risks involved in a job
- take precautions to minimise these risks
- provide protective clothing and equipment, and make sure it is well maintained
- provide any training needed to do a job safely
- provide toilets, drinking water and first-aid facilities
- record workplace injuries in an accident book

Employees have to:

- act responsibly, and take care of their and other people's safety
- carry out tasks as they've been trained to do
- report dangerous practices

This is to help identify hazards and prevent future accidents.

Computer Use can Cause **Health Problems**

Computers look pretty safe, but they can cause various health problems.

1) Repetitive strain injury (RSI) means aches, pains and muscle or tendon damage resulting from overuse of a keyboard or mouse. And circulation, fitness and back problems might result from sitting all day in front of a computer. These are long-term health problems.
2) Spending too long in front of a computer screen can cause eye strain and headaches. The Display Screen Equipment Regulations 1992 set out rules concerning the use of computers.

Employers must:

- Analyse workstations and reduce risks.
- Plan work routines so that employees can take periodic breaks from using a computer.
- Provide health and safety training and information.
- Provide free eye-tests to all staff who regularly use computers as part of their job.

Employers and **Employees** Have Responsibilities

1) Employers should allow employees to take regular breaks from computer work. Employees should use these breaks to walk around and exercise their fingers and hands.
2) Employers have a responsibility to provide suitable equipment, e.g. desks, chairs, keyboards and screens. (A 'suitable' screen, for example, would allow staff to adjust its brightness and position.)
3) Employers also have to provide training in how to use this equipment (e.g. how to arrange it properly, how to sit without straining your back). Employees then need to follow this training.
4) Employers and employees have to take precautions to reduce risks to everyone's safety. For example, they should make sure electrical cables aren't in places where people can trip over them.

Health and Safety laws are all about looking after workers...

Employers and employees need to be aware of health and safety. Draw a table with the problems ICT can cause in one column and the solutions in another column. Careful with that pen, though — it looks sharp.

Warm-up and Worked Exam Questions

Warm-up Questions

1) What is "induction training"?
2) Write down a formula for working out a person's total wage if you know their pay rate and the amount of work they've done.
3) What is a fringe benefit?
4) Give one advantage and one disadvantage of hot-desking.
5) According to the Health and Safety at Work Act (1974), who is responsible for health and safety at work?

Worked Exam Questions

There's plenty to learn in this section — loads of theories and definitions. You have to make sure you can apply them all to the real world, though, because that's what you'll have to do in the exam.

1 GeeWhizzz is a computer retailer with branches nationwide. Each shop has a manager and a number of sales assistants. Shop managers are paid a salary. Sales assistants receive a weekly wage worked out using a time-rate of £6.20 per hour.

a) State one difference between a salary and a wage.

A salary is a fixed payment, ✔[1 mark] *but a wage can change depending upon how much work is done.* ✔[1 mark]

(2 marks)

b) Calculate how much a full-time member of the sales staff would earn in one week if they worked 37 hours.

Total wage = hourly wage x number of hours worked ✔[1 mark]

= £6.20 per hour x 37 hours = £229.40 ✔[1 mark]

(2 marks)

2 KillAllPests plc uses various training methods for its workforce of pest control operatives.

a) Distinguish between on-the-job training and off-the-job training at KillAllPests plc.

On-the-job training is learning to do the work by being shown how, and then practising ✔[1 mark] *e.g. by accompanying existing KillAllPests employees as they work.* ✔[1 mark] *Off-the-job training means learning away from the workplace,* ✔[1 mark] *e.g. attending courses on health and safety.* ✔[1 mark]

Make sure you apply your answer to KillAllPests plc.

(4 marks)

b) State one problem associated with each type of training.

On-the-job training is often taught by a colleague, so bad habits can be passed on. ✔[1 mark] *Off-the-job training can sometimes be too general, and not linked directly to the job the employee will be doing.* ✔[1 mark]

It's usually more expensive as well.

(2 marks)

Exam Questions

1 Read **Item A** and then answer the questions that follow.

Item A

Heath Insurance Services is a medium-sized business that employs several office staff. The office staff are currently paid the national minimum wage. The board of directors has noticed that profits are falling.
Several of the office staff say that their motivation is at a very low level.

a) One director suggests that all the office staff should undertake some training.
Explain **two** benefits to *Heath Insurance Services* of training their employees.

....

....

....

....

(4 marks)

b) A different director thinks that introducing teleworking might increase profits.
Explain how teleworking might lead to higher profits.

....

....

....

(3 marks)

c) Discuss the potential risks of introducing teleworking.

....

....

....

....

(4 marks)

d) The directors decide they should pay their staff more in an effort to increase their motivation. One director thinks the firm should increase wages. Another thinks it would be better to introduce a bonus scheme.

Recommend which method the firm should use to increase the motivation of its office workers. Explain your answer.

....

....

(Continue your answer on a separate piece of paper) *(8 marks)*

Revision Summary for Section Four

Human resources aren't like other resources. Humans have feelings, so they don't like working 100 hours a week in a freezing cold box with no lights and no-one to talk to. Businesses have to treat their employees reasonably well, which can create extra costs — but it's nice when everybody's happy.
Speaking of happiness, here are some questions. Don't come out of your box till you've answered them all.

1) Why might some people choose to work part time? Why might other people need to work full time?
2) Why might a business want to employ workers on temporary contracts?
3) Describe one problem that temporary contracts cause for employees.
4) List eight bits of information that should be included in a contract of employment.
5) What's the main purpose of a job description? What information should it contain?
6) Explain the difference between a job description and a person specification.
7) What information should a job advert include?
8) Give three advantages and two disadvantages of advertising a job internally.
9) Describe the main features of CVs and application forms.
10) What's the difference between skills and attitudes?
11) Give a reason why most firms ask short-listed candidates to an interview.
12) Explain the drawbacks of interviews as a way of selecting candidates.
13) What information is contained in a firm's discipline procedure?
14) It's illegal to discriminate against employees because of their sex.
    Give five other illegal grounds for discrimination.
15) Under what circumstances is it legal to make staff redundant?
16) Explain one problem that employment laws can make for a business.
17) What benefits can employment laws bring to a business?
18) When does induction training take place? What should it include?
19) Give one advantage and one disadvantage each of on-the-job training and off-the-job training.
20) Give four benefits that training staff has for employers.
    Now give three benefits that training can bring to employees.
21) What's the difference between a time rate and a piece rate?
    What kind of work is each rate best suited to?
22) A shop assistant is paid a time rate of £7 per hour. He works 35 hours per week.
    Calculate his weekly wage.
23) Explain the difference between a commission and a bonus.
24) A factory worker is paid a piece rate for packing boxes. Last week, she earned £225.
    This week, she packed 8% more boxes. How much will she earn for this week?
25) Describe seven types of fringe benefit.
26) Describe how flexitime works, and give one advantage that it has for employees.
27) Explain what teleworking and hot-desking are.
28) Give one advantage and one disadvantage of teleworking to: a) Employers b) Employees
29) Give one advantage of teleconferencing.
30) Give three things that employers can do and three things that employees can do
    to reduce health and safety risks at work.
31) Explain three problems that can be caused by using computers for long periods of time.
32) Give a brief description of what employers must do according to
    the Display Screen Equipment Regulations 1992.

22. £245
24. £243

Data Processing Systems

First off in this Section is a page about data-processing systems.

Businesses Need to Collect and Process **Data**

1) Business data can come from all sorts of sources.
2) Primary data is collected first-hand by the business itself.
   Secondary data is information that's been collected by someone outside the firm.
3) But whatever the source, data needs to be relevant and accurate.

See p15 for more about primary and secondary research.

Data Systems Can be **Paper-Based** or **Computer-Based**

Data is stored, processed and communicated using a data system.
Two very important things to know about any data system are the purpose and the medium.

1. PURPOSE What a data system needs to do. You need to know this before you can design or evaluate a data system.

2. MEDIUM Data systems can be paper-based or computer-based.

You need to know the pros and cons of both paper-based and computer-based systems.

PAPER-BASED SYSTEMS
- These are useful when hard copies (i.e. paper versions) of documents are needed.
- These systems don't need computer equipment, and staff won't need computer training.
- But paper documents can take up a lot of storage space.
- And paper-based systems don't allow for easy data processing — it has to be done by hand.

COMPUTER-BASED SYSTEMS
- These require less storage space — a single PC can store as much data as many stacks of paper.
  And it's easy to create backup copies of electronic files.
- Data can be processed quickly and accurately.
  Files can also be viewed and changed on-screen, so it's easier to edit documents.
- Computers can be linked together in networks. This makes it easy to share data.
  But it can also mean that confidential data needs to be very carefully protected (see p57).

Most of this section is about computer-based data systems. They're made up of hardware and software.

3. HARDWARE Hardware means the bits of kit you can actually touch (e.g. keyboards, printers and so on).

Most of this section is all about hardware and software.

4. SOFTWARE Software means the programs used on the computer — the operating system (e.g. Windows® or Linux) and applications (e.g. word processors, spreadsheets).

All businesses rely on data these days...

A data-processing system is the methods and equipment a business uses to deal with information.
Computer-based systems are now most common, but keeping paper copies is still important to many firms.
A lot of the time the purpose of your data system will involve communicating information from one person or place to another — there's a lot more about communication in Section 6, so come back to this page and have another look once you've read that. For the moment, just get ready to see a load of hardware and software.

Computers and Input Devices

This is the first of a few pages all about hardware. First off, the computer itself.

Computers Can be **Desktop** or **Portable**

1) Desktop computers are relatively large and are designed to be used in a single place.
2) Laptops are smaller and portable. Netbooks are smaller still.
3) Handheld computers include Personal Digital Assistants (PDAs), e.g. Smartphones. They often have a touch-sensitive screen or a small keyboard. Most PDAs also include a mobile phone and internet access.
4) Computers can be connected together to form a network. This makes it possible for them to communicate with each other.
5) A network file server is a powerful computer that stores files users have made and 'runs' the network. Network workstations give users access to the network.

The choice of computer will depend on...

1) Where the computer will be used: desktop PCs are perfect for an office. But if you're going to be moving around, you'll need something more portable.
2) The tasks that need to be done: desktops with large monitors are ideal if you're going to be creating detailed documents all day long. A smartphone wouldn't be so good for this.
3) The cost: technology is expensive — firms have to live within their means.

Keyboards are the Most Common Input Devices

An input device is any hardware that's used to enter data onto a computer — a keyboard, for example.

1) Qwerty keyboards are based on the way typewriters were designed. The name comes from the first row of letters on the keyboard.
2) Keying in can be slow unless the user has been trained to type, but QWERTY keyboards are so standard that most people can use them pretty well.
3) Long-term keyboard use can sometimes cause repetitive strain injury (RSI) (see p44).

Concept keyboards and touch-sensitive screens

Concept keyboards are most often found in shops and restaurants. Each key has a symbol (or word) on it, representing a piece of data stored in the computer (e.g. a price).

They're great if you want to key in similar data over and over again. But they're only designed for inputting very limited types of information.

Touch-sensitive screens are a bit like concept keyboards — but instead of pressing a key, you touch the picture or word on the screen. Again, they're easy to use. And you can have different options each time the screen display changes. But they're more expensive than a keyboard.

A **Mouse** is Used for **Pointing** and **Clicking**

1) Mice tell the computer the direction and speed they're being pushed in — this is used to control a pointer.
2) A mouse can make using a computer much quicker than a keyboard alone, but, again, using a mouse for long periods can cause repetitive strain injury.

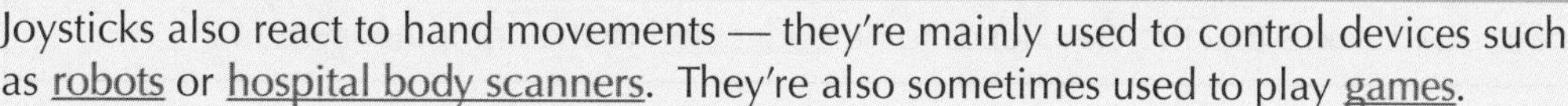
Joysticks also react to hand movements — they're mainly used to control devices such as robots or hospital body scanners. They're also sometimes used to play games.

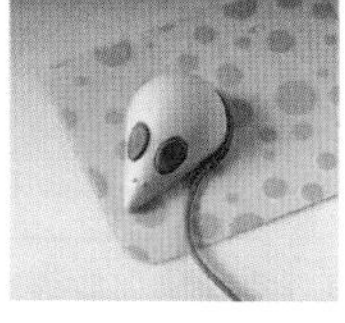

Most of this is probably familiar — but read it carefully just in case...

Providing a specialised input device is one way that an employer might be able to adapt the workplace to allow a person with a disability to work more easily (see the Disability Discrimination Act on p37). For example, a head-wand allows someone with limited mobility in their arms to use a keyboard.

More Input Devices

If you like input devices, then you'll love this page. It's got data capture forms on it too.

Digital Cameras and Scanners Convert Images into Data

1) Digital cameras capture real images and convert them into data which can then be uploaded onto a computer and edited.
2) Images can then be posted on the internet or sent as email attachments.
3) Scanners are similar to digital cameras, except they digitally capture images of paper documents.
4) OCR (Optical Character Recognition) software can then turn scanned text into text that can be edited using word-processing software.

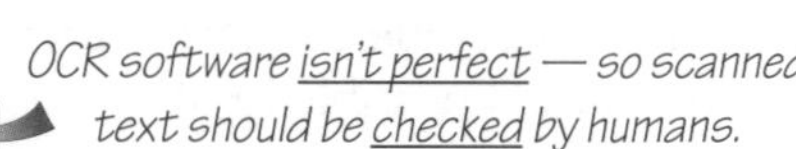

OCR software isn't perfect — so scanned text should be checked by humans.

> Many retailers, especially supermarkets, use EPOS (Electronic Point of Sale) devices such as laser scanners. These scanners read product bar codes which the store's computer system uses to automatically add up prices and adjust stock records.

5) Webcams are basically digital cameras. But they're usually used to take pictures (and record video footage) for streaming (showing) over the internet.

Microphones are an Increasingly Common Input Device

1) Microphones are used to capture sounds, which can be stored digitally or streamed over the internet.
2) They can also be used with voice-recognition systems, which convert speech into text or into commands for the computer. This means you can use dictation instead of having to type (but the systems aren't always 100% reliable).

This is another way that employers can adapt the workplace to allow people with certain disabilities to work more easily.

Data Capture Forms are Used to Collect Data

Data capture forms are also used for inputting data — but they're not hardware like the other input devices. They're paper forms, or computer software — data is written or typed onto them.

MANUAL DATA FORMS — the information is collected by hand, usually on paper.

- For example, a customer might write down information on an order form and post it to a business.
- The main drawback is that the information then needs to be entered into a computer by another person. This can lead to mistakes — e.g. by misreading the information on the form.

ELECTRONIC DATA FORMS enable users to enter information directly into the computer system.

- For example, a form on a website might enter data into a database (see page 105).
- The data is entered directly by the user (i.e. no one else has to read the form and type the data in) — this should mean fewer mistakes. Most systems also carry out validation checks — e.g. if there's information missing, you won't be able to move on to the next part.
- The main drawback is that the user needs to be connected to the computer system.

Read the page — don't assume you already know it all...

A page all about input devices — should be easy enough. But make sure you actually know it — don't just skim over it and assume you could answer any questions about this stuff just because you've used a digital camera.

Data Storage

Businesses can have huge amounts of data that need to be stored securely and accessed easily — often by lots of people. Luckily, there are plenty of options to choose from when it comes to data storage.

Storage Devices Can be *Internal* or *External*

1) There are two main types of computer storage devices...

- Internal devices are built into a computer (e.g. a hard disk).
- External devices can be removed from a computer (e.g. a USB stick).

2) Some smaller companies use their computer's hard drives (internal devices) as the main form of storage. This can work fine, but it's best to back up data regularly as well (see p52).
3) Larger firms tend to store information on a central server on their network so that all staff have access to it. This centrally held data can easily be backed up onto an external device.
4) Portable storage devices can be used for backing up, or transferring files between different computers.

Hard Disks are Usually *Internal* Storage Devices

1) Most computers have an internal hard disk.
2) Storage capacity of hard disks is usually measured in gigabytes (GB). One gigabyte is the same as 1024 megabytes (MB).
3) The storage capacity of hard disks gets larger all the time. But desktop computers generally have more storage space on their hard drives than laptops (it's to do with the lack of physical space inside a laptop).
4) If a hard drive fails all the data on it can be lost. So it's sensible to keep back-ups of data files on an external storage device (see next page).
5) You can also get external hard disks. These portable devices plug into a computer to provide even more storage capacity — they're also useful for backing up hard drives.

Memory Cards and *Memory Sticks* Store Data on *Chips*

1) Memory cards and memory sticks can't hold as much data as hard disks. But they're small enough to be carried in a pocket or purse.

- Memory cards (e.g. SD cards or Compact-Flash cards) fit into small memory slots in digital cameras, smart phones or computers.
- USB sticks fit into USB slots on a computer.

2) They allow you to easily transfer data between electronic devices, since they can be unplugged from one computer and plugged into another.
3) They can create security problems though. They're easily lost, for example. It's also easy to copy confidential information onto them or transfer viruses onto company networks. Some businesses don't allow their employees to use them.

Make sure memory sticks stick in your memory...

Memory sticks and hard disks are common ways of storing data, but they're not perfect for all purposes. Small memory sticks are easy to accidentally lose/flush down the toilet, and hard disks can be corrupted. Given this, there's nowt like backing up all your data... just in case. See the next page for more...

Data Storage and Back-Up

A second page about data storage, plus some info about backing up.

CDs and DVDs Can Be *Read-Only* or *Rewritable*

Compact Discs (CDs)

CDs hold about 700 MB of data. There are several different types:

1) **CD-ROM** — these are read only — the data held on them can't be altered. ROM = Read-Only Memory
2) **CD-R** — you can write data to a blank CD-R. But... once you've written the data, you can't change it. R = Recordable
3) **CD-RW** — these have the advantage that data on the disk can be erased, and the disk reused. RW = ReWritable

Digital Versatile Discs (DVDs)

DVD — these are like CDs but hold more data — about 8 GB.
And like CDs...

- some DVDs are read-only,
- some can be written to once,
- some can be written to and erased.

1) CDs and DVDs are great for storing audio and video to use at home, but aren't ideal for most business data.
2) This is because it takes a relatively long time to write data onto them. And there's no quick way to edit a file and save the changed version onto the disc. It's also easy to scratch the discs, making them unreadable.

Magnetic Tape and *Web-Based* Storage

1) Magnetic Tape is cheap and it has a huge storage capacity compared to DVDs. Companies often use magnetic tape to back up their electronic data. But accessing data on magnetic tape can be slow.
2) Web-based file storage services allow data to be uploaded to the internet, and downloaded again when it's needed. This is an example of remote storage — the data is stored in a completely separate place from the computer that writes the data.

Storage Devices Can be Used to *Back Up* Data

1) Any storage device can be lost, stolen, damaged or destroyed. Data can also be corrupted (accidentally or by viruses) or lost.
2) For this reason, it's important for businesses to back up their data (i.e. make a copy).
3) Backing up data can cost a business time and money, but losing all their data could be much more costly. Making back-up copies of a company's data can take a long time — it's often done overnight.
4) Back-ups are usually stored in a different location (in case the firm's main building is burgled or damaged by fire). Ideally the backed-up data should be stored in a locked fireproof room.

Backed-up files are often compressed (reduced in size) to save space.

Plan A — always have a back-up plan...

There are all sorts of ways that a business can store its data. But whatever storage devices it uses, it's vital to make sure that data is backed up and stored safely — that way, any data that gets lost can be retrieved.

Warm-Up and Worked Exam Questions

Warm-up Questions

1) What's the difference between hardware and software?
2) What kinds of things might you consider when deciding whether a desktop or a laptop computer would be best?
3) What's a concept keyboard?
4) What's meant by "OCR" (when said in the same breath as "scanner")?
5) What's the difference between an internal storage device and an external one?

Worked Exam Question

You know what to do... try the questions on this page and the next, and compare your answers to ours.

1 An accountant is introducing a new computerised data system to store his clients' records. For security reasons, he will need to store a back-up copy of the data on separate premises.

a) Explain **two** advantages of using a computerised system instead of paper records.

A computerised system will be able to hold larger amounts of data in a given amount of space. ✔[1 mark] *It will also be much easier to back up the data.* ✔[1 mark]

(2 Marks)

b) Recommend a data storage medium for the backed-up data. Give reasons for your answer.

I would recommend using magnetic tape. ✔[1 mark] *Magnetic tape is cheap,* ✔[1 mark] *can hold vast amounts of data,* ✔[1 mark] *and is easily transported to separate premises.* ✔[1 mark]

Web-based storage might also be a possibility, but the data would need to be encrypted before it was transferred over the Internet.

(4 Marks)

c) The first time a new client visits the accountant's office, the accountant needs to collect a lot of detailed information. The accountant is unsure whether to use:

- manual data forms, whose information can be transferred onto a computer later, or
- electronic data forms so new clients can type information onto the computer themselves.

Evaluate these two methods, and recommend which the accountant should use.

With manual forms, mistakes can occur as data is transferred from the form to a computer, ✔[1 mark] *either as the information is being typed in by hand,* ✔[1 mark] *or because OCR software has not interpreted writing correctly.* ✔[1 mark] *I'd recommend electronic forms are used as the client can type directly onto the system, and the computer can instantly check that all necessary details have been input.* ✔[1 mark] *However, people might need to consult their own financial records, so it could be more convenient to fill in a form at home or work.* ✔[1 mark] *One possibility might be to type the data onto a secure website.* ✔[1 mark]

(6 Marks)

Exam Questions

1 Clare is about to collect some market-research data because she wants to open a shop.

a) Clare has been told she could use either primary data or secondary data.
Explain the difference between primary and secondary data.

....

....

(2 marks)

b) Briefly discuss the advantages and disadvantages for Clare of these different types of data.

....

....

....

(4 marks)

2 Clare is going to use a computer to keep track of her business's sales and purchases.
She is currently investigating input devices that she could use with her computer system.

a) Clare is considering buying an EPOS system. What is meant by the term "EPOS"?
Explain how an EPOS system might be useful for Clare.

....

....

....

(Continue your answer on a separate piece of paper) *(5 marks)*

b) Identify **two** other input devices Clare will find useful.
Explain what each could be used for.

1. ....

2. ....

(2 marks)

3 Clare knows that her business's data will be very important.

a) Explain why it is important for Clare to back up her data.

....

....

....

(3 marks)

b) Clare is told that memory sticks are a great way to transfer data between computers.
Explain one danger of using memory sticks for this purpose.

....

....

(2 marks)

Output Devices — Printers

An output device is any hardware used to communicate results of processing data. First, printers....

Businesses Often Need Hard Copies

1) Printers produce hard copies of documents (a hard copy means it's printed out on paper).
2) Businesses often need to produce hard copies — sometimes to create a permanent record, but sometimes because it's the most appropriate way to communicate with customers.
3) But printing documents out on paper usually works out more expensive than looking at them on screen. (There's the cost of the paper and ink, as well as the cost of maintaining the printer.)

There are Different Kinds of Printer

Laser Printers are Fast and High Quality

Laser printers are the best choice for larger businesses that print a lot of documents.

Advantages of Laser Printers

- They can print high-quality documents.
- They're fast — usually over 10 pages per minute (ppm).
- Laser printers are very quiet.

Disadvantages of Laser Printers

- They can be quite expensive.
- They contain a lot of complex equipment — so they're expensive to repair.
- They can't use continuous or multi-part stationery.

Ink-Jet Printers are Cheap and Reasonable Quality

1) These cost less to buy than laser printers, but they're not quite as slick.
2) Small jets of ink are sprayed through tiny nozzles onto the paper.
3) Ink-jet printers are great for small businesses that don't make loads of printouts — they provide good quality at a reasonable price.
4) For larger businesses, they're just too slow, and the quality isn't top-notch.

The resolution of a printer (the detail it can print) is usually measured in dots per inch (dpi)

Advantages of Ink-Jet Printers

- Good resolution — although usually not as good as a laser printer.
- Can be cheaper to buy than laser printers.
- Small — so ideal for home or office desk use.

Disadvantages of Ink-Jet Printers

- Slow(ish) — colour printing is often less than 4 pages per minute.
- Quite expensive to run — the ink costs more (per page) than laser cartridges.

Dot-Matrix Printers are Old-Fashioned and Slow

Dot-matrix printers use pins and an inked ribbon to create patterns of dots — these dots form characters.

- Dot-matrix printers are slow, noisy, and have poor resolution.
- But they're cheap to run and very reliable.
- And they can print onto long rolls of paper — useful for, say, printing long invoices.

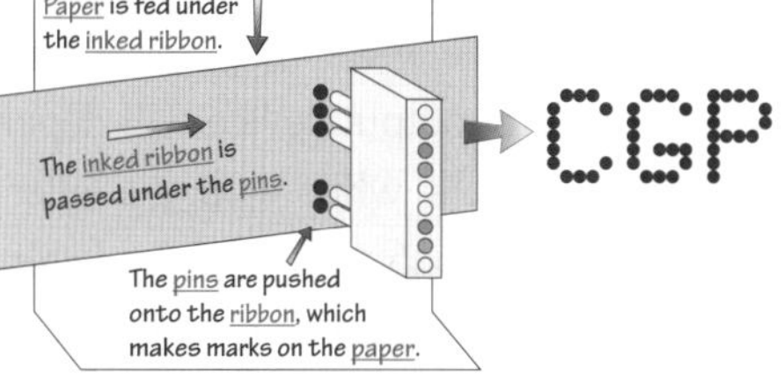

Nowadays, dot-matrix printers are only really used for printing till receipts and ATM statements.

Don't go hard copying other people's work in the exam...

If you want your electronic data put onto paper, you're going to need a printer. The type of printer that'll suit you best depends on how much printing you need to do, and the level of print quality you need.

More Output Devices

Output isn't just about printing onto paper. Here are some different types of output device.

Monitors are the Most Common Output Device

1) The monitors used by businesses depend on the type of work being carried out. For example, design work needs large, clear screens.
2) More straightforward work like word processing or entering data into a database can be done on cheaper, smaller screens with a lower resolution.
3) Monitors have changed over the years. In the old days, all monitors used a cathode-ray tube — these monitors were really heavy, took up loads of space on a desk and could damage your eyes.
4) Most computers these days have LCD flat screens. These take up less space on desks and are lightweight — making them easier to move. They also have low power consumption. However, they're easier to damage.

LCD Projectors Make Presentations Much Easier

See pages 113-114 for more about presentations.

1) LCD projectors are another type of output device. They can be connected to a laptop or desktop computer.
2) Whatever appears on the computer monitor is projected onto a screen so that it can be viewed by an audience.
3) They're used for training, sales presentations and meetings.

Advantages of LCD Projectors

1) Video images can be displayed. (In fact, they can display anything a normal computer screen can.)
2) Fairly light and portable.

Disadvantages of LCD Projectors

1) Can be quite delicate and easy to break.
2) Need a screen to project images onto.
3) Need dimly lit conditions (not always convenient).

Speakers Output Sound

Speakers are used to output audio (sound, to you and me).

1) Most computers come with speakers built in, but they may not be very good quality. New speakers can usually be connected to improve sound quality or volume.
2) Speakers are needed for audio-conferencing and video-conferencing (see p75) — they allow people's voices to be heard during the meeting.
3) Computers usually have sockets for headphones, too — useful if the user needs privacy, or needs to work quietly (e.g. using a laptop on a train).

Different Output Devices Have Different Functions

The choice of output device will depend on the situation.

1) For example, while writing a letter, you'll probably view it on a monitor so you can see changes instantly.
2) But once you've finished the letter, you might need to print it out and post it.
3) For a presentation, a projector may be best (so the audience won't have to gather round a small screen).

Need audio output? Speakers would be a sound idea...

More output devices you need to know everything about. But the good news is that you probably know a bit about most of these things already. But don't get complacent — make sure you learn everything properly.

Keeping Data Secure

All businesses face threats to their data's security. This includes traditional burglars breaking in and stealing their computers, and more modern criminals who like to commit their crimes electronically...

It's *Vital* to Keep Business Data *Secure*

Lots of business data is confidential (e.g. personal or financial data). This needs to be kept safe.

1) Stolen data can be used to commit identity theft, or steal money from bank accounts and credit cards.
2) Some data could reduce a firm's competitiveness if it leaked out to competitors.
3) Data that's been corrupted or altered by unauthorised users is useless to a business.

Physical Security Means Locks and Alarms

1) One type of security risk is having equipment and data physically stolen from buildings.
2) A decent alarm system and quality locks should be used in buildings where valuable equipment and data are stored.

Access Security Involves Usernames and Passwords

Unauthorised access to data (by people inside the firm, or hackers from outside) is potentially very serious.

1) All authorised users of a network should be given usernames and create their own passwords. This will limit unauthorised access to the network.

And users should change their password frequently to be on the safe side.

2) If people leave their computers for a short time, screen-savers (especially ones that need a password before the computer can be used again) can prevent people seeing what's displayed on the screen.
3) A firewall is a software application that increases the protection of a network from external threats. It works by examining all the traffic moving through a network, and denying access to unauthorised users (e.g. hackers). Firewalls increase security, but they can't provide total protection.
4) Encryption software converts data into the form of a code — a key (similar to a password) is needed to decode the data and read it. So even if someone does gain access to your data, as long as they don't know the key, the data won't make any sense. Whenever data is transmitted anywhere (e.g. over the internet), there's a risk that it might be 'captured' by baddies — encryption stops it being read.

Spam, Spyware, Viruses — Dangerous and/or Annoying

Malware (malicious software) means any software that's been designed to damage a computer system or its data. You need to know about different kinds, and how a business can protect itself against them.

1) A virus is a program that can corrupt files and even operating systems. Viruses can copy themselves and spread to other computer systems by attaching themselves to emails, for example. Anti-virus software reduces the risks. But it's important to download updates regularly — new viruses are detected practically every day.
2) Spam emails (electronic junk mail) take up storage space, and checking through them wastes time for staff. Anti-spam software tries to detect junk mail, and block it from an inbox.
3) Similarly, anti-adware can help to block unwanted pop-up advertisements.
4) Spyware is software that collects information about the user without their knowledge. It can also install unwanted software and change settings. Anti-spyware packages help to defend computers against it.

Data security is a big problem these days...

It's not hard to see why security is important to businesses — they have a lot to lose if their data is stolen. Learn the stuff on the page, then write down what you can remember about potential threats to a business's data and what a business can do to prevent problems. If you get anything wrong, you'll need to do it again.

Data Protection and the Law

Businesses and other organisations keep data on customers, patients, students and other individuals — whether on paper or on computer files. There are laws to control how the data is used.

The *Data Protection Act* Controls How Data is *Kept* and *Used*

The Data Protection Act (1998) basically says two things...

1) Any business or organisation that holds personal data about individuals ("data subjects") must comply with the 8 data protection principles below.
2) Data subjects have various rights to see, correct and prevent their personal data being processed or used for marketing without their permission.

There are *Eight Principles* of Data Protection

1. Data must not be processed unless there is a specific lawful reason to do so.
   E.g. a firm would be able to check if someone usually pays back money on time — that's legal.

2. Data can only be obtained and used for specified purposes.
   E.g. businesses can use names and addresses to deliver goods — but if they want to use the data for advertising in the future, they have to ask the data subject's permission.

3. Data should be adequate, relevant and not excessive for the specified use.
   E.g. if a business needs to deliver goods, they shouldn't ask for someone's national insurance number.

4. Data must be accurate and kept up to date.
   E.g. an employee's examination results must be updated each time they sit extra exams — otherwise incorrect information could be given in a reference to another college or potential employer.

5. Data should not be kept longer than is necessary for the specified purpose.
   But this will be different depending on why the data is being kept. E.g. financial information can be kept by certain institutions for up to seven years, but medical records are kept for the life of a patient.

6. Data processing should meet the legal rights of the data subjects (see below).
   E.g. some information must not be passed on without the permission of the data subject.

7. Data holders must protect the data against loss, theft or corruption.
   It's the duty of the business to back up data, and to dispose of it properly when no longer needed.

8. Data should not be transferred abroad, except to certain other European countries.
   This is so that businesses can't just send data abroad to a country where the Data Protection Act doesn't apply.

The Data Protection Act (1998) gives these rights to data subjects:

1) The right to view data held about them (but they must give notice and maybe pay a small fee).
2) The right to prevent the processing of data if it might cause distress or damage to themselves.
3) The right to compensation if damage or distress has been caused.
4) The right to have any inaccurate data changed or deleted.
5) The right to prevent data being used to send junk mail.

Data Protection — learn the eight principles...

There are a few exceptions to the Data Protection Act — e.g. data used for national security purposes, solving crime, or for tax assessment is exempt from some of the data protection principles.

Warm-Up and Worked Exam Questions

Warm-up Questions

1) What's meant by the term "hard copy"?
2) Explain the pros and cons of: a) laser printers b) ink-jet printers.
3) What's the point of having a password on your screensaver?
4) What's meant by the term "malware"?
5) When you're talking about the Data Protection Act, what is a "data subject"?

Worked Exam Question

You should know what to do by now... read the questions and answers below, and see the kind of answers that get you marks. Then try the exam-style question on the next page yourself.

1 Read **Item A** and then answer the questions that follow.

Item A

A doctor is about to modernise his medical surgery. As part of the modernisation, he is having a new computer system installed. This computer system will be used for:

- storing patient information
- printing prescriptions
- consulting online medical texts

The doctor has been advised that data security is extremely important, and that he will need to have a firewall installed.

a) State with reasons **two** output devices that the doctor will need.

1. *He will need a monitor* ✔[1 mark] *to make entering and editing information easier.* ✔[1 mark]

2. *He will need a printer* ✔[1 mark] *to print prescriptions.* ✔[1 mark]

(4 Marks)

b) What is meant by the term "firewall"?

A firewall is a software application that monitors data going into and out of a computer. ✔[1 mark] *It's designed to block harmful 'network intrusions'.* ✔[1 mark]

(2 marks)

c) Recommend **two** other precautions the doctor should take in order to ensure the security of his data. Explain why you would recommend these precautions.

The doctor should make sure he has anti-virus software ✔[1 mark] *installed and running, since viruses could corrupt his data or operating system.* ✔[1 mark]
He should also make sure that his data is password-protected ✔[1 mark] *so that unauthorised users cannot easily gain access to it.* ✔[1 mark]

(4 marks)

Exam Questions

1 Terry, the owner of a building business, has decided to store personal data about his staff on a computer system. Terry knows that his business must comply with the Data Protection Act. However, Terry knows little about the details of the Act.

a) The Data Protection Act describes eight principles of data protection. State **three** of these Data Protection principles.

1. ....

2. ....

3. ....

(3 Marks)

b) For each of your principles above, explain one practical step Terry could take in order to comply with that principle.

1. ....

....

2. ....

....

3. ....

....

(6 Marks)

c) A member of Terry's staff asks to see the information that Terry is holding about her. Terry is not sure whether he should allow employees to see his computer records.

Use your knowledge of the Data Protection Act to explain to Terry what he should do.

....

....

....

(3 marks)

2 Sarah owns a company that offers financial advice. Part of her job involves visiting other companies and giving presentations to large groups of employees on financial matters. Sarah is considering buying a projector which she will be able to attach to her computer.

Evaluate the advantages and disadvantages of such a projector for Sarah.

....

....

....

....

(Continue your answer on a separate piece of paper) *(9 marks)*

Revision Summary for Section Five

Here you go — a whole heap of questions about data processing systems.
Potentially, one of the problems you might have with this section (maybe) is thinking, "I know about computers — I'll not bother reading it or doing the questions." And that would probably be a mistake.

Okay, you might know lots about computers, but that doesn't necessarily mean that you'll know all about the use of computers in business — the 8 principles of the Data Protection Act, and all that.

The best thing to do is try these questions. If you get them all right, then good for you — move on to Section 6. But if it turns out there's something you weren't sure about, you can go back and look it up. Makes sense to me.

1) What's the difference between primary and secondary data sources?
2) Explain the main features of paper-based and computer-based systems.
   Give some advantages and disadvantages of each type of system.
3) What is meant by 'hardware'? And 'software'?
4) Describe the main pros and cons of: a) a desktop PC b) a laptop PC.
5) What is meant by 'input device'?
6) Give one advantage and one disadvantage of a QWERTY keyboard.
7) Explain what a concept keyboard is, and give an example of a business that might use one.
8) Give two situations where a joystick might be used.
9) What does EPOS stand for? What do EPOS systems do, and where are they usually used?
10) Give one benefit and one drawback of voice-recognition systems.
11) Explain the differences between manual data forms and electronic data forms.
12) What's the difference between internal and external storage devices? Give one example of each.
13) Give two benefits and two drawbacks of memory sticks.
14) Explain the differences between CD-ROMS, CD-Rs and CD-RWs.
15) What advantages do DVDs have over CDs?
16) Why should firms always create back-up copies of their data?
17) Why might businesses want to store data at a different site?
18) Explain the differences between laser, ink-jet and dot-matrix printers.
    What types of business might want to use each of these types of printer?
19) Describe what an LCD projector does, and when you might use one.
20) Give three reasons why firms need to keep their data secure.
21) What does physical security protect against? Give two examples of physical security measures.
22) Explain three things that can be done to protect data on a network of computers.
23) Explain what the following security threats are, and name the software that protects against them.
    a) Spam; b) Spyware; c) Viruses.
24) What does the Data Protection Act control?
25) Explain the eight principles of Data Protection.
26) What five rights do data subjects have under the Data Protection Act?
27) Give two examples of data that may be exempt from the Data Protection Act.

Purposes of Communication

Communication. It's a big part of this subject. But what actually is it...

Communication Involves the **Exchange of Information**

1) Communication involves transmitting (sending) information from a sender to a receiver. The information that's sent is called the message.
2) Messages are sent using a particular medium. Examples of media include: email, letter, phone...
3) The receiver of the message can send feedback to show they've received it and understood it. Feedback is important for judging how successful the communication has been.

One medium, but two media etc.

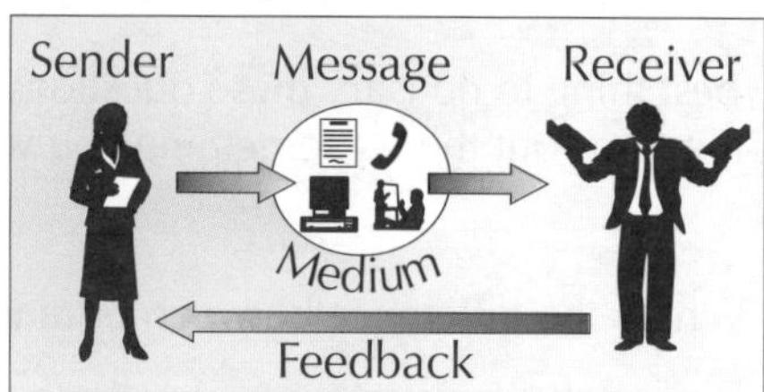

Before **Sending** a Message, You Need to **Choose** a **System**

The main things that will decide how a message is sent are...

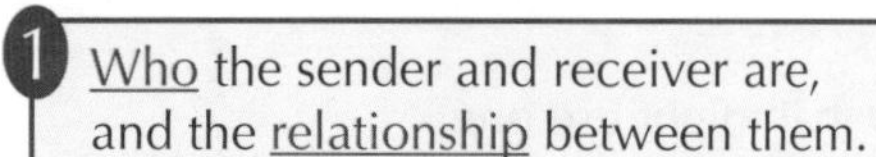
1 Who the sender and receiver are, and the relationship between them.

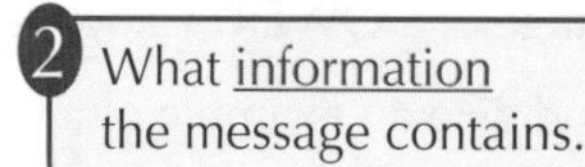
2 What information the message contains.

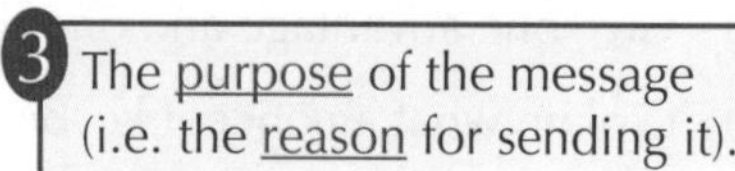
3 The purpose of the message (i.e. the reason for sending it).

Based on these factors, the sender will choose the best communication system for sending the message. A communication system is made up of a method, a channel and a medium of communication.

Choose the Best **Method** of Communication

Methods

- **WRITTEN** messages can be kept and read many times, so they're good for complex information.
- **ORAL** messages are spoken — they're more personal, and good for getting immediate feedback.
- **VISUAL** methods involve images or body language — they express meaning quickly without words.
  - Pictorial methods use pictures (e.g. ☺ is a quick, informal way to express happiness).
  - Graphical methods use graphs, charts and diagrams to show technical information and data.

Choose the Right **Channel** of Communication

Types of channel

- **Internal and external** — Messages that don't leave the business go through internal channels. Messages sent to receivers outside the firm are sent through external channels.
- **Formal and informal** — Formal channels are used for official business (e.g. formal letters sent to suppliers, or job applicants). Informal channels are less official — e.g. word-of-mouth messages.
- **Confidential and non-confidential** — Confidential messages (e.g. financial data) need to be private.
- **Urgent and non-urgent** — Urgent channels are used to deliver important messages quickly.

Choose the Best **Medium**

The medium means the 'equipment' you use to send the message — this will depend on the method and the channels of communication.

If your exam's tomorrow, this is an urgent communication...

There's a lot of jargon on this page (see p64 for more about that). You'll need to use these technical terms to talk about how communication works. The rest of this section should make it clearer what all this actually means.

Internal and External Communication

Good communication is good. Bad communication is bad. Easy so far. Now for the details...

Internal Communication Happens *Inside* the Firm

Internal communication can be between different layers of a hierarchy, or between people on the same level.

Communication between different layers of the hierarchy:
- Managers and supervisors need to communicate with operatives to give them tasks.
- Operatives can give feedback to their managers.

Hierarchies are covered on p23.

Communication across the same level of the hierarchy:
- Team members need to exchange information to complete tasks effectively.
- Different departments need to communicate with each other to coordinate their activities.

1) The media that staff use to communicate (e.g. email, telephone, meetings) may depend on their positions in the company. For example, not everyone may have access to a computer.
2) Good internal communication means staff will be better informed about what's going on in the firm, improving their motivation. Communication between staff should also mean that they work together better and make fewer mistakes. These things should increase efficiency, productivity, and levels of customer service. An efficient business with happy customers should make more profit.
3) Poor internal communication can lead to employees feeling alienated — that their opinions are misunderstood or ignored. This isn't good for staff morale, productivity, the company, or its customers — profits could suffer.

External Communication is With People *Outside* the Firm

1) Businesses need to exchange information with a wide range of stakeholders in the outside world.

- Businesses communicate with their suppliers to agree the size, cost and delivery dates of orders.
- Businesses communicate with their customers in order to improve sales.
  E.g. market research to find out what customers want, and advertising to promote their products.
  Customer care is also important — e.g. dealing with complaints and questions about products.
- Customers can also provide feedback — e.g. by filling in questionnaires, or phoning a helpline.

2) When communicating externally, firms need to make sure that the messages they send are delivered in an appropriate form for each type of receiver (as well as being clear and accurate).
3) Businesses also need to think carefully about the image (see p76) they want to create for themselves.

For example, the firm might take part in environmental schemes. Or the firm might do something to benefit the local community. If people are aware of this, it might generate trust and good will.

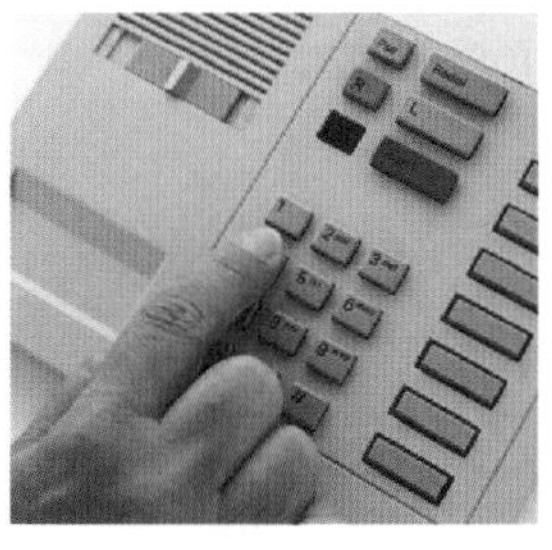

4) Good communication with customers is vital if a business is having a problem. For example, if a company won't be able to deliver something on time, it's usually best to tell the customer. If the customer knows the delivery will be late, they can make other plans instead of waiting in for something to arrive.
5) Bad external communication can cause misunderstandings, which could be pretty serious. For example, suppliers might deliver goods late (or the wrong goods) if they've misunderstood an order. Similarly, customers will be upset if their orders are delivered late, or if they feel they're not being listened to.

Internal — Inside, External — Outside. Simple...

Poor communication can have a big impact on businesses — inefficient, badly motivated employees and dissatisfied customers are likely to result in fewer sales, less profit and conflict with stakeholders.

Barriers to Communication

So... you know what information you want to communicate, and how you're going to send the message. But there are still factors that can affect the receiver's interpretation — you need to keep these in mind, too...

Barriers Can **Prevent** Good Communication

- JARGON — this is technical language to do with a particular subject. People who aren't experts in that subject may not understand.
- NOISE — this could be traffic noise making it hard to hear a phone call. Or it might be visual noise — e.g. too much information on a page can make it hard to pick out the important points.
- POOR CHOICE OF CHANNEL OR MEDIUM — e.g. an urgent letter sent by second-class post may not get there in time. And complex information might be best written down, rather than spoken, so that the receiver doesn't forget any of it.
- INAPPROPRIATE PRESENTATION — a message's presentation should be suitable for the audience. E.g. an advert should be easy to understand — if it's too complex, customers might lose interest.
- EMOTIONAL INTERFERENCE — e.g. if the sender and the receiver don't get on personally, it can affect how the communication is understood.
- TRUST AND HONESTY — if the receiver thinks the sender is dishonest, they may be suspicious about the content of the message.
- CULTURAL DIFFERENCES — communicating internationally can be tricky. Foreign languages can easily be mistranslated. Also, what seems polite in one country may be rude in another.
- THE STATUS OF THE SENDER People outside a business are often more likely to trust information if it comes from somebody who's high up in the organisation.

Checking Documents for **Errors** is a **Good Idea**

Errors can also be a barrier to communication — they can make messages misleading and confusing. Luckily, written and visual messages can be checked for errors before they're sent.

1) Errors in spelling, punctuation and grammar — In formal business documents, this looks unprofessional — the firm may lose respect if words aren't spelt correctly.
2) Errors in tone — This will depend on the sender, message and receiver. A formal business letter to a customer needs formal language. If the tone is too chatty, it can seem disrespectful.
3) Factual errors — Factual errors can cause big problems — e.g. putting the wrong prices in a catalogue could damage a firm's reputation. Giving out misleading information could even be a criminal offence.
4) Problems with graphics and diagrams — Graphics are supposed to make information clearer. But if they're not properly labelled, they could just add to the confusion.

- Checking business documents for errors can save embarrassment, confusion, and more serious problems.
- The main drawback of checking for mistakes is that it takes time and money to do it properly. But it's usually time and money well spent.

You can trust this page — I'm very high status...

When sending a message, it's important to think about how the receiver will interpret it — if the message is unclear, confusing, or full of mistakes, your point might not across come the way you meant it to. Capisce?

Warm-up and Worked Exam Questions

Warm-up Questions

1) What is communication?
2) What type of communication channel should be used to send a customer's financial details?
3) Why might poor internal communication affect a company's profits?
4) Give one reason why businesses communicate externally.
5) Why is it a good idea to check business documents for errors?

Worked Exam Question

Read through the questions and answers below and think about how you would have answered them in an exam. Then have a go at writing your own answers to the questions on the next page.

1 Part of an email that was sent to a member of staff working at Kold Kallers is shown below.

> Hi Tom,
>
> Sorry I've not spoken to you about this in person — I've been snowed under! Basically, I need to say two things:
>
> a) Unfortunately, after a lot of consideration, I have decidedd that your post is no longer required in the company.
>
> b) We'll need to chat about your redundancy package — it's a bit complicated, but I'll call you later on and talk you through it.
>
> Cheers,
> Hannah

a) Describe **two** ways in which the message is unsuitable for its purpose.

The tone of the email is inappropriate ✔[1 mark] *for a serious matter like redundancy.* ✔[1 mark] *The email also has a spelling error,* ✔[1 mark] *which makes it look unprofessional.* ✔[1 mark]

(4 marks)

b) What method(s) would you recommend using to communicate the above two pieces of information? Explain your answer.

I would have told Tom about his redundancy in a face-to-face meeting. ✔[1 mark] *Oral messages are more personal* ✔[1 mark] *and this would be more suitable when dealing with a sensitive topic like redundancy.* ✔[1 mark] *I would then send the details on Tom's redundancy package in an email.* ✔[1 mark] *There may be lots of detailed information,* ✔[1 mark] *so an email might be more useful than a phone call because Tom could print the email and refer back to it.* ✔[1 mark]

(6 marks)

Questions that ask for your opinion don't usually have one correct answer — most of the marks will come from justifying your opinion.

Practice Exam Questions

1 Read **Item A** and then answer the questions that follow.

Item A

Stallion Sneakers is a company that sells horseshoes. The company produces an annual report that is communicated internally to all staff. The report contains an analysis of monthly sales figures and the results from a customer satisfaction survey.

The company has also been communicating with some of its customers. The deputy manager of Stallion Sneakers recently wrote an article for a local newspaper about the racecourse regeneration project that the company is involved with. Shorter versions of the customer satisfaction survey results, along with the newspaper article, were emailed to Stallion Sneakers' overseas customers.

a) What is meant by the term "internal communication"?

....

....

(2 marks)

b) Explain **two** potential benefits of sending the annual report to the staff of Stallion Sneakers.

....

....

....

....

(4 marks)

c) i) Suggest **one** potential benefit to the firm of producing an article for the local newspaper.

....

....

(2 marks)

ii) Describe any potential barriers to communication that may affect how the message to Stallion Sneakers' overseas clients is understood.

....

....

....

....

....

....

(6 marks)

Written Communication — Letters

Written communication is very important to businesses.
Business letters are a very common form of written communication.

Business Letters are Used for External Communication

1) Letters are one of the main ways that businesses communicate externally. They're sometimes used for formal internal communication as well. They're used when:

- A formal message is needed — e.g. to confirm an order with a supplier.
- A permanent record of the message is needed — e.g. if the terms of a contract are being changed.
- A message is complicated or a lot of information needs to be given.

2) Formal business letters are usually presented in a standard format. There's no need for flashy graphics, just neatly presented text that uses straightforward formal language to get the facts across.

Some firms also send informal letters to promote products and special offers. The idea with these letters is that customers will be encouraged to make more purchases if the firm seems friendly and trustworthy.

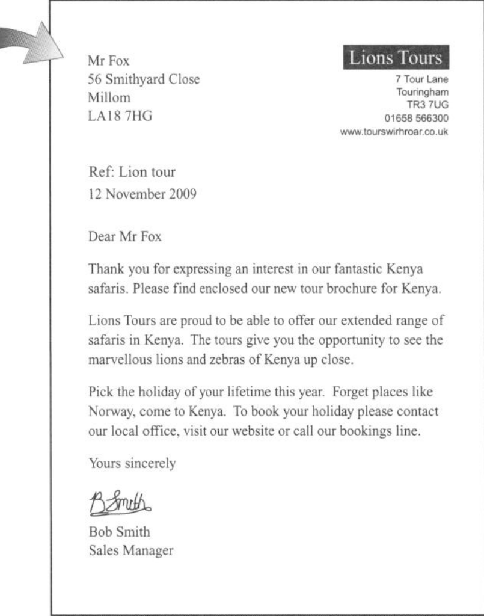

Mr Fox
56 Smithyard Close
Millom
LA18 7HG

Lions Tours
7 Tour Lane
Touringham
TR3 7UG
01658 566300
www.tourswirhroar.co.uk

Ref: Lion tour
12 November 2009

Dear Mr Fox

Thank you for expressing an interest in our fantastic Kenya safaris. Please find enclosed our new tour brochure for Kenya.

Lions Tours are proud to be able to offer our extended range of safaris in Kenya. The tours give you the opportunity to see the marvellous lions and zebras of Kenya up close.

Pick the holiday of your lifetime this year. Forget places like Norway, come to Kenya. To book your holiday please contact our local office, visit our website or call our bookings line.

Yours sincerely

B Smith

Bob Smith
Sales Manager

3) Word-processed letters can be mail-merged. This means that very similar letters can be sent to large numbers of individual receivers, with their personal details slotted in automatically.

Mail merge makes it easy for firms to send out thousands of letters, even if customers haven't asked for them — it's often seen as junk mail.

See p94-95 for more about business letters and mail merge.

Sending a Letter has Benefits and Drawbacks

Benefits of business letters

1) The business can keep a copy of a letter it sends (either electronically, on paper, or both). This can be used as proof that the message has been sent and of what the message said.
2) Both the sender and receiver can keep the letter and use it for future reference. This can be helpful if the information is important or complicated.
3) The business can get proof that the message was delivered if they use recorded delivery. Fax machines (see p70) also give receipts to show that a faxed letter has been received.

Drawbacks of business letters

1) Posted letters take at least a day to be delivered — so they're not suitable for urgent messages. Faxing a letter is much quicker though.
2) Posted letters can get lost or stolen in the post. There are more secure channels you can use (e.g. Royal Mail's Special Delivery™ service), but these are more expensive.
3) The sender gets no immediate feedback from the reader.

Business — it's a mail-dominated world...

Business letters are perfect for formal communication, but they're not usually very eye-catching. If a firm really wants to dazzle its customers, it may be better to use a more visual method, like a flyer or a brochure (see p69). Learn when business letters are used, and what makes a good business letter. Got it? Good.

Internal Written Communication

Employees of a business often like to write internal messages to each other.
It means there's a written record of the information, and it can be an effective way to communicate.

Memo is Short for Memorandum

1) A memorandum (or 'memo') is a formal written message (printed on paper) sent to people inside an organisation. Nowadays, emails are often sent where memos were used in the past. But a memo is more formal than an email (it can even seem a bit 'stuffy').
2) The main advantage of memos is that there's a hard copy of the message that can be kept.
3) But emails are quicker and don't use any paper.

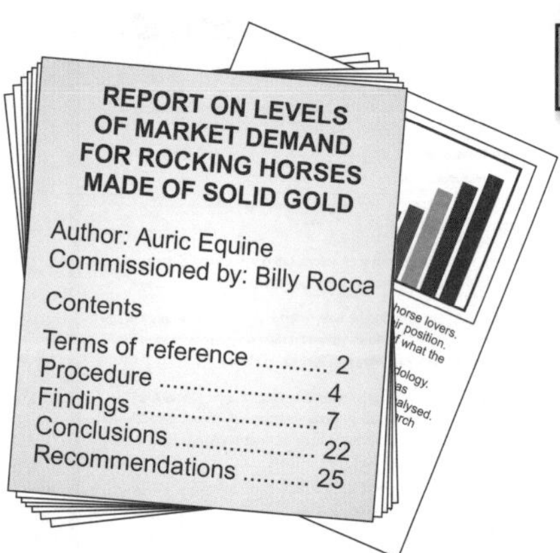

REPORT ON LEVELS OF MARKET DEMAND FOR ROCKING HORSES MADE OF SOLID GOLD
Author: Auric Equine
Commissioned by: Billy Rocca
Contents
Terms of reference 2
Procedure 4
Findings 7
Conclusions 22
Recommendations 25

Reports are Written After Investigations

1) Reports are written when somebody has been asked (or commissioned) to investigate a topic and give detailed advice and recommendations.
2) Written reports usually follow a set format. There are sections that explain the methods used, the information that was found, and the writer's conclusions and recommendations.
3) Reports are formal documents — they're usually aimed at staff within the business who have specialist knowledge of the subject, so they often contain complex data.

Company Newsletters Keep Staff Informed

Newsletters can also be used to send information to customers.

1) Internal newsletters are often a bit like mini-newspapers that report on events and developments within the business. They can be formal or informal, depending on the company.
2) Newsletters can be used to keep staff informed — this can help to boost motivation and productivity (see p63).
3) But they can also be expensive to produce — especially if paper copies are sent to every member of staff. And there's no guarantee that staff will read them, so they shouldn't be used to send important messages.

GlassCo Gazette
Skylight sales go through the roof!
Employee does something clever/funny

Notices are Put Up Where All Employees Can Read Them

1) Notices are meant to be read by the whole staff, so they're put in places where all staff can see them.
2) They're often used for publicising events or changes to company policy.
3) Notices can be on display for a long time, giving all staff the chance to see them, possibly many times.
4) Notices are easy to ignore — some staff might not see them, so they're no good for important messages. And since they're displayed in public, they're also not suitable for confidential information.

Take notice and commit this page to memo(ry)...

These documents all have their uses, but most modern firms rely heavily on electronic forms of communication now. If you want to write a message to someone you work with, it's quicker and easier to send an email.

More Written Communication

Businesses often send out written documents to their customers to keep them informed about their products. Sometimes, people outside the firm will send written messages (like CVs) to the business.

Brochures, Leaflets and Flyers are Posted to Customers (mostly)

All these forms of written communication are types of advertising. Traditionally, they were all printed on paper, but it's now common to send flyers by email and make brochures available to download from the internet.

BROCHURES are like glossy magazines — they're used to publicise new products or give customers an overview of the existing product range.

CATALOGUES are similar, but they usually contain more information about individual products. This might include product descriptions, prices, and details of how to order.

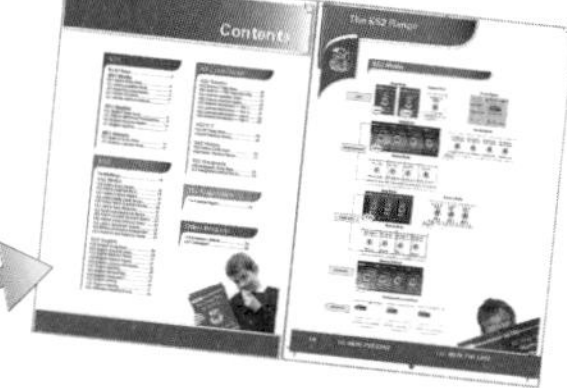

FLYERS are usually single-page advertisements containing a basic message about a product or event. Flyers are often quite visual — pictures are used to make the page more eye-catching.

LEAFLETS usually contain a more detailed message.

Financial Documents Need to Be Clear and Accurate

1) Businesses must keep accurate records of all the money being spent and received. To do this, firms use a variety of financial documents.
2) One example is an invoice — this is a request for payment from a customer. Invoices include details of who the customer is, what they've bought, the discount they're entitled to, and how much they owe the firm.
3) Financial documents must be accurate and clear. Invoices usually just contain addresses, product names, prices, and dates. The figures are often laid out in columns so that the details can be checked quickly.
4) A financial report might use tables and charts to help explain financial data.

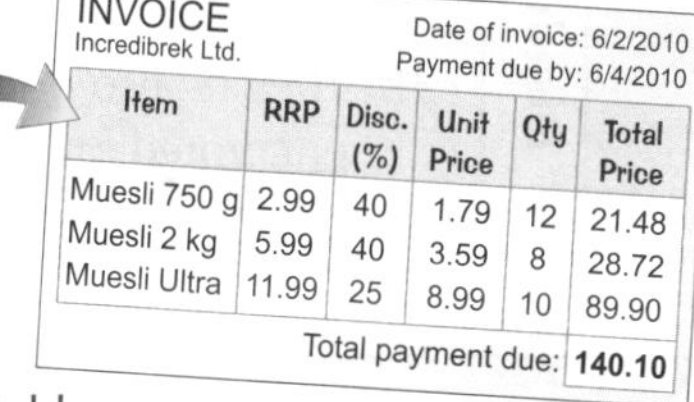

INVOICE
Incredibrek Ltd.

Date of invoice: 6/2/2010
Payment due by: 6/4/2010

Item	RRP	Disc. (%)	Unit Price	Qty	Total Price
Muesli 750 g	2.99	40	1.79	12	21.48
Muesli 2 kg	5.99	40	3.59	8	28.72
Muesli Ultra	11.99	25	8.99	10	89.90
				Total payment due:	140.10

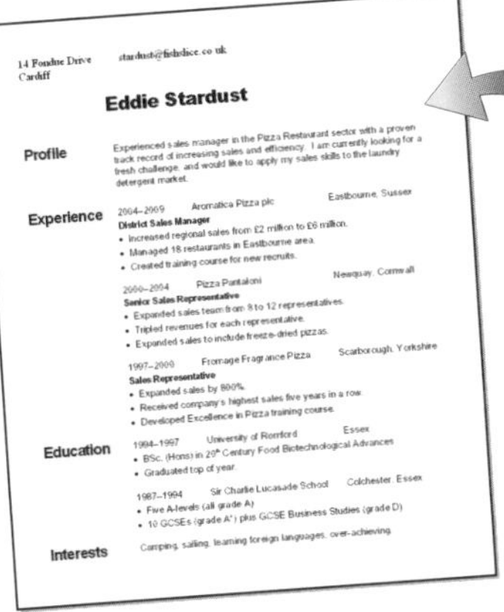

14 Fondue Drive
Cardiff

stardust@fishdice.co.uk

Eddie Stardust

Profile
Experienced sales manager in the Pizza Restaurant sector with a proven track record of increasing sales and efficiency. I am currently looking for a fresh challenge, and would like to apply my sales skills to the laundry detergent market.

Experience
2004–2009 Aromatica Pizza plc Eastbourne, Sussex
District Sales Manager
- Increased regional sales from £2 million to £6 million.
- Managed 18 restaurants in Eastbourne area.
- Created training course for new recruits.

2000–2004 Pizza Pantaloni Newquay, Cornwall
Senior Sales Representative
- Expanded sales team from 8 to 12 representatives.
- Tripled revenues for each representative.
- Expanded sales to include freeze-dried pizzas.

1997–2000 Fromage Fragrance Pizza Scarborough, Yorkshire
Sales Representative
- Expanded sales by 800%.
- Received company's highest sales five years in a row.
- Developed Excellence in Pizza training course.

Education
1994–1997 University of Romford Essex
- BSc. (Hons) in 20th Century Food Biotechnological Advances
- Graduated top of year.

1987–1994 Sir Charlie Lucasade School Colchester, Essex
- Five A-levels (all grade A)
- 10 GCSEs (grade A*) plus GCSE Business Studies (grade D)

Interests
Camping, sailing, learning foreign languages, over-achieving.

CVs are Used When Applying for a Job

1) A curriculum vitae (CV) is a summary of a person's personal details, skills, qualifications, experience and interests. Employers use them to assess how suitable someone is for a job.
2) CVs should be broken up into clear sections so that an employer can find the information they want easily.
3) A CV is designed to impress a potential employer, so good spelling, punctuation and grammar are important for making a good first impression.

Written communication — it has prose and cons...

A few bits and pieces to think about on this page. All these written documents are usually printed on paper so that they're easy to refer to, but they can also be sent and received electronically. Grand.

Electronic Communication

Most of what you've seen so far in this section has been paper-based communication. But thanks to ICT, information can be exchanged without using paper at all.

Paper Documents can be Sent by Fax

1) Fax machines send and receive copies of paper documents using a telephone line.
2) They're useful when the sender needs to make sure the receiver gets a document quickly. (Fax machines give you a 'receipt' to show that a document you've sent has been received.)
3) Faxes are quick and cheap, but not as quick or cheap as email (see below). Faxes can look a bit scruffy, so they're not ideal if presentation is important.

Faxes usually record the date and time they were sent.

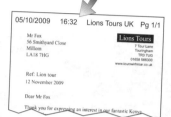

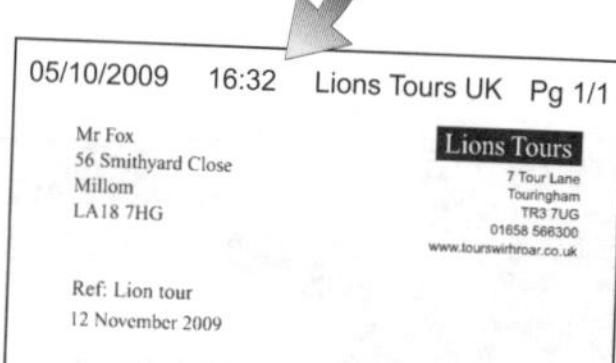
05/10/2009 16:32 Lions Tours UK Pg 1/1

Mr Fox
56 Smithyard Close
Millom
LA18 7HG

Lions Tours
7 Tour Lane
Touringham
TR3 7UG
01658 566300
www.tourswirhroar.co.uk

Ref: Lion tour
12 November 2009

Dear Mr Fox

Thank you for expressing an interest in our fantastic Kenya

Email is Quick and Easy

Email is now the main way most firms send written messages quickly.

Advantages

1) Emails can be sent all over the world using the internet, or between a firm's staff over an intranet. It usually only takes a few seconds for an email to get from the sender to the receiver.
2) It's easy to send copies of the same email to lots of people, and cheaper than a phone call.
3) The receiver can either print the document themselves or just view it on screen, so unnecessary paperwork can be avoided.
4) Other files and documents can be attached to emails and sent at the same time.

Disadvantages

1) Both the sender and the receiver need access to a computer (or a suitable phone).
2) Emails are usually less formal than business letters — they're not usually well suited to serious messages like staff warnings.
3) They're also not very confidential — but some emails can be encrypted for extra security (see p57).

Internet Websites Can be Used to Exchange Information

Posting messages on a website can be a good way of making them available to the general public.

Advantages

1) Anyone with internet access can view the website. This means that messages can reach large audiences all over the world.
2) Some parts of a website can be restricted so that only authorised users with passwords can access them — this means businesses can control who is able to receive certain messages. E.g. a firm could post a report for shareholders without customers being able to read it.
3) Customers can also send messages and feedback to businesses through their websites. E.g. they might be able to order products online, or leave comments in a guestbook.

Disadvantages

1) People who don't have internet access may miss out on information (e.g. special offers).
2) It can be difficult to get people to look at your website.

Electronic communication leads to net gains...

Most modern businesses use email and the internet to send and exchange information. These media are quick and convenient, and they can reach a large audience without using three forests' worth of paper.

Electronic Communication

Here's some more methods of electronic communication...

Mobile Phones Can Send Text Messages Using SMS

1) Mobile phones can be used to send SMS text messages (SMS stands for Short Message Service). Single messages can be up to 160 characters long (if you need to say more, you can pay for extra texts).
2) SMS messages are usually cheaper than a phone call.
3) But they're fiddly to type, and people often abbreviate words using textspeak. This makes them most useful for short, informal messages.

Electronic Notice Boards Can be Regularly Updated

Electronic notice boards display information in the same way as a computer monitor.

Electronic notice boards are used a lot at airports and railway stations — to deliver messages to large groups of people.

The screen can cycle through many pages of information, displaying each one for a short time.

The information can be easily edited and displayed straight away. But they're expensive.

Loyalty Cards, RFID Tags and Satnavs — All Very Clever

1) Many shops and supermarkets use loyalty cards to collect data about customers electronically.
2) Customers often collect points on their cards whenever they shop. These points can then be used to earn money off future purchases.
3) But the cards also collect data about the customers' shopping habits. This data can be used to produce a profile of each customer, so that they can be sent marketing materials that will interest them.
4) This targeted marketing is more efficient than sending out the same promotions to all customers.

RFID (Radio Frequency IDentification) tags can be recognised by a radio receiver. RFID tags can be attached to:

- vehicles — to automatically pay tolls for tunnels, bridges, and so on.
- products — so shops and delivery companies can track individual items.

Satnavs (Satellite navigation systems) also involve electronic communication.

1) A satnav system in a vehicle picks up signals from satellites orbiting the Earth. It uses these to calculate its position very accurately.
2) It can then use data stored in its memory to give directions.

Electronic Systems — Good, but Not Cheap

Electronic communication systems are generally very quick and efficient if they're used the right way. But...

1) ICT equipment can be expensive to buy and maintain.
2) Staff may need training before they can use a system properly. This takes time and money.

ICT is useful, but not all systems go...

Remember, just because ICT systems are often expensive to buy, that doesn't mean they're not cheaper in the long run. Buying a computer and sending a million emails might be cheaper than buying a million stamps.

Warm-up and Worked Exam Questions

Warm-up Questions

1) Why do business letters not usually contain flash graphics and lots of fancy fonts?
2) Give one advantage of sending a memo instead of an email.
3) State two characteristics of an effective CV.
4) Why are text messages most useful for short, informal messages?
5) What are sat nav systems? How do they work?
6) Give two disadvantages of using electronic communication systems.

Worked Exam Question

Here's another worked exam question to read through. And on the next page there's a couple of practice questions for you to answer. Check your answers at the back of the book when you're done.

1 The Amazium Gymnazium posted sign-up packs to 100 people. Each pack contained an informal covering letter, details of three special offers, and gym membership forms.

a) The covering letters were created using mail-merge.

i) Explain **one** advantage of using mail-merge to create letters.

Mail-merging makes it easy to send similar letters to lots of individual receivers ✔[1 mark] *by slotting personal details into the letters automatically.* ✔[1 mark]

(2 marks)

ii) Suggest **one** reason why the covering letter may have been written in an informal tone.

The informal tone may make the gym seem friendly, ✔[1 mark]

which could encourage more people to sign up to the gym. ✔[1 mark]

(2 marks)

b) A flyer advertised the gym's special offers. Explain **one** characteristic of an effective flyer.

It would be eye-catching ✔[1 mark] *to draw the readers' attention to the flyer.* ✔[1 mark]

(2 marks)

c) The packs were expensive to produce and to post, but only 8 people joined the gym as a result. Suggest how electronic methods of communication could be used to reduce costs and increase the number of people signing up. Give reasons for your answers.

The gym could send sign-up packs by email ✔[1 mark] *or put them on a website.* ✔[1 mark] *Both of these methods reduce costs because the packs don't need to be printed or posted.* ✔[1 mark] *Emails can be sent cheaply to many more people than letters,* ✔[1 mark] *so you'd expect more people joining the gym overall.* ✔[1 mark] *The membership form could be filled in and processed on the website, which might speed up the joining process and reduce costs for the business.* ✔[1 mark]

(6 marks)

Exam Questions

1 Lacquer Luster is a company that supplies wood varnish. It has a website that it uses to display information about its products. The website also includes the company's phone number, email address and postal address in case anyone wants to contact the company.

a) Describe one advantage of using a website to display information.

....

....

(2 marks)

b) Lacquer Luster always send out invoices with customers' orders.
State **two** details that might be found on an invoice.

1. ....

2. ....

(2 marks)

c) Terry, a carpenter, has recently received several incorrect deliveries from Lacquer Luster. He wants to complain, so he looks at Lacquer Luster's website to get their contact details.

Suggest a suitable method of communication for Terry to use to send his complaint to the company. Give **two** reasons for your answer.

Method of communication ....

1. ....

....

2. ....

....

(5 marks)

d) After investigating Terry's complaint, Lacquer Luster discovered that the incorrect orders were due to some staff members not following the correct procedures when processing orders.

The manager of Lacquer Luster wants to remind all staff about the correct procedure.

i) Suggest **one** suitable way for the reminder to be communicated.

....

(1 mark)

ii) Describe **one** advantage and **one** disadvantage of the method suggested above.

Advantage ....

....

Disadvantage ....

....

(4 marks)

Face-to-Face Meetings

Electronic communication is great, but sometimes it's more effective to meet other people in a room for a chat.

Face-to-Face Meetings Involve *Oral Communication...*

1) Face-to-face meetings involve a group of people getting together in the same place to discuss business.
2) Informal meetings can be like a conversation — without any written record.
3) Formal meetings are more carefully organised and recorded. They involve various protocols (see below).
4) In face-to-face meetings the sender (i.e. a person who says something) gets instant feedback. The sender can check that their message has been understood by asking questions (the listener can also ask questions to clarify anything they didn't understand).

...and *Silent Communication*

Humans communicate silently all the time — even if they don't always realise they're doing it.

1) Body language and facial expressions can be a giveaway (people can look bored, happy, angry...) Listeners may interpret a message in a particular way as a result of the speaker's body language.
2) Touch can also make a difference — e.g. people are sometimes judged on their handshakes.

Protocols are Rules Followed in Meetings

Protocols are rules and conventions that people agree to stick to when communicating.

1) In informal meetings, protocols are often the same thing as manners. For example, it's often considered rude to interrupt, or not listen to others.
2) Formal meetings usually have many protocols. For example:
   - The agenda outlines the topics that will be discussed. This should be sent to people in advance so that they can plan what they want to say.
   - A chairperson controls the discussion — people may have to ask for permission to speak.
   - Minutes are a written record of what has been discussed in the meeting.

Appraisals and *AGMs* are Face-to-Face Meetings

1) APPRAISAL MEETINGS — a manager and a worker discuss the worker's performance over the previous year. They then set performance targets for the worker for the next year.
2) Appraisal meetings are usually private and face-to-face. This makes it easier to raise personal issues and concerns.

1) ANNUAL GENERAL MEETINGS (AGMs) are held once a year by many limited liability firms (see p3). The directors invite all shareholders to attend.
   - The business provides a report on its performance to the shareholders.
   - The directors can be asked questions about their performance by the shareholders.
2) AGMs are a good opportunity to inform shareholders of developments in the business.
3) They also allow the directors to get feedback from the owners of the business about their performance. Shareholders may be able to vote on the way the business is run.

Face it — you're just going to have to learn this page...

Meetings involve a lot of talking (or oral communication, if you prefer). Talking face to face with people can get quite emotional, especially if there's a disagreement. It's a lot more personal than all those letters.

Other Oral Communication

Sometimes it isn't practical to have a face-to-face meeting. Fortunately, there is technology which allows oral communication between people who aren't in the same room.

Telephones Allow Long-Distance Oral Communication

1) Telephone conversations allow instant feedback. But you can't see body language, which can make it harder to interpret the message.
2) Mobile phones allow people to be contacted even when they're not in the office. This is great for people who travel a lot as part of their job (as long as they can get a signal).
3) Voicemail can be used to leave messages. This means oral messages can be delivered at any time (though the sender won't get instant feedback this way).
4) Businesses often use protocols for telephone conversations (e.g. when they answer a call, staff usually give their name and the company's name).

Teleconferencing Links People in Different Places

Teleconferencing is when several people in different locations communicate as though they're in a meeting — usually using either phone or internet technology. There are two main types of teleconferencing.

AUDIO CONFERENCING allows the people to communicate orally.
- Each person has a microphone to talk into, and a speaker that outputs what other people are saying.
- Audio conferences can be held using fairly basic telephones, so it's not too expensive.
- On the downside, you can't see people's body language, so messages are easier to misunderstand.

VIDEO CONFERENCING allows oral and visual communication.
- It uses speakers, microphones, video cameras and monitors to transmit sound and images.
- You can see people during the meeting, so it's more human and personal.
- But the equipment is more expensive than normal telephones.

See p43 for more on teleconferencing.

Teleconferencing has become more popular in these globalised days. But it's not perfect.
1) There's always the risk of technical failure — if the machinery breaks down, then the meeting's over.
2) There can also be delays as messages are transmitted — this can make conversation difficult.

The Internet Can be Used to Transmit Oral Messages

The internet is used these days to carry all sorts of business communication.
1) Webcasts are a bit like normal TV broadcasts, except they're on the internet. E.g. companies that provide training often use webcasts.
2) Podcasts are audio or video files that people can download from a website and play on a computer or a portable device. Businesses use them to provide information about the company, or to promote new products.
   People who subscribe to podcasts automatically receive updates, so they can be a good way to keep people in touch with what your company is doing.
3) Webinars are like presentations, but over the internet. They're held at prearranged times, and people who want to take part have to log on to a particular website. The audience can usually participate in webinars (e.g. by typing questions or comments for everyone else to see).

The wonders of modern (and Victorian) technology...

Make sure you know how telephones, audio and video conferencing and the internet affect oral communication. And remember — a lot of this technology can be very expensive, so it might not always be appropriate for a firm.

Visual Communication

Some forms of communication can say a lot, even if it doesn't look like they are...

Names, **Logos** and **Designs** Can Help Build a **Brand Image**

1) Businesses try to give themselves trading names that are unique, catchy and easy to remember. They want you to think of them whenever you need a plumber/shampoo/bank/...

2) A logo is a visual representation of the business. It might include the trading name and some visual images summing up key messages about the business — to help it create an identity.

Some brands are so well known they can use a really simple logo (e.g. Nike's 'swoosh').

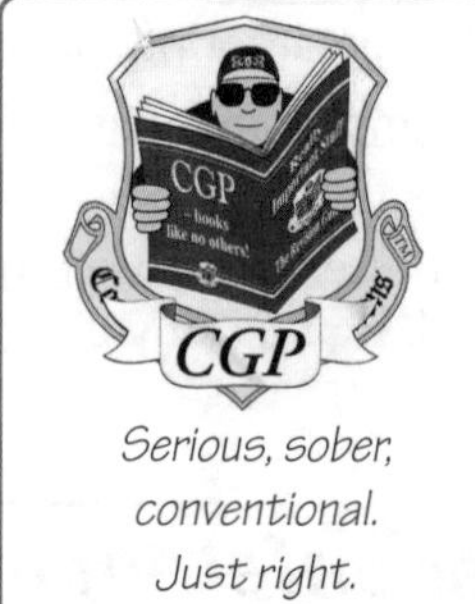

Serious, sober, conventional. Just right.

3) For example, a legal firm will probably want its logo to look neat, formal and professional (because this might make people think the firm is professional and reliable too — important for a legal firm).
4) Logos usually appear on all a business's written communications (letters, envelopes, brochures, adverts...), so it's important to get it right.
5) Even things like using the same colour scheme in all its communications can help a business create an identity — eventually customers might connect those colours with the business.

Advertisements Promote Products **And** Create an **Image**...

Adverts need to fit in with the overall message that a firm wants to communicate.

- Some adverts aim to communicate specific information about products and services.
- Some use images of attractive people to link the product to a glamorous lifestyle.
- Others can be plain weird — these aim to get people thinking and talking about the brand, even if no-one really understands what's going on.

...as do **Celebrity Endorsements** and **Slogans**

1) **CELEBRITY ENDORSEMENTS**
   - Large companies often ask famous people to endorse their products by appearing in advertising campaigns and smiling a bit.
   - This can really boost sales — so a really popular celebrity can be paid huge amounts for their services.
   - But if the celebrity gets involved in a scandal, it can make the firm look bad too.

2) **SLOGANS AND STRAPLINES**
   - Slogans are phrases that are designed to be catchy. Sometimes they're even set to music (in which case they're called jingles).
   - Straplines are captions that appear next to company logos.
   - Both of these are a bit like a logo, only in words — they can help a firm project a certain image of itself, even though they're usually pretty short.

For example, CGP's strapline used to be "Buy Our Books, They're Ace."

It's all about creating a brand image for the business...

Visual communication (in logos, design, adverts etc.) can be a great way for businesses to reinforce the image they're trying to convey. And if they can rope in a celeb to say something nice, then all the better.

Changing a Communication System

Over recent years, communications technology has developed fast. Firms have to constantly assess whether they're communicating in the most effective ways. And if not, they need to change things.

Systems Need to be **Developed** and **Improved**

There are a couple of reasons why a business might want to change a communication system.

1) **EFFECTIVENESS** — All systems are designed for a particular purpose (e.g. providing customer service, communicating with suppliers). If the system is no longer doing its job effectively, it'll need to change.

2) **COST** — An efficient system should deliver good results for a low cost. As the needs of the business change and new technology becomes available, the old system may no longer be the cheapest option.

Systems Go Through a **Continuous Cycle** of Change

There are several stages involved in changing a communication system. But it's not enough to go through them once — the process goes round in a constant cycle.

1 Set objectives for the improved system

- What does the system need to do?
- What needs to be improved about the old system?

2 Plan the creation of the improved system

- Make an action plan for improvements.
- This should say what needs to be done, by when, and what resources will be needed.

3 Implement the improvements

- Put the plan into action.
- This might mean buying new hardware, or installing more modern software or cabling.
- Test and refine the new system so that it works as intended.

4 Evaluate the impact of the improved system

- Has the new system had the desired effect?
- Have there been any negative effects?
- Are employees using the equipment in the most efficient ways? Is any training needed?

But eventually problems are bound to emerge, so you go back to the beginning...

Updated Systems May Have an **Impact** on the Business

New and improved systems can have big effects — good and bad. Businesses need to stay alert...

1) Costs need to be monitored to make sure the new system is good value for money.
2) Staff may need training and re-skilling to get the best out of the new system. Some workers' new jobs might be very different from their old ones.
3) Multi-tasking may become possible — this means staff could have several tasks on the go at once.
4) New ways of working might become possible — e.g. hot-desking and working from home (see p43).
5) Some workers might be made redundant if the new system needs fewer people. On the other hand, a new system can bring employment opportunities in new areas of the business.

I recommend a continuous cycle of revision and practice...

Change in a communications system doesn't have to involve new technology, but very often it does. Technology moves fast — sparkly new communication systems start to go out of date as soon as they're plugged in. Businesses need to constantly review and improve their systems, and assess their impact.

Warm-up and Worked Exam Questions

Warm-up Questions

1) What is a face-to-face meeting?
2) Why are appraisal meetings usually held in private?
3) Give one advantage and one disadvantage of voicemail.
4) Describe what a podcast is. Why might a business produce a podcast?
5) Give one disadvantage of a celebrity endorsement.
6) What is a slogan?

Worked Exam Question

Cover up the answers below, think how you would answer the questions, and then see how your answers compare to ours. Then have a go at the exam question on the next page.

1 Read **Item A** and then answer the questions that follow.

Item A

S&D Deliveries have used the computer program InvoiceGen Pro to create their invoices for the last 8 years. The finance manager has told the director of S&D Deliveries that the company should upgrade to a more modern program. However, the director wants to consider the impacts of such an upgrade before purchasing any new software.

a) Explain **two** reasons why InvoiceGen Pro may need to be upgraded.

InvoiceGen Pro may no longer do the job S&D Deliveries need it to do, ✔ [1 mark]
e.g. it may not be compatible with other software that the firm uses. ✔ [1 mark]
Newer programs may have new features which make invoicing faster and more efficient. ✔ [1 mark] *This could reduce costs for S&D Deliveries.* ✔ [1 mark]

(4 marks)

b) Describe one potential **negative** impact on S&D Deliveries of a new invoicing program.

Some staff may need training to use the new invoicing program. ✔ [1 mark]
This will cost S&D Deliveries both money and time. ✔ [1 mark]

(2 marks)

c) Suggest two ways that the impacts of a new invoicing program could be evaluated.

Check that the department's costs have fallen. ✔ [1 mark]
Ask staff using the new system for feedback. ✔ [1 mark]

(2 marks)

d) The process of upgrading communication systems is often seen as a "continuous cycle". Explain why this is the case.

Communications technology advances all the time. ✔ [1 mark] *Firms need to assess constantly whether new technology could improve their efficiency.* ✔ [1 mark]

(2 marks)

Exam Questions

1 Read **Item A** and then answer the questions that follow.

Item A

Every Friday, the branch managers of Blut Bank plc meet at the company's main office. However, it takes some of the managers an hour and a half to reach the main office and many of the managers do not like the informal nature of the meeting. It is often rowdy, with no clear focus, and many of the managers don't take notes.

The director of Blut Bank plc wants to improve the weekly meeting. He has decided to purchase some teleconferencing equipment and to introduce certain protocols to the meeting to make it more formal.

a) i) What is "teleconferencing"?

....

....

(2 marks)

ii) Video conferencing is a type of teleconferencing that could be used in the weekly meeting. Explain **one** advantage and **one** disadvantage of video conferencing.

Advantage ....

....

Disadvantage ....

....

(4 marks)

b) Describe three protocols that may be suitable for the weekly meeting at Blut Bank plc. Explain the advantages of each.

....

....

....

....

....

....

....

....

....

(9 marks)

Revision Summary for Section Six

You know the drill by now... try all the questions below. And if you don't know the answer to any of them, go back, revise that page again and have another go. You really need to be able to answer them all without any mistakes.

1) What's the purpose of communication? What two roles are involved in a communication?
2) Give three methods of communication. Give an advantage of each.
3) List eight channels of communication.
   Think up an example of a message that might be sent through each channel.
4) What is internal communication? Describe two benefits of good internal communication.
5) Give four examples of communication between a business and external stakeholders.
6) Describe three ways that poor external communication can cause problems for a business.
7) List eight barriers to communication. Give a quick explanation of each.
8) Explain four types of error that can be made in business documents.
   Why is it important to check documents for errors before sending them?
9) List three situations when a business letter might be used to send a message.
10) Give three advantages and three disadvantages of business letters.
11) Describe these methods of internal written communication: memos, reports, newsletters, notices.
    Give an advantage and a disadvantage of each.
12) What's the difference between a flyer and a brochure?
13) What's an invoice? Give four pieces of information that an invoice will contain.
14) What kind of information does a CV contain?
15) Are faxes quite good, or a bit rubbish? Discuss.
16) Give four reasons why email is great. Then give three problems with it.
17) How can a business restrict access to some parts of its website?
18) What does SMS stand for? What kind of message is SMS useful for?
19) Explain why supermarkets are so keen to give their customers loyalty cards.
20) What does RFID stand for? What can an RFID tag be used for?
21) Give two examples of how people can communicate silently in meetings.
22) Describe three protocols used in formal meetings.
23) Explain the purposes of appraisal meetings and AGMs.
24) What advantage does teleconferencing have over normal telephone calls?
25) Give an advantage and a disadvantage of video conferencing.
26) Describe the main features of webcasts, webinars and podcasts.
27) What's the purpose of a company logo? Why is it important to have a good logo?
28) What is a strapline?
29) Give two reasons why a firm might want to change one of its communication systems.
30) Draw a diagram showing the four stages involved in updating a communication system.
31) Explain five ways that a new communication system might have an impact on a business.

How Businesses Use the Internet

The internet and the World Wide Web have changed the way firms communicate.
Long gone are the days when communication was done during office hours only.

The *Internet* Creates All Sorts of *Opportunities* for Firms

1) The internet is basically a huge network of computers covering the whole world.
2) The World Wide Web (www) is a huge collection of websites that can be viewed by accessing the internet. To view these websites, you need a web browser.
3) Anyone can make a website — it can then be accessed by other computers elsewhere in the world, 24 hours a day.
4) Most modern businesses have their own website these days.

Websites Can Provide *Customer Services*...

The Internet is a really powerful tool for businesses. Used wisely, it can provide all sorts of customer services.

1) E-commerce (see next page) means buying and selling over the internet. Loads of firms these days let customers order goods online 24 hours a day. The goods can then either be posted to the customer or, for things like software and music, they can be downloaded straight away.
2) Websites can also provide technical support. For example, a lot of software updates are provided over the internet.
3) Some companies let customers set up an online customer account. This allows customers to access services on the web (for example, bank websites let their customers pay bills online, mobile phone companies let customers top up their calling credit, and so on...).
4) Firms can also provide answers to frequently-asked questions (FAQs). This can be convenient for customers (since the information's available all the time). It also means the firm doesn't have to have employees answering the same questions over and over.

...and *Give* and *Receive* Information

The internet's also good for more general communication.

1) Websites can provide detailed information about products and services. It's cheaper for the firm than printing catalogues on paper.
2) Company websites can also give positive messages about what the firm does and how it does it. This might include the company's mission statement, or details of its social and environmental policies.

Read the story of CGP's early years, for example.

Good communication goes both ways...

1) Customers can provide feedback via a firm's website. The firm can then react to this — maybe by answering questions, dealing with complaints or providing information that a customer's asked for.
2) Firms can also use feedback to make improvements to their products or customer service — firms often ask for opinions using online surveys.
3) And guestbooks allow customers to leave messages for the firm and other website visitors to read.

Websites help firms keep in touch with their customers...

Websites have become a very important way for firms to communicate with their customers and other stakeholders. They can reach a wide audience, and messages can be exchanged quickly and easily. None of this information probably comes as a surprise, but make sure you know it, all the same.

Business Websites — Benefits and Costs

Buying and selling products and services online is called e-commerce.
Businesses need to think about the potential costs and benefits of e-commerce.

Websites Can be Used to Reach *Wider Markets...*

The internet provides extra marketing possibilities...

1) The internet can be accessed all over the world — this makes it possible to target potential customers in foreign countries.
2) A company can put marketing material on its own website, or pay to advertise on other websites.
3) Internet adverts can be animated and interactive — great for catching people's attention. And they usually contain a direct link to the company's own website.

*...And **Sell** to These Markets **24/7***

A good website can really help a firm's competitiveness and increase its market share.

1) Firms can market and sell goods through their websites 24 hours a day, 7 days a week (or '24/7').
2) 24/7 marketing and selling can give e-commerce firms an advantage over traditional 9 to 5 businesses. Customers shop from home at a time that's convenient for them.

*Websites Can **Reduce Costs** — But They're **Not Free***

E-commerce can reduce costs in lots of ways. For example...

1) Putting product information online saves the cost of printing and distributing catalogues and brochures.
2) Online customer services (e.g. FAQs) may mean that fewer customer service staff need to be paid.
3) Businesses that only sell online rather than in High Street shops save money on rent.

But for some businesses, the costs of the website could be greater than the savings.

1) Setting up a website costs money. Firms often need the help of specialist website designers. And things like online payment facilities can be expensive to set up.
2) Once the website is up and running, staff will be needed to maintain and update it.
3) The internet is always available, so staff may need to work outside normal office hours to maintain it or offer customer support. These staff will need to be paid for their extra time.

*Websites Can Give Businesses More to **Worry About***

1) E-commerce firms collect confidential data from their customers (e.g. phone numbers, credit card details).
2) Firms need to protect this information from unauthorised users by making their websites secure. Customers who have money and information stolen may sue. The firm may also be prosecuted and could easily get a bad reputation.
3) The internet can help a firm reach wider markets. But it also means that competitors from all over the world can compete in the firm's 'home' market.

Customers can now shop till they drop, 24/7...

For most large businesses, having a website is essential to compete in the market. But for some more traditional firms, a website may not be what their customers want — the costs could outweigh the benefits.

Domain Names and Hosting

There are a few technical details on this page. It's all useful, though.

Domain Names Have to be **Bought** and **Registered**

Any computer on the internet has an Internet Protocol address (IP address) — e.g. 87.106.176.53. These long strings of numbers are fine for computers, but aren't very human-friendly. That's why we have domain names.

1) Domain names are used to help make these IP addresses more memorable to humans.
2) Companies choose their own domain name, but all domain names have to be registered with an organisation called a domain name registrar.
3) Companies need to choose their domain name carefully. For example, a short, catchy domain name is probably more memorable than a really long, obscure one that won't mean anything to anybody.
4) A domain name registrar can tell you whether a domain name you've chosen for your firm is already being used by someone else, or whether it breaks any naming rules (e.g. spaces aren't allowed).

(1) There are a few rules about this last bit of a domain name...

(2) But this bit here... you can have more or less what you like (unless someone's registered it before you).

- You can't just use ".uk" (e.g. www.cgp.uk wouldn't be allowed).
- ".ac.uk" is reserved for academic institutions (e.g. universities), and ".gov.uk" is for local or national government.
- But you could have, for example:
  .co.uk — usually used by commercial firms
  .org.uk — usually used by non-profit organisations
  .plc.uk — usually for public limited companies
  .sch.uk — usually for schools etc.

5) In the UK, domain name registrars are usually commercial businesses — so they'll charge you a fee when you register a domain name.
6) Once you've registered a domain name, nobody else can use it. But registration doesn't last forever. You have to pay a fee (every two years, usually) to carry on using the domain name.

Domain registrars often provide web hosting facilities too — see below.

Websites are **Hosted** on **Servers**

1) A website is basically a load of computer files. All these files are stored on computers called web servers.
2) These web servers are managed by companies called web hosts.
3) Web-hosting businesses charge a fee if you want them to host your website. For the customer, this is usually less expensive than buying the equipment themselves, though.
4) Large firms often prefer to have their own servers — this gives them more control of their websites.
5) You use a website address to find computers on the World Wide Web. The address is usually 'www.' followed by the company's domain name (e.g. www.cgpbooks.co.uk).
6) Websites don't have to be on the internet. Firms often have internal websites hosted by a web server on an internal network — these are called intranets. Only users of the firm's network can look at these websites.

Website developed by the business... ...and uploaded to a web server.

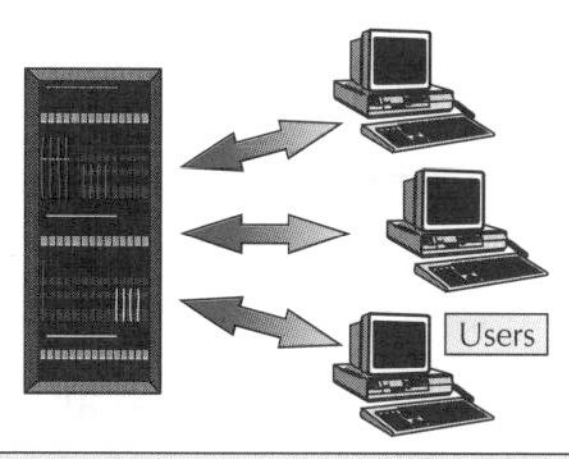

The web server then sends pages from the website to users who request them.

Make sure you learn domain points on this page...

Okay... not the easiest page in the world. Don't get domain names and IP addresses confused. They're similar, but a domain name is 'human-friendly' (since it's easy-to-understand words), whereas an IP address is a load of hard-to-understand numbers, but which is more useful to a computer. That's the basic difference really.

Websites and the Law

There are laws even in cyberspace. It's hard for the law to keep up with cybercrime, though.

Personal Data Collected on Websites Must be Protected

Not surprisingly, your old pal the Data Protection Act (1998) (see p58) applies to websites.

1) All UK-based websites that collect personal data from visitors have to obey the Act.
2) This includes protecting private information like email addresses, usernames and passwords.
3) E-commerce sites that collect financial data and customer addresses need to be especially careful — this means investing in good online security.

Websites Can't Copy Material Without Permission...

Websites are also subject to the Copyright, Designs and Patents Act (1988).

1) This Act means it's illegal to copy text, data or images, without permission from the copyright holder.
2) So businesses need to be careful about what they put on their website — if they want to use somebody else's material, they have to ask permission and they may have to pay a fee.
3) Website owners breaking this law could face an unlimited fine — especially if they've profited from it.

...Must Sell Products Legally...

1) Websites selling goods and services have to follow the same laws as High Street shops, including the Supply of Goods and Services Act (1982) and the Sale and Supply of Goods Act (1994).
2) These laws state that every product (including products sold online) must:

   i) be fit for its purpose — i.e. it should do the job it's designed for.
   ii) match its description — so all online product information must be accurate.
   iii) be of satisfactory quality — it should last a reasonably long time, and not have other faults that cause problems for the buyer (e.g. a fridge that buzzes loudly).

3) If products don't come up to scratch, customers are legally entitled to an exchange or a replacement. For e-commerce businesses, this can be expensive — they may also have to pay the costs of postage.
4) Businesses must also do all they can to make sure their websites are accessible to people with disabilities.

...And Follow Distance-Selling Laws

1) Distance selling means selling where there is no face-to-face contact between buyer and seller.
2) The Consumer Protection (Distance Selling) Regulations 2000 give customers three main rights:

   i) Websites must provide clear information about the firm and its products before customers buy.
   ii) They must give customers written confirmation of any orders placed — usually by email.
   iii) Customers have a seven-day cooling-off period when they can cancel the order without penalty.

3) Firms should always use an encrypted part of their website to collect payment.
4) As usual, businesses that break these rules can be fined. Serious fraud can lead to prison sentences.

An encrypted web page has "https://", rather than just "http://" in the address — the 's' stands for 'secure'.

Businesses can't use the internet to hide from the law...

They may be online, but e-commerce businesses deal with real people, real money and personal information. It can cost money to obey the laws, but breaking them can lead to fines and damage the firm's reputation.

Success of Business Websites

Businesses need to know how successful their websites are to make sure they're worth the investment. There's no point splashing out cash on a fancy website that doesn't achieve anything except to look pretty.

Firms Need to **Measure** the **Success** of their Websites

There are different ways for a firm to do this. For instance, they can measure:

- how many 'hits' they get — i.e. how many times the page is viewed,
- how long people look at their website for,
- how many repeat visitors they get.

A firm can even track where people linked to their site from (so if the firm placed an advert on another website, it can see how successful it was).

This is all very nice, but what a company is really interested in is whether their website has helped to:

1 Increase Brand Awareness

1) A firm's website is a good place to tell potential customers about their brand (see p9).
2) Brand awareness can be measured by surveys (often online) that ask people where they heard about various different businesses.

2 Increase Overall Sales and Market Share

1) It's easy to track how many sales are made online — if these are increasing, then that's a good sign. But customers may just be buying through the firm's website instead of through shops or mail-order.
2) So a good website (like any other promotion) will ideally increase a firm's overall sales.
3) A successful website should help a firm increase its market share (market share is the percentage of all sales in the market that a firm receives — see p8).

3 Reduce Costs

1) A firm might be able to reduce the number of stores it operates if online business really takes off.
2) If online customer support is effective, there should be fewer calls to the company's telephone helpline.
3) Online product information should lead to less demand for paper catalogues and brochures.

But remember that none of these measures is totally reliable in measuring the website's success. Other factors might also be affecting these measures (e.g. sales might be increasing because of other marketing campaigns, or because customer habits have changed).

Websites **Won't** be Vital For **All** Businesses

1) Websites don't allow face-to-face contact. Some firms might decide a website wouldn't really help them (e.g. if they make a point of providing personal advice in a traditional way).
2) Some businesses will feel they need to have a website as part of their general marketing 'presence' — it's what customers expect. They may choose just to have a basic, inexpensive website that provides information and contact details, but not worry too much about anything fancy.

Firms need to keep an eye on how successful their website is...

Most businesses now have a website of some sort, but some firms will benefit much more than others. If a website isn't earning its keep, it may need to be redesigned and relaunched.

Creating a Website

So you now know everything about websites. Well, almost.
You also need to know a few things to consider when actually making a website.

Plan the Website Around the Budget, Content and Users

Budget

1) The more ambitious the website, the bigger the budget a firm will need. Or to put it another way, if you don't have a big budget, keep your ambitions realistic. A really fancy website might have loads of interactive content and look really professional. But it all costs.
2) Secure e-commerce facilities also cost — so firms with a small budget need to work out whether they're likely to earn the money back through internet sales.

Content

1) Think about the purpose of the website — this will decide the content.
2) You might be able to provide information using mainly simple text and diagrams. But if you want to thrill or entertain, you might go for videos and interactive content — this is more complex, more expensive and takes up more memory.

Users and their equipment

The site's content needs to meet the needs of the people who'll be using it.

1) For example, children will prefer sites that have plenty of bright colours, games and animations.
2) Sites designed for adults (e.g. news sites) will probably be very different in tone.
3) You also need to think about the different equipment people might be using...

- The speed of internet connections varies from place to place. Website designers need to make sure that most users will be able to download content at a reasonable speed. If a website runs too slowly, many users will get tired of waiting and go elsewhere.
- There are also many different internet browsers available — the site should be compatible with as many as possible. If it's not, some users won't be able to use the site.

Develop, Test and Roll Out the Website

TECHNICAL DEVELOPMENT

1) Once the planning's done, the website needs to be constructed.
2) This can be done using specialist web-authoring software (see p115). Web designers may be employed to set up the website — depending on how complex the design is.
3) When the development is finished, it needs to be tested for bugs and other problems. This should include testing on different browsers, internet connections and hardware. This helps to make sure that all users will be able to get good access to the site.

ROLL-OUT AND MAINTENANCE

1) Businesses roll out their websites by uploading them to an internet server.
2) Sometimes complex websites are rolled out one section at a time — e.g. a few initial bits may be published first, and links added to it once any technical glitches have been ironed out.
3) Once the site is up and running, it needs to be maintained. Content needs to be kept up to date, and links to other websites need to be checked to make sure they still work.

Roll out, roll out — step this way to revise website development...

Making a website is a creative process, but web designers should keep all the factors on this page in mind. Different businesses will need different things from their sites, but all websites should serve a purpose.

Warm-Up and Worked Exam Questions

Warm-up Questions

1) Give two ways that a website can collect customer feedback.
2) Describe how companies can use the internet for marketing.
3) What action might a customer take against a company if their confidential data was stolen from the company's website?
4) What is an intranet?
5) Give one reason why having a website wouldn't really help some businesses.

Worked Exam Question

The following question has been answered already — but there are other possible answers to some parts, so have a think about what you would have written down. After you've done that, it's time for another exam question.

1 Totems To You is a retailer that currently sells its goods through High Street stores. The business is now considering introducing e-commerce facilities onto its website.

a) i) What is meant by the term "e-commerce"?

It's the buying and selling of products or services online. ✔[1 mark]

(1 mark)

ii) Describe how e-commerce can allow businesses to reach wider markets.

A website can be accessed by people all over the world, ✔[1 mark] *meaning that anyone with Internet access is a potential customer, wherever they are.* ✔[1 mark]

(2 marks)

b) Companies using a website for e-commerce in the UK must follow certain legal requirements. Describe **two** such legal requirements.

The companies have to follow distance-selling laws, ✔[1 mark] *e.g. they must provide written confirmation of any orders placed.* ✔[1 mark]

Any goods sold must also be accurately described and of satisfactory quality, ✔[1 mark] *otherwise customers are entitled to an exchange.* ✔[1 mark]

(4 marks)

c) The manager of Totems To You wants to use e-commerce if it will save the company money. Describe **three** ways that e-commerce might reduce the firm's costs.

Displaying product information online saves printing catalogues, ✔[1 mark] *which will reduce the firm's printing costs.* ✔[1 mark] *Totems To You may reduce the number of stores it owns if an online shop is successful,* ✔[1 mark] *which may reduce rent costs.* ✔[1 mark] *Online customer services, e.g. FAQs,* ✔[1 mark] *may reduce the number of customer service staff needed and so reduce staff costs.* ✔[1 mark]

(6 marks)

Exam Questions

1 Read **Item A** and then answer the questions that follow.

> **Item A**
>
> Dynamo Dynamics Ltd. sells alternating current generators. The company is setting up its first website, which will include an online shop and product support documents. Eleanor, the company's founder, has suggested 'generating.ac.uk' as the domain name for the website. The website will eventually be hosted by HTMLHoldings, a private web-hosting firm, but it is currently in the planning stage.

a) i) Explain the term "domain name".

....

....

(2 marks)

ii) Describe **one** difficulty that might be encountered when Dynamo Dynamics Ltd. tries to register the domain name 'generating.ac.uk'.

....

....

(2 marks)

b) Suggest **one** reason why some companies might prefer to use web-hosting firms instead of hosting websites on their own computers.

....

(1 mark)

c) Explain **two** factors that should be considered when planning a website.

....

....

....

....

(4 marks)

d) Describe **three** ways for Dynamo Dynamics Ltd. to measure the success of its website.

....

....

....

....

....

(Continue your answer on a separate piece of paper) *(8 marks)*

Revision Summary for Section Seven

There's quite a lot to say about websites...

There's the business side (all the costs and benefits), for example. Then there's all the technical stuff (domain names, servers, development). Try these revision questions to make sure that everything has stuck in your memory.

1) What is the World Wide Web, and what kind of software do you need to view it?
2) Give four types of customer service that can be provided on a website.
3) Describe two types of information that a firm might put on its website.
4) What is e-commerce?
5) What is 24/7 marketing and selling, and why might it help firms with a website become more competitive?
6) List three ways that a website can reduce business costs, and three ways it could increase them.
7) How can a website cause problems for a business?
8) What is meant by the term 'domain name'?
9) Explain the process of getting a domain name.
10) What is web hosting?
11) Can all websites be viewed on the internet? Explain your answer.
12) List five types of personal data that a firm might collect on its website.
13) Explain how the Copyright, Designs and Patents Act 1989 affects website owners.
14) a) Give three criteria that all products sold on websites have to meet by UK law.
    b) What are customers entitled to if products don't meet these criteria?
15) What three rights do website customers have under 'Distance Selling' laws?
16) Why might increasing sales on a website not mean that sales are increasing overall?
17) Why might some companies choose not to have a website?
18) Give four ways in which content could be presented on a website.
19) Describe the different stages of developing a website.
20) What is meant by rolling out a website?
21) Give two things that need to be done during website maintenance.

Software Applications

This last Section is all about using software to make different types of business document.

- If you're doing AQA or OCR, this is all about getting ready for your computer-based assessment.
- If you're doing Edexcel, you won't have a computer-based assessment, but you do still need to know all about the various business documents mentioned — e.g. the important features of a business letter, and so on. So don't just skip over the pages thinking it's nothing to do with you.

You'll Need to **Practise Practise Practise**

Now then... learning how to use a piece of software isn't the kind of thing that's best done just by reading a book. You really need to:

- sit yourself down in front of a computer,
- find out how to use all the different features mentioned on these pages — using the software you'll be using for your computer-based assessment.

We don't know exactly what software you'll be using on your exam day — so we can't tell you in this book exactly what buttons to press to use all the different features (even different versions of the same piece of software can look very different).

BUT...

We've got some animated computer-based tutorials that will talk you through how to use some of the trickier features for some common pieces of software.

Have a look at the contents pages at the front of this book for more information.

Okay, now it's on with the show...

Open, **Save** and **Print** Using The **File** Menu

You'll probably need the File menu (or the 'Microsoft® Office Button' in Office 2007) several times in your exam — it's similar in most pieces of software. You can use it to Save, Print and Open documents.

Click on the File menu, then...

You might know quicker ways to do this stuff. If so, that's fine — do it the way you like best. But if in doubt, always head for the File menu.

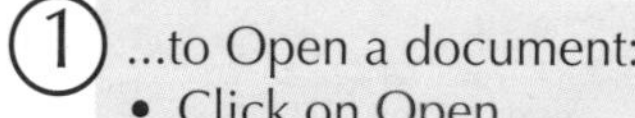

1. ...to Open a document:
   - Click on Open...,
   - Find your document and click on it,
   - Click on the button marked Open.

2. ...to save a document with a different name:
   - Click on Save As...,
   - Type the name you want to give to your document in the File Name box,
   - Click on the button marked Save.

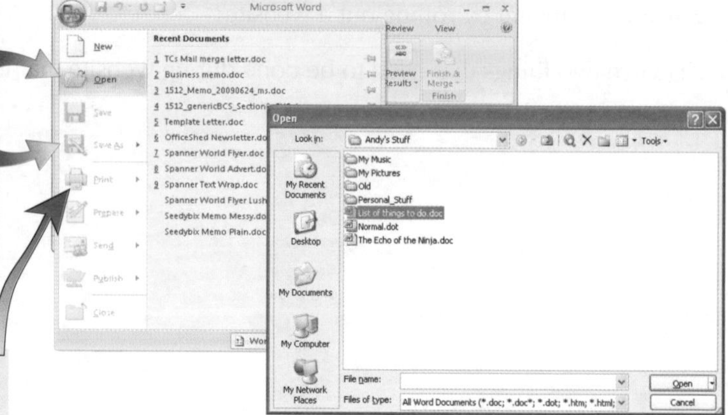

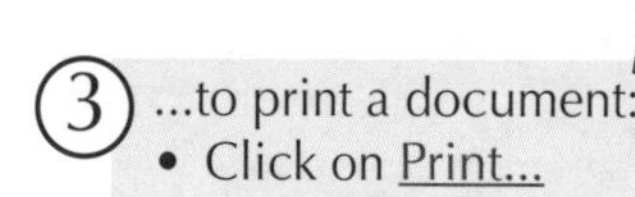

3. ...to print a document:
   - Click on Print...

Open your mind and save this info to your memory...

I know... maybe you know how to do all this stuff already. But don't get all complacent — you could easily lose marks in the exam if you save over a file you still need, or print in the wrong format. And if you're not confident about this stuff, try to find yourself a computer and practise.

Word Processors: Text Formatting

Word processors are designed specifically for editing text (words) — ideal for documents such as memos (p68). Word processors let you format text (change its appearance) in plenty of ways, but remember that no amount of prettiness will cover up for poor spelling, punctuation and grammar.

Formatting Can Make Text Attractive and Readable...

Memos are usually used for internal communication (see p63). They're not too fancy — they just contain the names of the sender and receivers, the date, the subject, and the message itself.

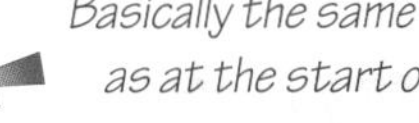

Basically the same information as at the start of an email.

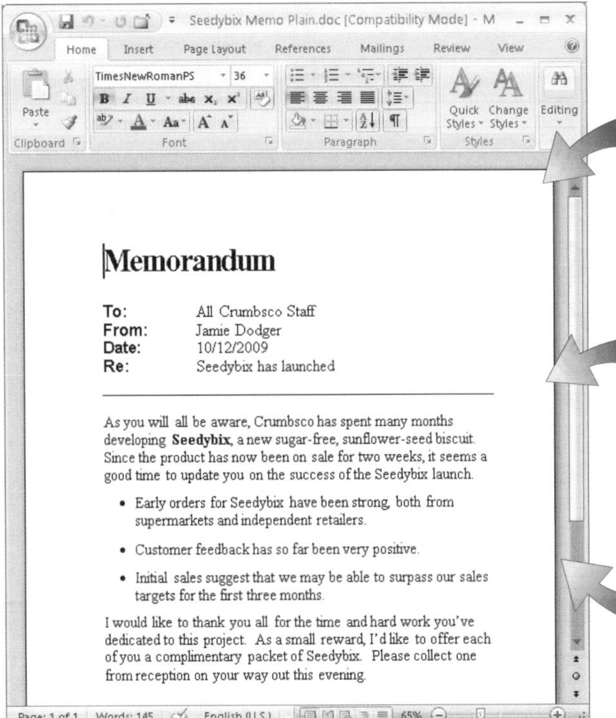

Memorandum

To: All Crumbsco Staff
From: Jamie Dodger
Date: 10/12/2009
Re: Seedybix has launched

As you will all be aware, Crumbsco has spent many months developing **Seedybix**, a new sugar-free, sunflower-seed biscuit. Since the product has now been on sale for two weeks, it seems a good time to update you on the success of the Seedybix launch.

- Early orders for Seedybix have been strong, both from supermarkets and independent retailers.
- Customer feedback has so far been very positive.
- Initial sales suggest that we may be able to surpass our sales targets for the first three months.

I would like to thank you all for the time and hard work you've dedicated to this project. As a small reward, I'd like to offer each of you a complimentary packet of Seedybix. Please collect one from reception on your way out this evening.

You can Change the Size of Text

- The font size of normal text is often between 10 and 12 points. Most people find that fairly easy to read.
- Headings are often printed in a larger size of text.

Fonts can be Formal or Informal

Word processors let you choose from various fonts. You should choose a font that's appropriate for the type of document, and the document's audience.

Formal business documents usually use neat, clear fonts. Most of this memo is in Times New Roman, but there's a bit of Arial in there at the top, too.

For informal documents, other fonts might be more **eye-catching**.

Bullet Points Draw People's Attention

- You can indent text so that the line starts further away from the margin.
- And bullet points can draw people's attention to things that are important.

...But Don't Go Crazy With It

This is the same memo as above, but with different formatting — it's ended up looking a bit of a mess.

Highlighting can Draw Attention to Text

You can highlight text using **bold**, *italics*, underlining and colour. It's best not to use these too much though (especially in formal documents) — they can make the page look childish and messy.

Paragraphs can be Aligned in Different Ways

Text can be aligned in different ways. Left-align and justify are the most common for normal text. This version of the memo uses a range, including centre- and right-alignment.

You can also adjust the line spacing of text. Increasing the space between lines can make text less crowded and easier to read.

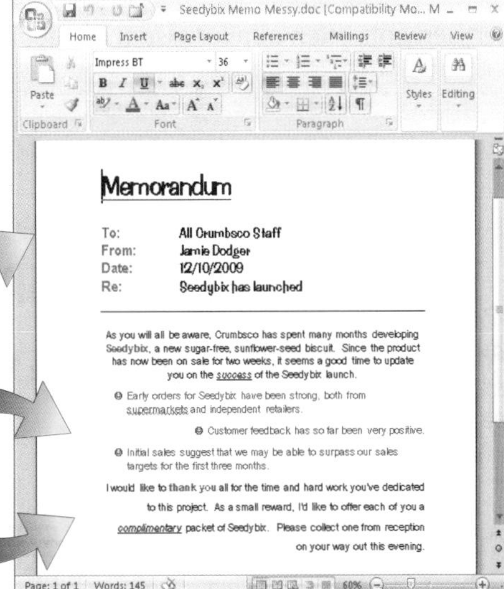

Memorandum

To: All Crumbsco Staff
From: Jamie Dodger
Date: 12/10/2009
Re: Seedybix has launched

As you will all be aware, Crumbsco has spent many months developing Seedybix, a new sugar-free, sunflower-seed biscuit. Since the product has now been on sale for two weeks, it seems a good time to update you on the success of the Seedybix launch.

- Early orders for Seedybix have been strong, both from supermarkets and independent retailers.
- Customer feedback has so far been very positive.
- Initial sales suggest that we may be able to surpass our sales targets for the first three months.

I would like to thank you all for the time and hard work you've dedicated to this project. As a small reward, I'd like to offer each of you a complimentary packet of Seedybix. Please collect one from reception on your way out this evening.

Underlining text — a word processing highlight...

You should be able to use all the techniques on this page, but don't throw them all in just because you can — keep the tone of your message in mind. In the exam, you might have to explain your formatting choices.

Word Processors: Text and Graphics

Sometimes a business will want to produce a document that contains more than just text.
Luckily, word processors can handle graphics too — you can use them to combine text and pictures.

Text Boxes and *Clip Art* Can Make a Page *Attractive*

Some business documents use a mixture of written and visual communication.
Flyers (p69) often combine text and graphics to make a big impact. Here's an example.

Text Boxes can be Dragged Around

Text boxes let you keep chunks of text separate from the main text on the page. You can give them borders and shading (like the heading on this page).

Clip Art is Ready-Made Pictures

Word processors often have their own collections of clip art (ready-made pictures) that you can insert into your documents.

You can Wrap Text in Different Ways

Text wrap lets you position text around objects in various ways (see below). You can also usually customise how the text wraps by dragging the 'wrap points' (like the ones around the spanner).

Square wrap: This text is wrapped square This text is wrapped square This text is wrapped square This text is wrapped square This text is wrapped square This text is wrapped square This text is wrapped square This text is wrapped square This text is wrapped square This

Tight wrap: This text is wrapped tight This text is wrapped tight This text is wrapped tight This text is wrapped tight This text is wrapped tight This text is wrapped tight This text is wrapped tight This text is wrapped tight This text is wrapped tight This text is wrapped tight This

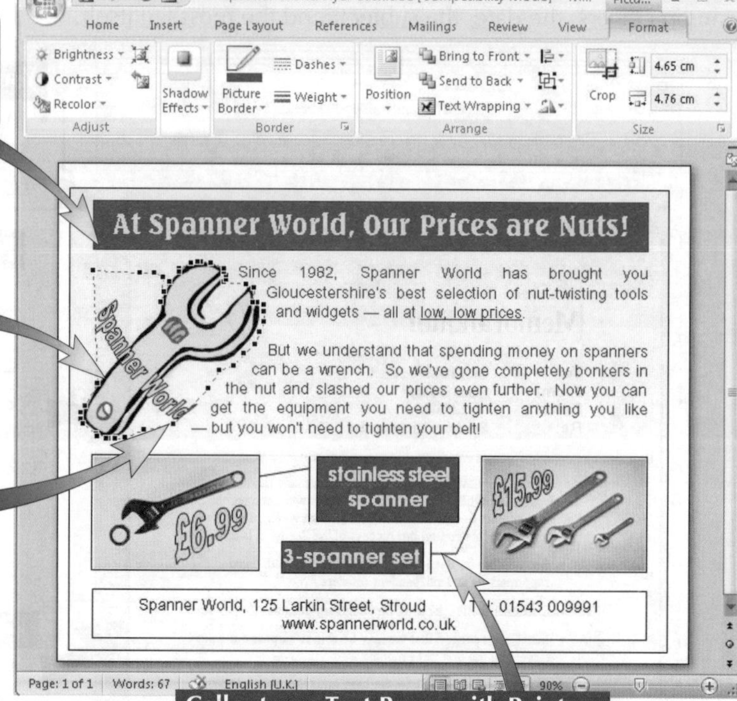

Callouts are Text Boxes with Pointers

Callouts are useful for labelling things and making speech bubbles. You can usually change the direction of the pointer.

You Can Also Put *Graphics* in the *Background*

Advertisements often aim for visual impact as well — not loads of information.

Spanner World has included its logo and its website address on its flyer and its advert.

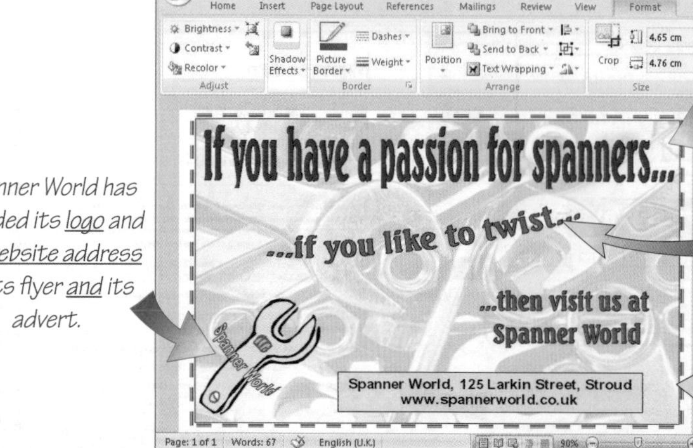

You can Overlay Text on Graphics

Putting text on top of a graphic is a really useful technique — it can make visual documents like adverts look a lot more interesting.

WordArt Makes Text Look Pretty

You can use WordArt to bend text into shapes, give it shading, and add borders to the letters.

Borders can help things to Stand Out

You can put borders around most objects in a word processor, including the page itself. You can change the style, thickness and colour of borders.

Learnt the stuff on this page? That's a wrap...

Word processors are really useful for making basic flyers, leaflets, etc. But most firms would probably make their documents using specialist graphics packages — so they look a bit more snazzy and professional.

Word Processors: Text and Graphics

You need to be able to present data in an appropriate way — and that could well mean tables and charts. Make sure you can create all the effects in the newsletter below.

Newsletters Can Include Columns, Tables and Diagrams

Newsletters are often a bit like mini newspapers, with text laid out in columns. They may also include data in the form of charts, graphs and diagrams. Your word processor should be able to handle all this stuff.

This newsletter has a colourful and eye-catching banner. (WordArt is good for this.)

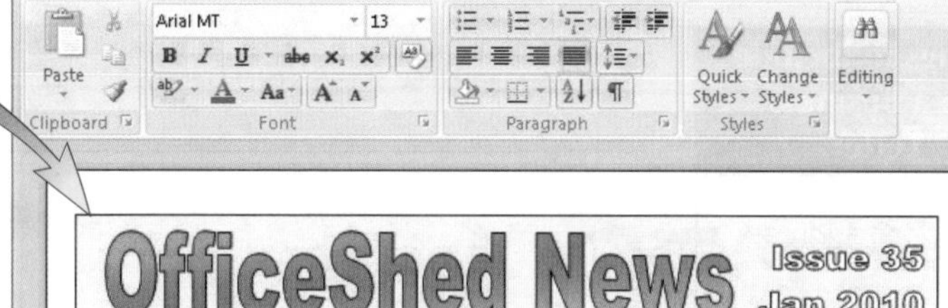

Large, bold headlines to draw attention. They should give the reader an instant idea of what the story is about.

Farewell to the Fax Machine

It's the end of an era for OfficeShed — after 25 years of selling fax machines, we've decided that there's just not enough demand to justify keeping them in stock any longer. Here are the sales figures for faxes and laptops since 2000:

Year	Laptop sales	Fax sales
2000	1236	954
2001	1470	920
2002	1510	765
2003	2013	590
2004	2465	424
2005	2953	311
2006	3730	230
2007	5005	157
2008	5660	92
2009	5840	66

As you can see, fax sales have dropped dramatically in the last ten years as more up-to-date electronic devices have taken over. Laptops have become some of our biggest-selling items, and have been boosted in recent years by the introduction of netbooks. Combined with email and efaxes, there's just no way the old-style fax machine can compete, so we've decided that the time has come to pull the plug on our paper-printing pal. We'll sell through our existing stock before discontinuing the range, so if you'd like to grab one, it could be now or never.

Derek Jacks, Sales Manager

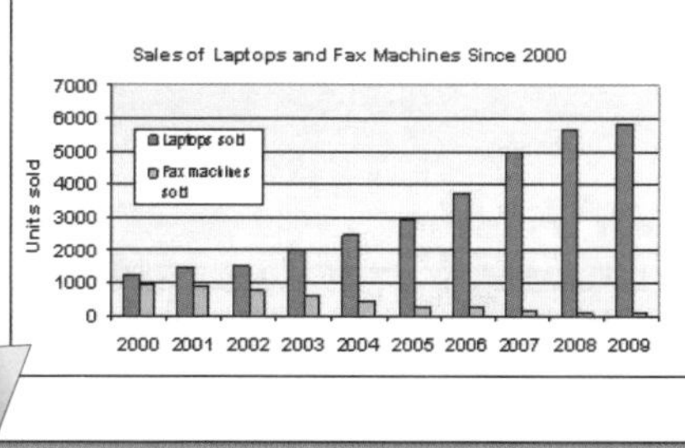

OfficeShed Loft Insulation Will Leave Competitors Lagging

OfficeShed has supplied stationery and other office equipment to its customers since 1977. But now we have exciting plans to expand our range of products into energy-saving office solutions, including loft insulation.

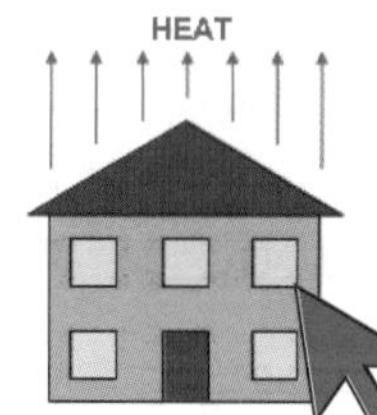

As the diagram clearly shows, hot air rises, so heat escapes rapidly through roofs that don't have insulation. Businesses can make massive savings on their energy bills simply by investing in the right materials, and we intend to target new and existing customers who we believe could benefit from this product.
More news on our marketing strategy for this in the next issue.

Lisa Kitt, Marketing Director

Page: 1 of 1 Words: 276 English (U.S.) 74%

Text Can be Split into Columns

Most word processors let you split the page into columns of text. This can make the text easier to read.

The text in the columns has been justified (the left- and right-hand edges are both aligned). This can make columns look tidy, but watch out for big gaps between words.

Tables are Good For Presenting Data Clearly

Word processors usually have a tool for making tables. You can change the number of rows and columns and tinker with the format till your table looks gorgeous.

You can also import tables from other places (see below), which can make life easier.

Graphs and charts can be a good way to represent data visually. Here, it's much easier to see the change on the graph than it is from the numbers in the table.

Charts and Graphs Can be Imported

Sometimes it's possible to use a diagram from another program (like a spreadsheet or a database) in a word processor document. (This graph was made in a spreadsheet, for example — see p101.)

Word Processors Often Have Simple Drawing Tools

Word processors often have some basic drawing tools — for example, you might be able to draw simple shapes like rectangles, triangles, arrows and so on. This house was made out of simple shapes (which were then grouped together).

Inserting graphics — it's a matter of great import...

For a change, I thought I'd lay out the text in this box in columns. But it's not really appropriate here. It's best not to do fancy things just because you can — leave it for times when it'll actually help.

Word Processors: Business Letters

A template is a standard document containing pre-set formats and layouts. Word processors usually come with a set of ready-made templates. But you can make your own from a document you've already made.

Business Letters Usually Follow a Standard Format

Businesses send different types of letters to different stakeholders (p7), but the formatting often doesn't change much. Here's an example of a letter responding to a job application.

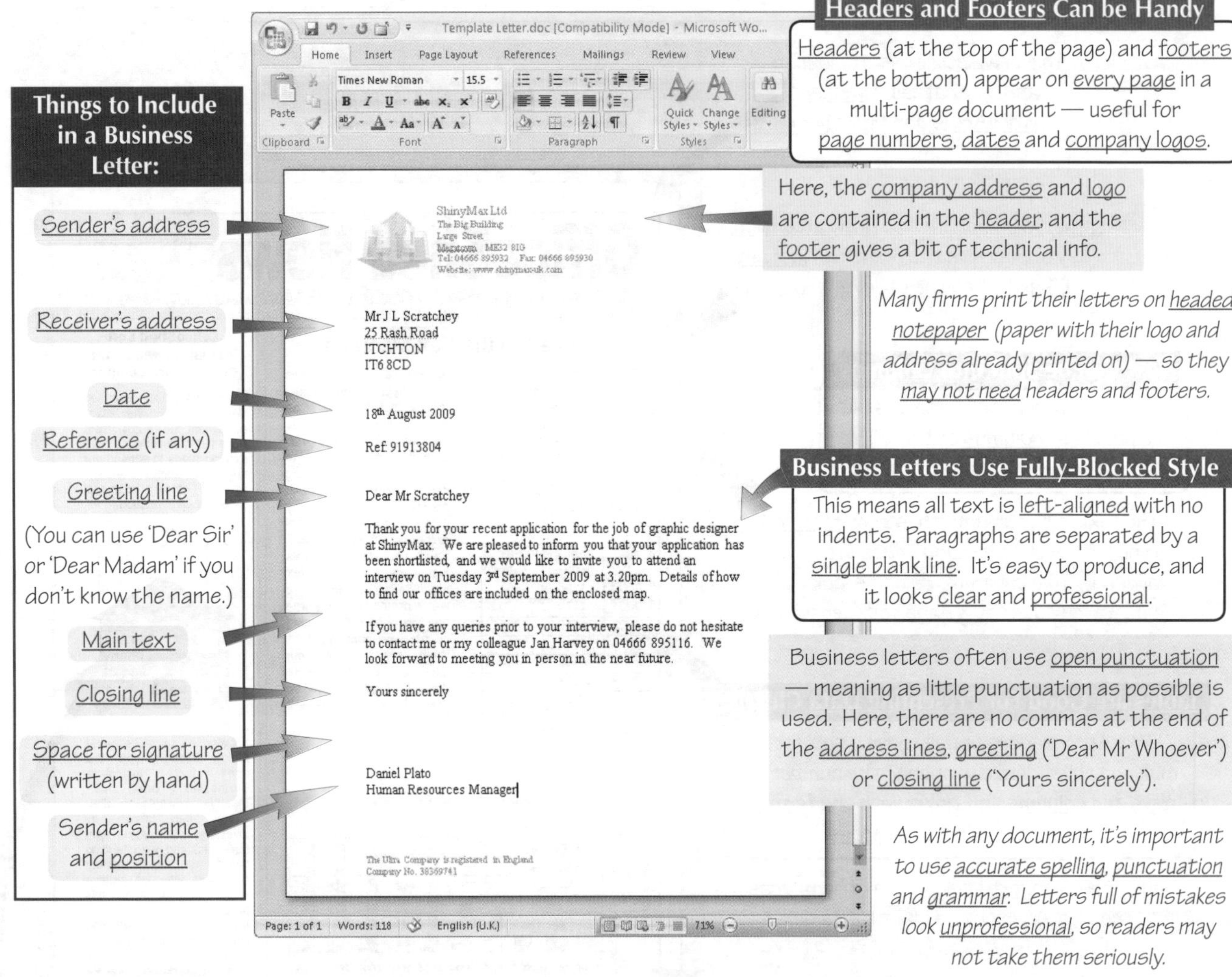

ShinyMax Ltd
The Big Building
Large Street
Maxxtown ME32 8IG
Tel: 04666 895932 Fax: 04666 895930
Website: www.shinymax-uk.com

Mr J L Scratchey
25 Rash Road
ITCHTON
IT6 8CD

18th August 2009

Ref 91913804

Dear Mr Scratchey

Thank you for your recent application for the job of graphic designer at ShinyMax. We are pleased to inform you that your application has been shortlisted, and we would like to invite you to attend an interview on Tuesday 3rd September 2009 at 3.20pm. Details of how to find our offices are included on the enclosed map.

If you have any queries prior to your interview, please do not hesitate to contact me or my colleague Jan Harvey on 04666 895116. We look forward to meeting you in person in the near future.

Yours sincerely

Daniel Plato
Human Resources Manager

The Ultra Company is registered in England
Company No. 38369741

Headers and Footers Can be Handy

Headers (at the top of the page) and footers (at the bottom) appear on every page in a multi-page document — useful for page numbers, dates and company logos.

Here, the company address and logo are contained in the header, and the footer gives a bit of technical info.

Many firms print their letters on headed notepaper (paper with their logo and address already printed on) — so they may not need headers and footers.

Business Letters Use Fully-Blocked Style

This means all text is left-aligned with no indents. Paragraphs are separated by a single blank line. It's easy to produce, and it looks clear and professional.

Business letters often use open punctuation — meaning as little punctuation as possible is used. Here, there are no commas at the end of the address lines, greeting ('Dear Mr Whoever') or closing line ('Yours sincerely').

As with any document, it's important to use accurate spelling, punctuation and grammar. Letters full of mistakes look unprofessional, so readers may not take them seriously.

Letters and Other Documents Can be Used as Templates

1) Once you've produced a letter you're happy with, you can save it as a template. Templates are 'starting points' for other documents. Templates allow a business to quickly produce letters with the right style and formatting without starting from scratch every time.
2) Some details (names, addresses etc.) will need to change for each receiver. This can be done manually, or by using mail-merge fields in the letter (see the next page).
3) You can set up templates for other types of document, too — e.g. memos, notices, agendas...
4) Word processors usually come with built in templates. These are often a good starting point for documents — they give you the basic layout, and you can change the details to suit your needs.

Better template than never...

Many businesses produce a lot of very similar documents (especially letters), day in, day out. Templates can save time, but make sure you know how to lay out a business letter from scratch too — examiners love it.

Word Processors: Mail Merge

Mail merge lets you merge data from a data source (e.g. spreadsheet or database) into a word processor document. This is incredibly useful when you need to send out stacks and stacks of standard letters with just a few details (like the name and address) changed each time.

First, You'll Need Some **Data** to Merge...

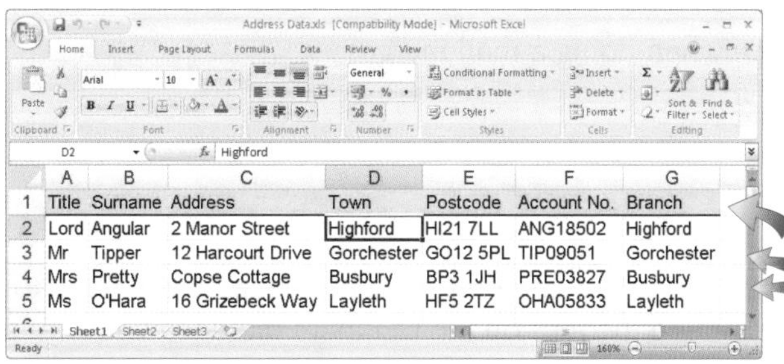

	A	B	C	D	E	F	G
1	Title	Surname	Address	Town	Postcode	Account No.	Branch
2	Lord	Angular	2 Manor Street	Highford	HI21 7LL	ANG18502	Highford
3	Mr	Tipper	12 Harcourt Drive	Gorchester	GO12 5PL	TIP09051	Gorchester
4	Mrs	Pretty	Copse Cottage	Busbury	BP3 1JH	PRE03827	Busbury
5	Ms	O'Hara	16 Grizebeck Way	Layleth	HF5 2TZ	OHA05833	Layleth

Organise Your Data

You'll need the source of the data that you want to merge into your letter. Here, the data's in a spreadsheet (p98).

The first row shows the names of the data fields.

Other rows each contain one complete record (see p105).

...Then You Need a **Letter**, Complete with **Merge Fields**...

Write the Letter and Add the Fields

Here's the standard letter that needs to go to all the customers whose details are in the above spreadsheet.

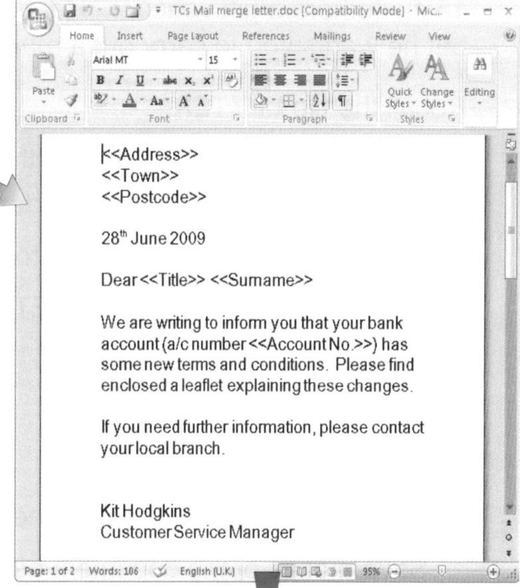

<<Address>>
<<Town>>
<<Postcode>>

28th June 2009

Dear <<Title>> <<Surname>>

We are writing to inform you that your bank account (a/c number <<Account No.>>) has some new terms and conditions. Please find enclosed a leaflet explaining these changes.

If you need further information, please contact your local branch.

Kit Hodgkins
Customer Service Manager

But there are some details missing that will be different for each customer — the name, address and account number, for example. Instead of filling these details in, fields have been inserted — these are the things inside <<double angled brackets>>.

Inserting the field names can be a bit fiddly, and usually involves a few different menus — like this, for example. But the basic idea is always the same — you're creating links from your letter to a field in your data source.

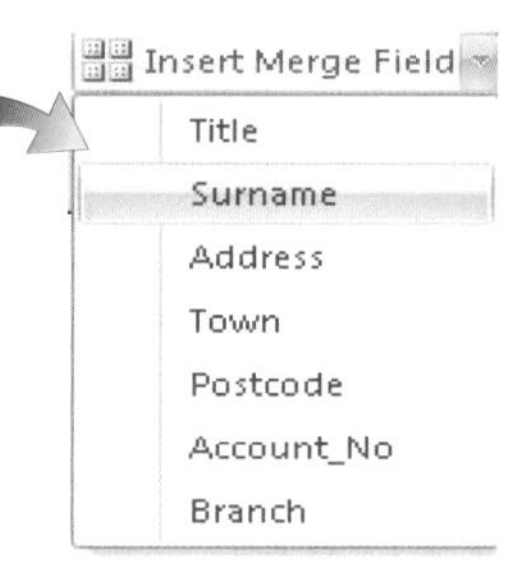

The animated tutorial will talk you through all this in more detail. See the Contents pages for more info.

...Then **Merge** Data And Letter

You've done the hard bit — this bit's pretty easy.

Merge the Data

It's pretty straightforward to merge the data and print your letters. But you should preview your letters first — just to make sure all's well.

When you preview the letters, the field names are replaced by data from one record in your data source. You can flick through all the letters (i.e. use data from each record in turn) to check they're all okay.

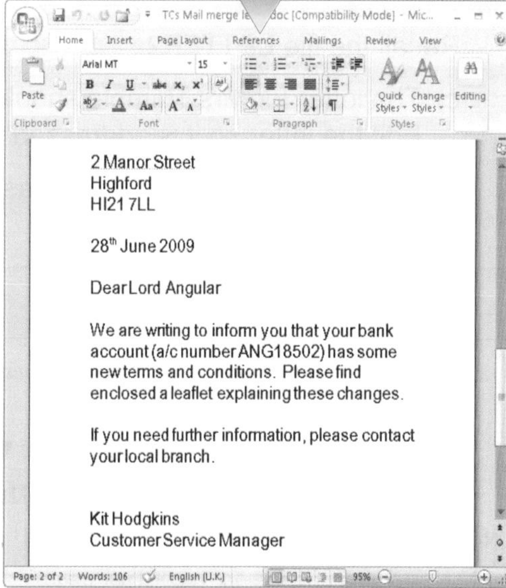

2 Manor Street
Highford
HI21 7LL

28th June 2009

Dear Lord Angular

We are writing to inform you that your bank account (a/c number ANG18502) has some new terms and conditions. Please find enclosed a leaflet explaining these changes.

If you need further information, please contact your local branch.

Kit Hodgkins
Customer Service Manager

Check your letters carefully before you print them.

If you're happy that all the different letters look okay, you can finish the mail merge and print the letters (or email them).

You can even edit the individual letters if they need to be customised somehow.

Well done, <<Title>> <<Surname>>, another page done...

Mail merge looks more fiddly than it actually is — the key is practice. So on your birthday, why not use mail merge to write standard thank-you letters to all your friends and relatives. They'll be so impressed.

Warm-Up and Worked Exam Questions

Warm-up Questions

1) Give five pieces of information that are usually found on a memo.
2) Describe what callouts are for.
3) Describe five details that should be included in a business letter.
4) Name two file types that can be used as a data source when doing a mail merge.

Worked Exam Question

The following exam question has been done for you — the answers are at the bottom of the page. If you want to try the question yourself (which would be a very good idea), you'll find the files on the CD that's included with this book.

Task One: Mail Merge

To celebrate the 10th anniversary of the opening of Harold's Emporium, Harold Lock is sending 15 customers a gift voucher. Harold has typed a standard letter to accompany the gift voucher but he wants you to carry out a mail merge to add the name and address of each recipient.

Recall the file **LETTER.**

a) Insert the following fields from the file **MERGE** into appropriate places in **LETTER**.

Title, Surname, Address_Line_1, Address_Line_2, Postcode.

Replace the word 'DATE' with today's date.

Save a copy of the letter as **LETTER1**.

Print one copy of **LETTER1**.

(7 marks)

Recall the file **LETTER1.**

b) Merge all 15 records into one new document.

Save a copy of the document as **LETTER2**.

(2 marks)

Recall the file **LETTER2**.

c) The letter for Mrs Thimble should be addressed to Mr Brown.
Edit the letter so it is addressed to the correct person.

Save a copy of the document as **LETTER3**.

(2 marks)

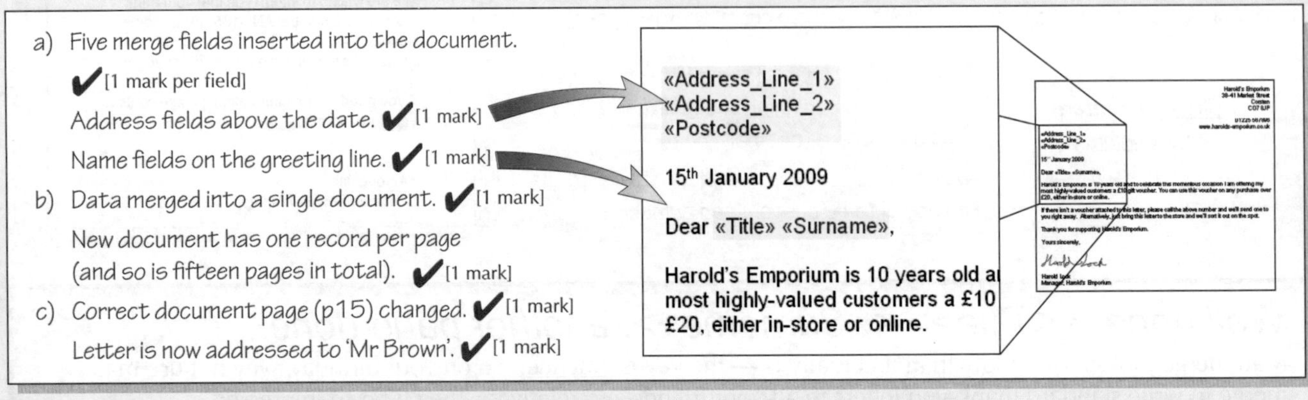

a) Five merge fields inserted into the document.
✔ [1 mark per field]
Address fields above the date. ✔ [1 mark]
Name fields on the greeting line. ✔ [1 mark]

b) Data merged into a single document. ✔ [1 mark]
New document has one record per page (and so is fifteen pages in total). ✔ [1 mark]

c) Correct document page (p15) changed. ✔ [1 mark]
Letter is now addressed to 'Mr Brown'. ✔ [1 mark]

«Address_Line_1»
«Address_Line_2»
«Postcode»
15th January 2009
Dear «Title» «Surname»,
Harold's Emporium is 10 years old a
most highly-valued customers a £10
£20, either in-store or online.

Exam Questions

Computer-based assessment — you'll need a **computer** to answer this question.

Task One: Advertisement

The department store Selfreezers is holding a half price sale in its stores. To make people aware of the event, Selfreezers wants to put an advertisement in local newspapers.

Recall the file **SALE**.

a) Using this text and a suitable software application, create an advertisement for the sale. You should not change the wording of the text.

The advertisement should be eye-catching and have a suitable layout.

The key points of the advertisement should be emphasised.

One appropriate clipart image should be placed on the advertisement.

There's some clipart on the CD for you to use, or you can pick out your own graphic.

Save your file as **ADVERTISEMENT**.

(9 marks)

Tim, the owner of Selfreezers, would like to know about the ideas behind the advert's design.

b) Use a word processor to write a note to Tim explaining the choices you made when you were designing the advertisement.

Save your file as **NOTE**.

(6 marks)

Written assessment — you'll need a **pen** to answer this question.

1 The employees of Ryter-Lettur plc, an insurance company, have to follow strict procedures when using written communication for business matters.

a) Business letters from Ryter-Lettur plc must be created from a standard template. Describe **two** advantages of using a template for written communication.

....

....

....

....

(4 marks)

b) All written communication from Ryter-Lettur plc must be checked for spelling and grammar errors. Explain **two** reasons why it is important to check for these errors.

....

....

....

....

(4 marks)

Spreadsheets

Spreadsheets are big grids full of fun. Assuming that your idea of fun is entering data (numbers or text), performing calculations, and producing charts and graphs, of course.

Spreadsheets Contain *Rows* and *Columns* of *Cells*

Each of the little boxes on a spreadsheet is called a cell.

Cells Belong to Rows and Columns

Cell references tell you which column and row a cell is in. For example, the cell in column A, row 2 has cell reference A2.

- To enter data, just click on a cell and start typing.
- To edit a cell's contents, click in the formula bar above the grid. (Double clicking on a cell sometimes works too).

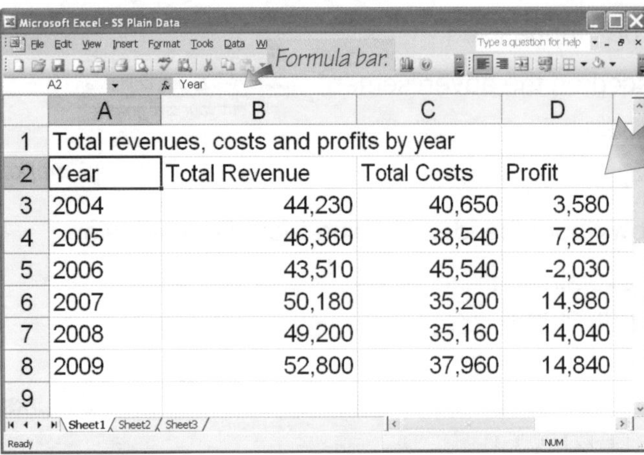

	A	B	C	D
1	Total revenues, costs and profits by year			
2	Year	Total Revenue	Total Costs	Profit
3	2004	44,230	40,650	3,580
4	2005	46,360	38,540	7,820
5	2006	43,510	45,540	-2,030
6	2007	50,180	35,200	14,980
7	2008	49,200	35,160	14,040
8	2009	52,800	37,960	14,840
9				

Use Titles and Headings

Spreadsheets should have a title in the first row to explain what the data shows. Each row and column should also be labelled. Each row or column of data is called a data series.

You can also put titles and other info into headers and footers (see p94). These only show up when you print.

You Can Change the Sizes of Cells

You can adjust the heights of rows and the widths of columns until your data fits neatly into the cells.

Validation rules control what data can be put into a cell, e.g. only text, or only numbers between 1 and 100, and so on.

Formatting Makes Spreadsheets *Clearer* and *Prettier*

Here's the same data, but with an extra column added, and some more formatting applied.

Text Can be Formatted as Usual

Data in cells can be formatted like in a word processor — e.g. you can make it bold, underlined and italic, and align it to the left, right or centre.

Cells Can Be Merged and Added

Here, cells B1, C1, D1 and E1 have been merged — they've become a single cell. Column A has also been inserted to add some extra information. The cells have been merged, and the text has been rotated to fit the space.

Microsoft Excel - SS Formatted Data

	A	B	C	D	E
1		**Total revenues, costs and profits by year**			
2		**Year**	**Total Revenue**	**Total Costs**	**Profit**
3	(Financial years ending 31st March)	2004	£44,230	£40,650	£3,580
4		2005	£46,360	£38,540	£7,820
5		2006	£43,510	£45,540	-£2,030
6		2007	£50,180	£35,200	£14[illegible]80
7		2008	£49,200	£35,160	£14,0[illegible]0
8		2009	£52,800	£37,960	£14,840
9					

Borders Help to Split Data Up

Borders help to keep sections of a spreadsheet separate. You can choose the thickness, style and colour of borders.

This sheet uses a coloured fill for titles and headings, but the cells containing data are left plain white.

Add a Splash of Colour and Set the Print Area

You can change the fill colour of cells, and the font colour within cells. This can make it easier to pick out particular types of data (and make the sheet look nicer). You can also choose which cells you want to appear on a printout.

You can use conditional formatting to set some colours to come up automatically — e.g. negative numbers can be highlighted in red.

Formatting — a fancy word for spreadsheet makeover...

Spreadsheets are a good way to organise data series (especially numerical data) into rows and columns. Formatting can help to make spreadsheets easier to read — as always, you're aiming for clarity.

Spreadsheets: Using Formulas

Spreadsheets are really useful for dealing with numbers — each cell can perform calculations. So using a spreadsheet is like having about a tonne of calculators on your desk.

Formulas Are Used for *Calculations*

The animated tutorial will take you through all this step by step.

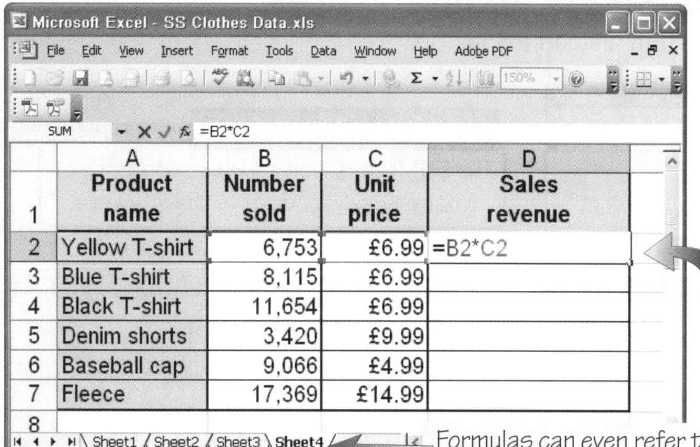

Microsoft Excel - SS Clothes Data.xls

SUM =B2*C2

	A	B	C	D
1	Product name	Number sold	Unit price	Sales revenue
2	Yellow T-shirt	6,753	£6.99	=B2*C2
3	Blue T-shirt	8,115	£6.99	
4	Black T-shirt	11,654	£6.99	
5	Denim shorts	3,420	£9.99	
6	Baseball cap	9,066	£4.99	
7	Fleece	17,369	£14.99	
8				

Sheet1 / Sheet2 / Sheet3 / Sheet4

Formulas Let You Do Calculations

Formulas are the key to doing calculations.
Type an equals sign (=), and then use these basic symbols:

+ (add) — (subtract) * (multiply) / (divide)

To calculate the revenue from yellow T-shirts, click in cell D2, and type = B2 * C2
Then hit return to see the answer.

revenue = quantity x price — see p17.

Using a formula means the answer will update itself automatically if you change B2 or C2.

Formulas can even refer to different sheets. Click on these tabs to see a different sheet.

Relative Cell References Can *Change*

Relative Cell References are Typed as Normal

In the example above, cell D2 contains the formula "=B2*C2" — this means "multiply the contents of the two cells on the left".

If you copy cell D2 and paste it into cell D3, the computer usually assumes you still want it to mean "multiply the contents of the two cells on the left" — so it'll actually change the formula to "=B3*C3".

B2 and C2 are called relative cell references.
When you copy and paste them, they change — so that they refer to the same place relative to the new cell.

So if you copy cell D2 and paste it into cells D3 to D7, the revenues from the other types of clothing will be calculated automatically.

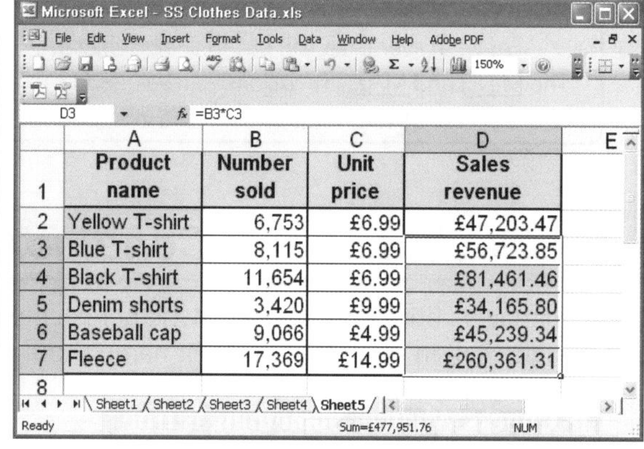

Microsoft Excel - SS Clothes Data.xls

D3 =B3*C3

	A	B	C	D
1	Product name	Number sold	Unit price	Sales revenue
2	Yellow T-shirt	6,753	£6.99	£47,203.47
3	Blue T-shirt	8,115	£6.99	£56,723.85
4	Black T-shirt	11,654	£6.99	£81,461.46
5	Denim shorts	3,420	£9.99	£34,165.80
6	Baseball cap	9,066	£4.99	£45,239.34
7	Fleece	17,369	£14.99	£260,361.31
8				

Sheet1 / Sheet2 / Sheet3 / Sheet4 / Sheet5

Sum=£477,951.76

Absolute Cell References Stay *Fixed*

Sometimes you won't want the computer to change cell references.

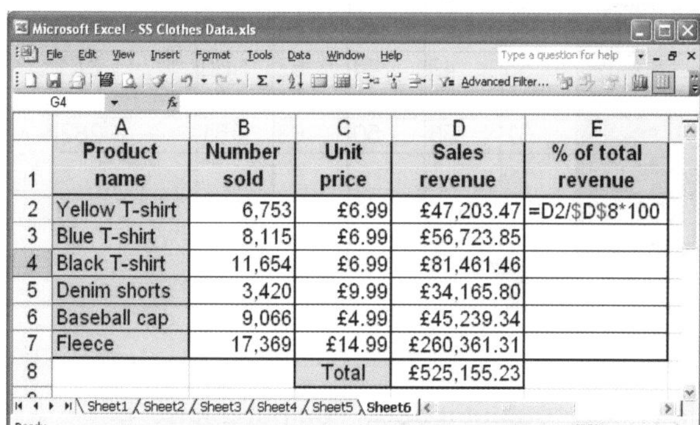

Microsoft Excel - SS Clothes Data.xls

G4

	A	B	C	D	E
1	Product name	Number sold	Unit price	Sales revenue	% of total revenue
2	Yellow T-shirt	6,753	£6.99	£47,203.47	=D2/D8*100
3	Blue T-shirt	8,115	£6.99	£56,723.85	
4	Black T-shirt	11,654	£6.99	£81,461.46	
5	Denim shorts	3,420	£9.99	£34,165.80	
6	Baseball cap	9,066	£4.99	£45,239.34	
7	Fleece	17,369	£14.99	£260,361.31	
8			Total	£525,155.23	

Sheet1 / Sheet2 / Sheet3 / Sheet4 / Sheet5 / Sheet6

Absolute Cell References Use the $ Symbol

Here, the total sales revenue has been calculated in cell D8, and cell E2 shows the percentage of total revenue made by Yellow T-shirts. So in cell E2 you could type "=D2/D8*100".

But... if you copied and pasted this into cell E3, it would become "=D3/D9*100") — the 'D3' is okay, but the 'D9' will cause problems.

To avoid this, type D8 instead — the dollar signs mean the cell reference will stay fixed — it's an absolute cell reference.

When you copy E2 and paste it into cells E3 to E7:

- D8 stays fixed — it's an absolute cell reference.
- D2 changes to D3, D4... — it's a relative cell reference.

Learning this page — a formula for success...

Formulas are great — if any cells in the formula change, the formula's answers will be updated automatically. Pasting formulas to other places is cool, but make sure you know when to use absolute cell references.

Spreadsheets: Using Functions

Spreadsheets can be used for basic arithmetic, but there are also functions that allow you to do more complicated calculations in a single step. As always, start with an equals sign '='.

SUM and AVERAGE are Common Functions

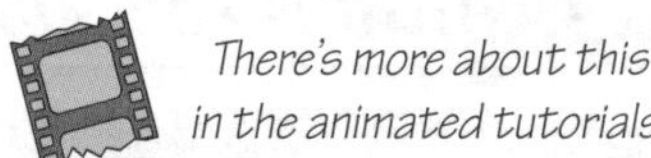

There's more about this in the animated tutorials.

This spreadsheet shows the output of five members of staff in a small toy factory.

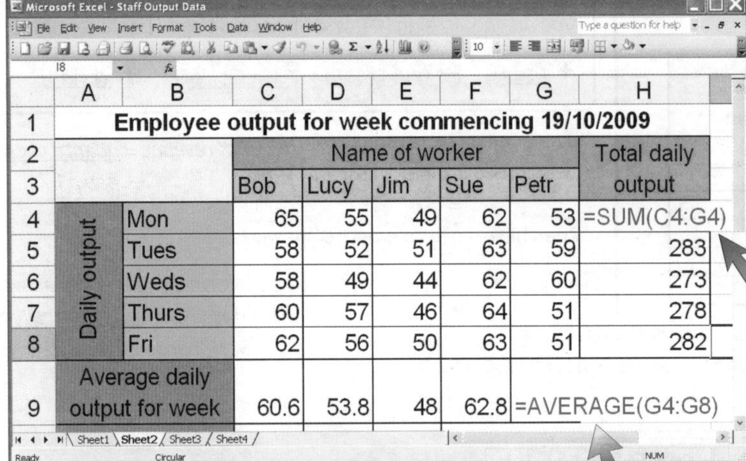

	A	B	C	D	E	F	G	H
1	Employee output for week commencing 19/10/2009							
2			Name of worker					Total daily output
3			Bob	Lucy	Jim	Sue	Petr	
4	Daily output	Mon	65	55	49	62	53	=SUM(C4:G4)
5		Tues	58	52	51	63	59	283
6		Weds	58	49	44	62	60	273
7		Thurs	60	57	46	64	51	278
8		Fri	62	56	50	63	51	282
9	Average daily output for week		60.6	53.8	48	62.8	=AVERAGE(G4:G8)	

SUM is Used for Adding

The SUM() function adds the contents of whatever cells you put in the brackets.

E.g. to find the total output of all five staff on Monday (row 4), you could enter:
= SUM(C4, D4, E4, F4, G4)

But it's quicker to type a range of cells using a colon (:). You could do the above calculation as:
= SUM(C4 : G4)

To find Petr's average daily output, enter:
= AVERAGE(G4 : G8)

AVERAGE, MIN and MAX — also useful

The AVERAGE() function finds the mean of whatever cells you put in the brackets.
The MIN() and MAX() functions can be used to work out the smallest and biggest numbers in a set of data.

If you use relative cell references, you can fill in the other totals and averages by pasting the functions (see the previous page).

IF Checks to See if Conditions Have Been Met

The managers now want to check whether each worker's average output is meeting the target of over 54 toys per day. If it is, the cell in row 10 under their name should say "Yes". If not, it should say "No".

IF Checks Whether Something is True

You can set the IF() function to output different results depending on whether a condition is true or false.

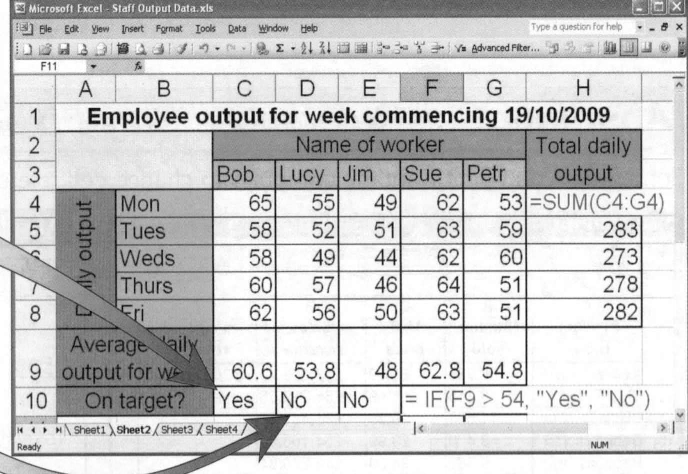

	A	B	C	D	E	F	G	H
1	Employee output for week commencing 19/10/2009							
2			Name of worker					Total daily output
3			Bob	Lucy	Jim	Sue	Petr	
4	Daily output	Mon	65	55	49	62	53	=SUM(C4:G4)
5		Tues	58	52	51	63	59	283
6		Weds	58	49	44	62	60	273
7		Thurs	60	57	46	64	51	278
8		Fri	62	56	50	63	51	282
9	Average daily output for week		60.6	53.8	48	62.8	54.8	
10	On target?		Yes	No	No	= IF(F9 > 54, "Yes", "No")		

To test whether Bob's average output (cell C9) is greater than 54, type in cell C10:
= IF(C9 > 54, "Yes", "No")
Bob's average is 60.6, so the output is "Yes".

But when you paste the function into Lucy's column (cell D10), the output is "No", since her average output for the week is less than 54.

This is a tricky one — the basic form is: =IF(condition to check, "output if true", "output if false")

I used the SUM function — now everything adds up...

Functions can look a bit off-putting at first, but once you've used them a couple of times you'll never go back to typing sums and averages the long way. Functions can use absolute and relative cell references, too. Just remember that you still need to use an equals sign before your function name. Practice is key here.

Spreadsheets: Graphs and Charts

Graphs and charts are ways of communicating data visually. Spreadsheets are great at turning dull numbers into colourful diagrams — they do most of the hard work for you.

Bar Charts are Often Called Column Charts

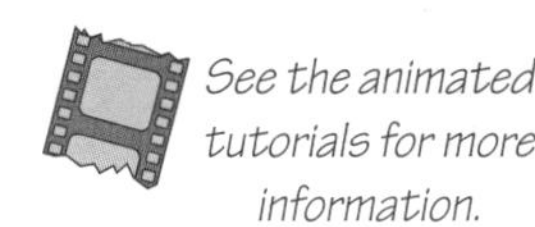

The owners of the Broken Chair café have made a spreadsheet of their drinks sales. They want to produce a bar chart to show how their sales of hot drinks compare over a year.

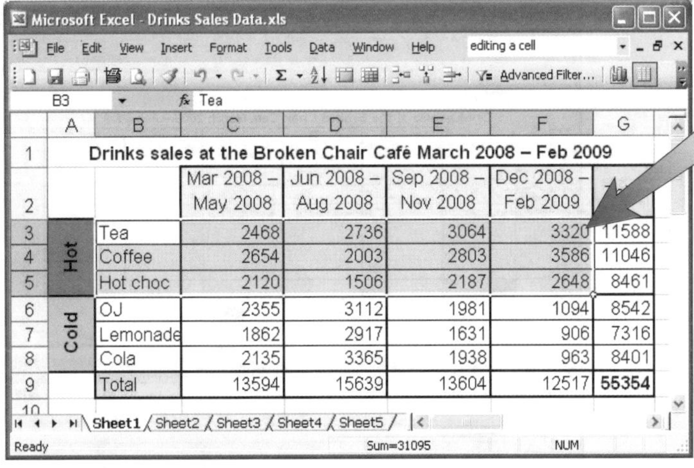

		Drinks sales at the Broken Chair Café March 2008 – Feb 2009				
		Mar 2008 – May 2008	Jun 2008 – Aug 2008	Sep 2008 – Nov 2008	Dec 2008 – Feb 2009	
Hot	Tea	2468	2736	3064	3320	11588
	Coffee	2654	2003	2803	3586	11046
	Hot choc	2120	1506	2187	2648	8461
Cold	OJ	2355	3112	1981	1094	8542
	Lemonade	1862	2917	1631	906	7316
	Cola	2135	3365	1938	963	8401
	Total	13594	15639	13604	12517	**55354**

First Select Your Data

Select the cells that contain the data you want to display in your chart. Include any headings.

You can sometimes select groups of cells that aren't next to each other by holding down the Ctrl key.

Then Create Your Chart

There will probably be loads of ways you could do this, and masses of options you can play with.

This is what you get using the basic bar chart (or column chart in some spreadsheets) option.

Your headings are used in the legend (or key) — this tells you which column is which.

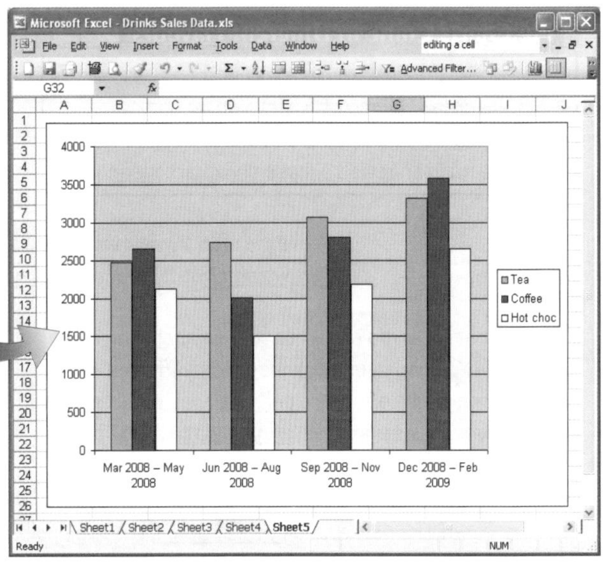

Finally, Edit Your Chart Till it Shines

You can adjust pretty much every part of a chart. Use the chart menus, or try right-clicking on different parts to see the options.

Remember to add a title and put labels on axes. You can choose the font, size and colour of the text.

You can also change the colours used, the style and thickness of lines, and the range of values shown on each axis.

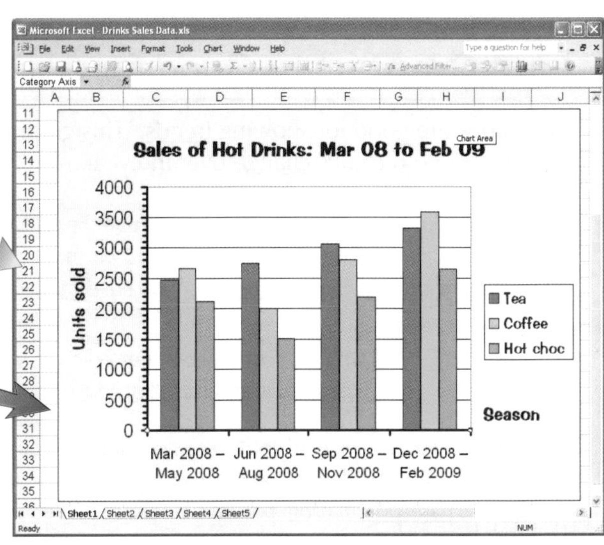

Don't get carried away with editing your charts. Remember that in business, it's more important to show data clearly than to make it look pretty.

Produce the best charts bar none...

A lot of spreadsheet programs have wizards that will help you draw graphs and charts. You normally have to answer a few questions, select some cells when it tells you to, and the wizard will sort out the rest. If you use the wizard to draw the chart in the first place, you can always customise it later to make it sparkle.

Spreadsheets: Graphs and Charts

Whatever kind of chart you want to make, the basic technique is the same — select the data series, choose the chart type, then edit it until it looks the way you want it to.

Pie Charts Show Proportions

See the animated tutorials for more about charts and graphs.

The owners of the café now want to look at their drinks sales for Dec 2008 – Feb 2009. They want to see what proportion of their total sales for this period came from each drink.

Select the Data You Need

Pie charts show data as slices of a round pie. To create one, highlight the data plus any headings.

If the data you need isn't in one block (like here, where the data is in columns B and F)... ...select the first group of cells (e.g. column B), then hold down ctrl and select the second group (column F).

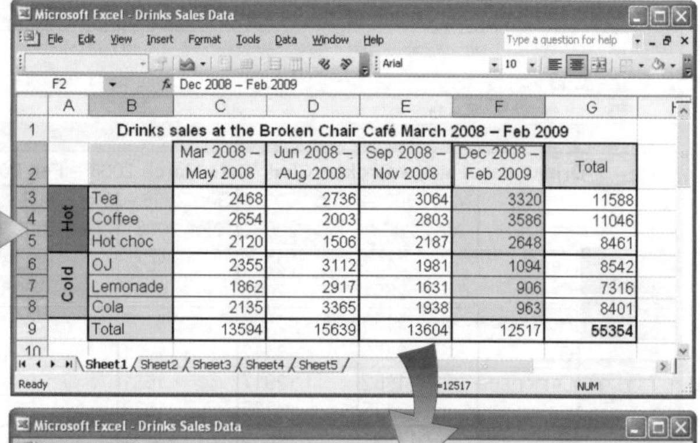

Drinks sales at the Broken Chair Café March 2008 – Feb 2009

		Mar 2008 – May 2008	Jun 2008 – Aug 2008	Sep 2008 – Nov 2008	Dec 2008 – Feb 2009	Total
Hot	Tea	2468	2736	3064	3320	11588
Hot	Coffee	2654	2003	2803	3586	11046
Hot	Hot choc	2120	1506	2187	2648	8461
Cold	OJ	2355	3112	1981	1094	8542
Cold	Lemonade	1862	2917	1631	906	7316
Cold	Cola	2135	3365	1938	963	8401
	Total	13594	15639	13604	12517	55354

Pie Charts Come in Different Flavours

Basic pie charts are circles split into sectors. But spreadsheets often let you go to town... ...and make 3D pies with slices exploding outwards. The main thing is to make the chart clear.

This pie chart was made using the chart wizard, but it's been tweaked a bit.

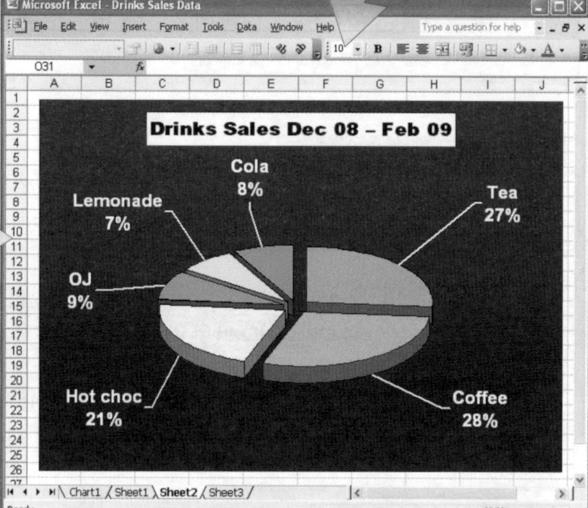

Sometimes, it's easier to read a label than use a legend. You can usually choose from different options — these labels show the percentages of total sales, but you could show the original data if you prefer.

You can also change things like the colours and sizes of the slices, and how far apart they've exploded.

Line Graphs are Good for Showing Changes Over Time

Line graphs are good for showing trends. This graph shows how sales of cold drinks change over the year.

You could show this information in a bar chart. But lines sometimes show the ups and downs a bit more clearly if you're looking at a long period, or you have lots of data points.

Here, it's pretty clear that sales of all three cold drinks peak in August, and fall steadily towards winter.

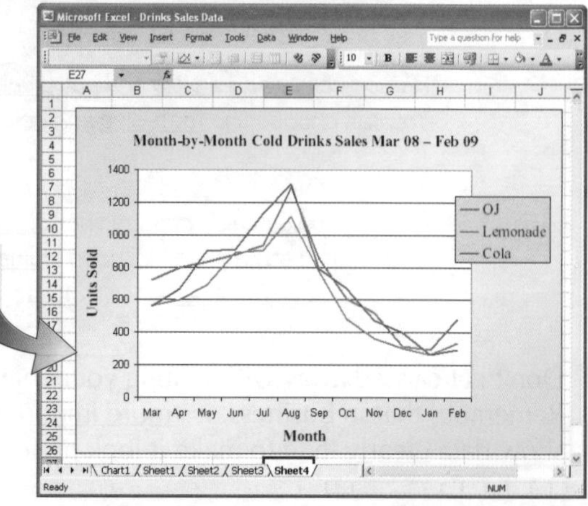

Before printing, an on-screen "print preview" will show you exactly how the printout will look. You can then:

- change the page orientation: 'portrait' — ▯, or 'landscape' — ▭,
- change where the page-breaks fall,
- include (or turn off) grid lines.

Put things into proportion — make a pie chart...

Once you've got data in a spreadsheet, producing professional-looking charts and graphs is a piece of cake. Or a slice of pie. The important thing is to make sure that your choice of chart is appropriate for your data.

Warm-Up and Worked Exam Questions

Warm-up Questions

1) Describe what happens when a selection of cells are merged.
2) What type of cell reference is C4? When is this type used?
3) What would be the output of the following function: =IF(6>4, "Yes", "No")?
4) Name three types of chart that could be produced from a spreadsheet application.

Worked Exam Question

Here's another computer-based assessment question to go through.
All the files used are on the CD — so you can try the question yourself.

Task One: Spreadsheet

Tiffany Bloom is the manager of the restaurant Bish Bash Fish. A spreadsheet is used to record bookings in the restaurant. Tiffany has given you part of the spreadsheet, which shows the bookings on a Friday night in December. The spreadsheet is incomplete.

Recall the file **BOOKINGS.**

a) Add the following data to the relevant bookings.

- The 19:00 booking was served by Tom and their bill came to £52.80.
- The 20:20 booking was for 6 people. They left a £6.00 tip.
- Format cells F4-F15 and G4-G15 so the amounts are shown with a £ sign, and to two decimal places.

Save a copy of the spreadsheet as **BOOKINGS1**.

(6 marks)

Recall the file **BOOKINGS1**.

b) For that Friday evening, Tiffany needs to know:

- The average party size.
- The total of all the amounts shown on the bills.
- The total tips left.
- Whether the total of the tips was 10% or more of the total of the bills.

Use functions to evaluate these results. Enter your functions in cells **E17:E21**.

Save a copy of the spreadsheet as **BOOKINGS2**.

(5 marks)

a) Data entered accurately. ✔ [1 mark per entry]

'Currency' / 'Accounting' format applied to 'Bill' and 'Tip' columns, showing £ sign and values to two decimal places. ✔ [1 mark per column]

	A	B	C	D	E	F	G
1	BISH BASH FISH - BOOKIN						
2							
3	Week	Day	Time	Party Size	Served By	Bill	Tip
4	52	FRI	18:10	14	Angela	£163.50	£16.35
5	52	FRI	19:00	4	Tom	£52.80	£3.80
6	52	FRI	19:10	4	Edward	£72.50	£3.40
7	52	FRI	19:15	2	Jessica	£23.00	£2.80
8	52	FRI	19:30	8	Tom	£101.90	£10.00
9	52	FRI	19:50	5	Angela	£82.60	£8.50
10	52	FRI	20:00	2	Richard	£18.00	£0.00
11	52	FRI	20:20	6	Jessica	£85.30	£6.00
12	52	FRI	20:30	3	Richard	£31.50	£3.50
13	52	FRI	21:00	3	Edward	£25.60	£1.50
14	52	FRI	21:10	5	Tom	£52.75	£2.75
15	52	FRI	21:30	4	Edward	£49.40	£2.00

b) Average party size =AVERAGE(D4:D15). ✔ [1 mark]

Total of all the bills =SUM(F4:F15). ✔ [1 mark]

Total of the tips =SUM(G4:G15). ✔ [1 mark]

Whether tips came to 10% or more of the bills, for example:
=IF(E19>=E18*0.1, "Yes", "No")
=IF(E19/E18*100>=10, "Yes", "No"). ✔ [1 mark]

Functions entered into the correct cells. ✔ [1 mark]

	A–D	E
17	Average party size	=AVERAGE(D4:D15)
18	Total amount on bills	=SUM(F4:F15)
19	Total tips left	=SUM(G4:G15)
20–21	Total tips left equals 10% or more of total amount on bills?	=IF(E19>=E18*0.1,"Yes","No")

Exam Questions

Computer-based assessment — you'll need a **computer** to answer this question.

Task One: Making a Chart

At the end of each month last year, Sundials 'R' Us asked 150 customers where they originally heard about the company. The manager of Sundials 'R' Us needs the survey results as a chart.

Recall the file **SURVEY**.

a) Create an appropriate chart to display the survey data.

The chart needs a title, a legend, and labels for the horizontal and vertical axes.

Save a copy of the spreadsheet as **SURVEY1**.

(8 marks)

Recall the file **SURVEY1**.

b) A full-page advert was put in the local newspaper at the beginning of May.

Indicate on the chart the effect the advert had on the customer survey results.

Save your file as **SURVEY2**.

(2 marks)

Recall the file **SURVEY2**.

c) Print a copy of your chart. The printout should show only the chart.

(2 marks)

Written assessment — you'll need a **pen** to answer this question.

1 Read **Item A** and then answer the question that follows.

> **Item A**
>
> Philip Scone is a science student. He currently keeps a record of the results from his experiments in hand-drawn tables.
> Philip then uses a calculator to analyse his data, although he finds this time-consuming. Every fortnight Philip has to present his data to the rest of his class. However, they find it hard to understand his results.

Suggest a suitable type of software application that Philip could use to record and analyse his data. Give reasons for your answer.

Software application ....

Reasons ....

....

....

....

....

....

(7 marks)

Databases

Databases are mostly used for storing a mixture of data — it might be names, addresses, reference numbers, dates, financial figures... you name it. The easiest way to think of a database is as a glorified table.

*Databases Store **All Kinds** of Data*

The animated tutorial will take you through this stuff step by step.

Flat-File Databases Store Data in One Table

Databases organise information in tables with rows and columns. A flat-file database contains one table.

Each row is a separate record. Each record contains data about one person or item.

Databases usually have a primary key field that uniquely identifies each record. Here there's a field called 'ID' — this is a different number for every record.

The column headings are field names — a field is just a particular category of data in the table (e.g. name, telephone number).

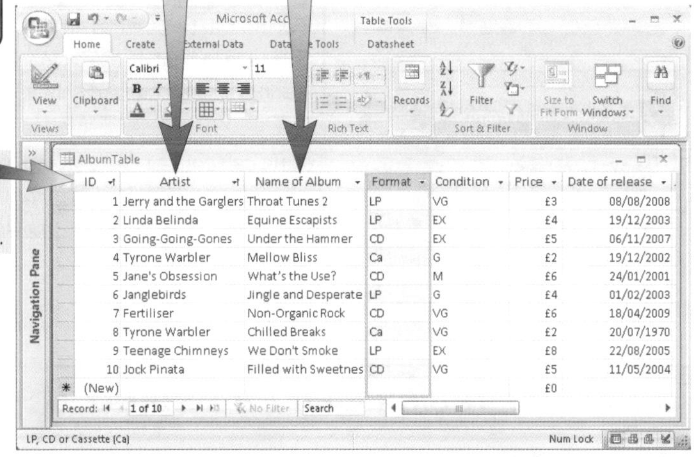

ID	Artist	Name of Album	Format	Condition	Price	Date of release
1	Jerry and the Garglers	Throat Tunes 2	LP	VG	£3	08/08/2008
2	Linda Belinda	Equine Escapists	LP	EX	£4	19/12/2003
3	Going-Going-Gones	Under the Hammer	CD	EX	£5	06/11/2007
4	Tyrone Warbler	Mellow Bliss	Ca	G	£2	19/12/2002
5	Jane's Obsession	What's the Use?	CD	M	£6	24/01/2001
6	Janglebirds	Jingle and Desperate	LP	G	£4	01/02/2003
7	Fertiliser	Non-Organic Rock	CD	VG	£6	18/04/2009
8	Tyrone Warbler	Chilled Breaks	Ca	VG	£2	20/07/1970
9	Teenage Chimneys	We Don't Smoke	LP	EX	£8	22/08/2005
10	Jock Pinata	Filled with Sweetnes	CD	VG	£5	11/05/2004
(New)					£0	

Relational Databases Contain Linked Tables

Relational databases organise data in several tables, where each table stores a different type of information. But links between related tables can be made by using fields which are common to both tables.

Relational databases are much more useful than flat-file databases. But they can be difficult to set up if you're not a database pro.

Records Can be Edited...

- To edit (change) a record, just click in a cell and type over the old data.

...and Deleted

- To delete a record, click somewhere in it and then click on the delete record button.

*You Can Set **Data Types** and **Options** in the **Design View***

Databases usually have a 'design view'. This is where you 'set up' your table.

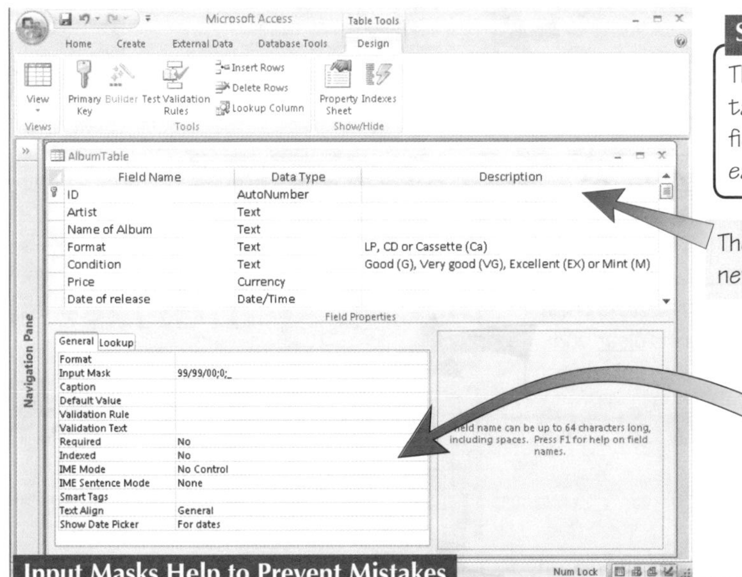

Field Name	Data Type	Description
ID	AutoNumber	
Artist	Text	
Name of Album	Text	
Format	Text	LP, CD or Cassette (Ca)
Condition	Text	Good (G), Very good (VG), Excellent (EX) or Mint (M)
Price	Currency	
Date of release	Date/Time	

Field Properties (General)	
Format	
Input Mask	99/99/00;0;_
Caption	
Default Value	
Validation Rule	
Validation Text	
Required	No
Indexed	No
IME Mode	No Control
IME Sentence Mode	None
Smart Tags	
Text Align	General
Show Date Picker	For dates

Set a Data Type for Each Field

This screen shows the design view of a database table. In this view you can change the names of your fields, and choose what type of data will be listed in each field (e.g. text, number, date, currency).

The Autonumber data type automatically gives each new record a different number — good for key fields.

There are Options for Each Data Type

You can set the maximum number of characters each entry can contain, and the way the data is displayed (e.g. the number of decimal places, or a currency symbol).

Input Masks Help to Prevent Mistakes

Sometimes data needs to be in a particular format (e.g. dd-mm-yyyy for a date) — input masks make sure that data can only be entered in this format.

Encoding Data Can Save Time

You can give data values a short code to save time typing them out in full every time. E.g. 'North' could be encoded as 'N'.

I can tell you're going to have a field day learning this...

Flat-file databases are great for simple sets of data — it's easy to handle data contained in a single table. But for a firm that stores more complex data, a relational database may increase efficiency.

Databases: Data Input Forms

Think of a database as being a bit like a swan. The tables are the bits that do all the work but which are not great looking (like a swan's legs). Forms are the pretty bits that are on show (the bit of a swan above the water). There... clear as anything.

Forms Are a User-Friendly Way to Enter Data

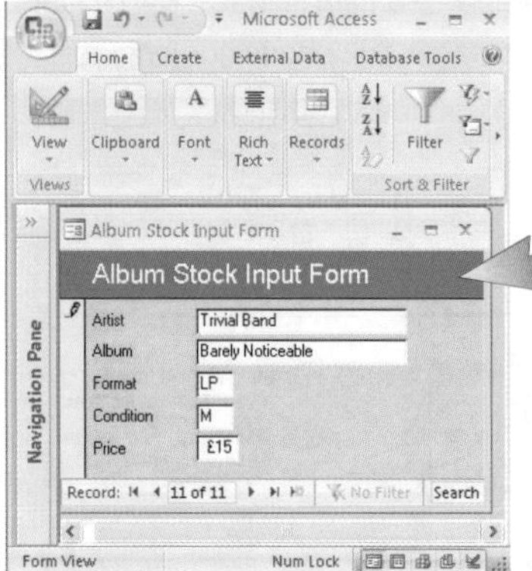

The animated tutorial will take you through designing a form step by step.

Forms Should be Clear and Simple

Forms can be used to enter data into a table. The idea is that they're clearly designed and user-friendly to make this as easy as possible.

Forms can contain text boxes (for typing into), or tick-boxes and 'option lists' for users to choose from. You can even display input masks in your text boxes.

When a user has entered their data, it's stored as a new record in the database table.

Forms and Tables Can be Linked

Choose a Table

When you create a form, you have to decide which table new data will end up in.

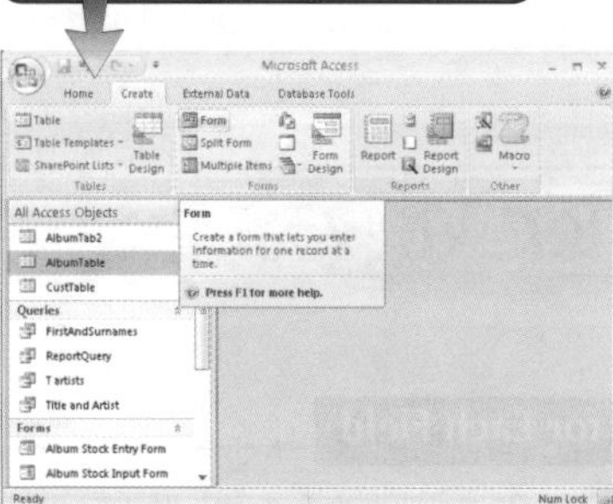

Here, the form has been used to enter a new record into the table. The details in this form will form the 11th row in this table.

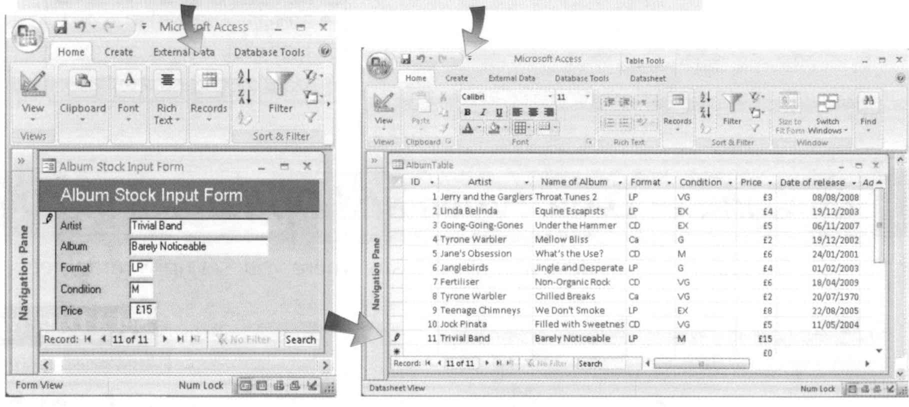

Use the Form Design View to Adjust Links and Layout

You Can Edit the Design of Forms

Like tables, forms have a design view where you can change their layout and appearance. You need to make your forms clear and logical so users know exactly what data they're being asked for.

You can add text boxes and labels using the design view.

- Text boxes are linked to fields.
- Labels are there just to help users understand the form.

You can also adjust the colours, fonts, and borders used on your form.

Text boxes need to be linked to fields in a table. But you don't have to include every field from the table in your form.

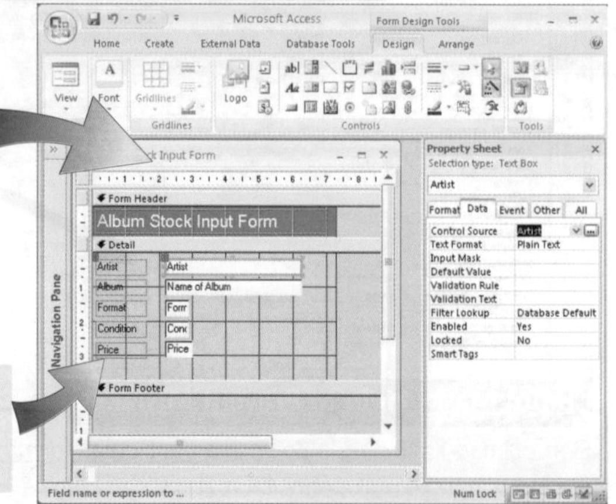

I'm a confused input form — can you fill me in?

Forms are supposed to be the friendly face of a database. A good form should make it obvious what data is needed, and be easy to use. If a form isn't clear, there's more chance that data will be entered incorrectly.

Databases: Simple Queries and Sorting

Databases can quickly <u>sort</u> data into <u>order</u>. They can also quickly find all the records that meet <u>certain conditions</u>.

*Data Can be **Sorted** Into Order by **Field***

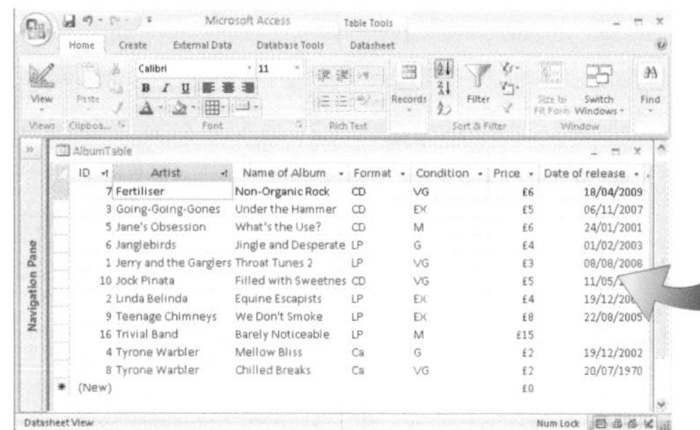

ID	Artist	Name of Album	Format	Condition	Price	Date of release
7	Fertiliser	Non-Organic Rock	CD	VG	£6	18/04/2009
3	Going-Going-Gones	Under the Hammer	CD	EX	£5	06/11/2007
5	Jane's Obsession	What's the Use?	CD	M	£6	24/01/2001
6	Janglebirds	Jingle and Desperate	LP	G	£4	01/02/2003
1	Jerry and the Garglers	Throat Tunes 2	LP	VG	£3	08/08/2008
10	Jock Pinata	Filled with Sweetnes	CD	VG	£5	11/05/
2	Linda Belinda	Equine Escapists	LP	EX	£4	19/12/20
9	Teenage Chimneys	We Don't Smoke	LP	EX	£8	22/08/2005
16	Trivial Band	Barely Noticeable	LP	M	£15	
4	Tyrone Warbler	Mellow Bliss	Ca	G	£2	19/12/2002
8	Tyrone Warbler	Chilled Breaks	Ca	VG	£2	20/07/1970
(New)					£0	

<u>Sorting</u> Data Means Changing its <u>Order</u>

When you add records to a database, they'll be listed in the <u>order you typed them</u>. But it's easy to <u>sort</u> data into a more useful order.

For example, the records in this table have been sorted into <u>alphabetical order</u> using the 'Artist' field. To sort your records, click somewhere in the field you want to put in order, and click on the '<u>sort ascending</u>' button. You can sort in the <u>opposite order</u> by choosing '<u>sort descending</u>'.

*Queries are Used to **Search** and **Filter** Data*

The animated tutorial will walk you through a query.

<u>Queries</u> Let You <u>Filter Out</u> the Data You Want

This is the <u>query design</u> screen. A query lets you look for records whose entries meet certain conditions — this is called <u>filtering</u>. Choose the <u>fields</u> you're interested in, and the <u>criteria</u> you want to search for.

You can also choose how you want the results to be <u>sorted</u>, and which fields you want to <u>show</u> in the results.

Query design

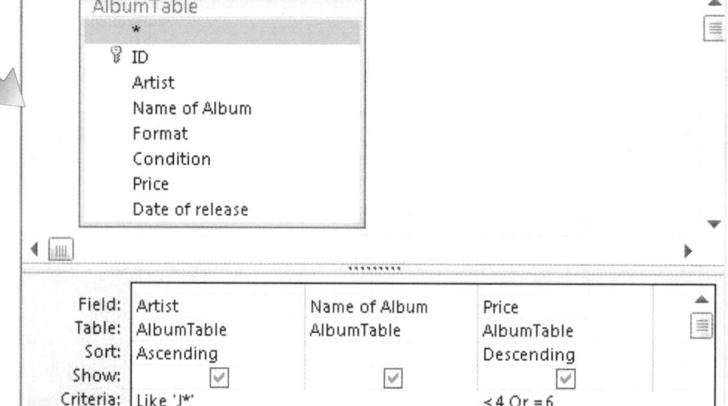

The <u>first column</u> of this query will search for albums by artists <u>starting</u> with the letter 'J'.

The <u>third column</u> searches for albums costing <u>less than £4</u> or <u>exactly £6</u>.

So the <u>query results</u> will display albums by artists starting with 'J' <u>and</u> costing either less than £4 or exactly £6.

Query results

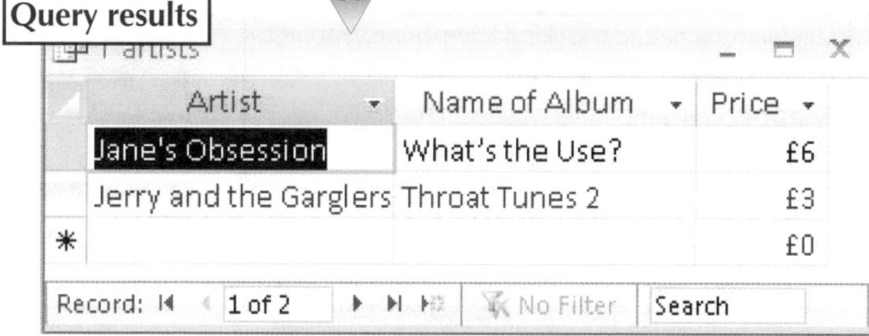

Artist	Name of Album	Price
Jane's Obsession	What's the Use?	£6
Jerry and the Garglers	Throat Tunes 2	£3
*		£0

Tips for Query Criteria

Use <u>'Quotes'</u> for <u>Words</u>

If you're searching for a <u>word</u>, put <u>quotes</u> around it in the criteria box — e.g. 'apple' or 'Smith'.

=, < and > are Useful for Queries

These symbols let you search for a <u>range</u> of data.
= (<u>equal to</u>) < (<u>less than</u>) > (<u>greater than</u>)
<> (<u>not equal to</u>) <= (<u>less than or equal to</u>)
>= (<u>greater than or equal to</u>)

Use <u>Like</u> and <u>*</u> for <u>Wildcard</u> Searches

A <u>wildcard search</u> is when only <u>part</u> of an entry has to match your search criteria.
For example, if you want to search for words <u>ending</u> with 'ity', you can type Like '*ity'.

Use <u>Logic</u> for More Complex Searches

When you're confident you can use the basics, you can use terms like <u>AND</u>, <u>OR</u> and <u>NOT</u> to search for several criteria at once. (See the next page too.)

If you've got a query about this page — have another read...

Queries are just <u>questions</u>. You can ask a database to display data that satisfies <u>particular criteria</u>, which saves loads of time wading through the records. Make sure you're happy with all this before your exam.

Databases: Producing Reports

You can fill a database with stacks of information, but reading from the table can be like solving a very big, very dull wordsearch. Reports can be used to display data in a way that makes it much easier to read.

Reports Are Linked to Tables or Queries

Reports can present data so it's both beautiful and easy to understand.
Reports can be designed to be viewed on screen or printed out.

Reports Display Data

You can base reports on either tables or queries.

It depends on whether you need to display all the records in a table, or just the ones that meet certain conditions.

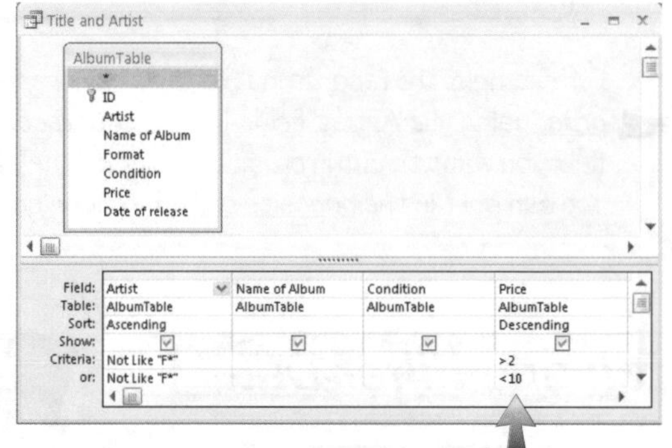

This query uses two lines to specify the search criteria instead of using 'OR'. You'd get the same result by putting ">2 OR <10" in the Price field.

This is the report based on the query on the left. There's a bit of colour and text formatting, and a title to make it clear what the report shows.

Design Reports to be **Clear** and **Attractive**

This is the design view of the report above.

Link Reports to Data Sources

Producing a report has a lot in common with producing a form (see p106).

1) Choose a data source (usually a table or a query).
2) Link the text boxes to fields in your data source (in the design view).
3) Make it look lovely.

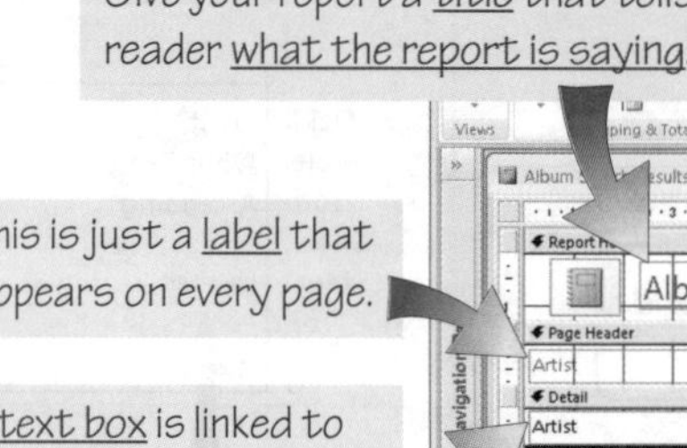

Give your report a title that tells the reader what the report is saying.

This is just a label that appears on every page.

This text box is linked to a field — the information shown in it will be different on every line of the report.

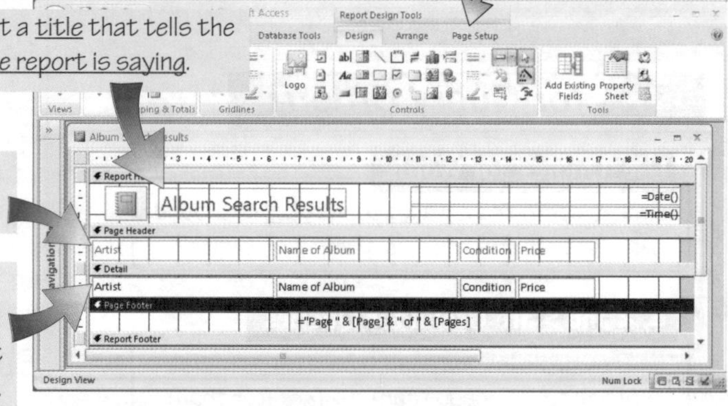

Wizards Can Make Forms, Reports and Queries **Easier**

Wizards Can Make Life Easier

Designing a decent-looking form/query/report from scratch can take time.
A lot of programs have wizards that help make the process less painful.

You usually answer a series of questions, and the wizard sorts out the technical details. You can always adjust the details afterwards using design view.

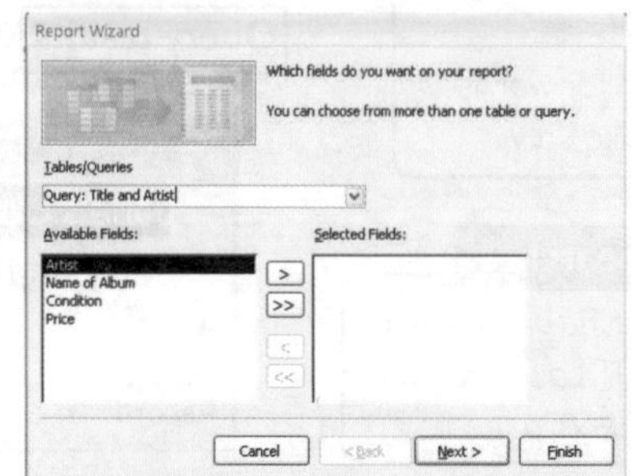

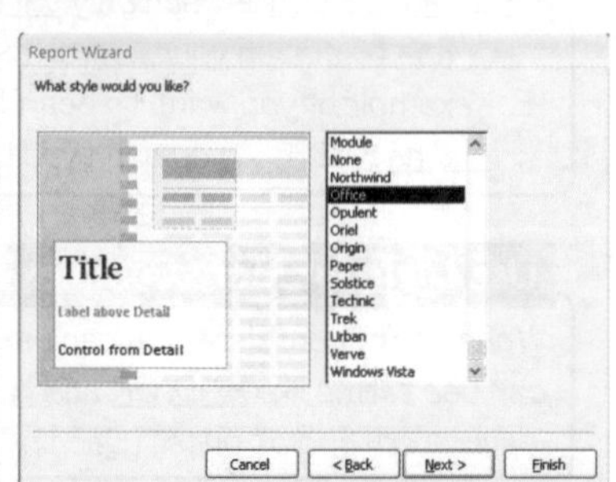

With a bit of practice you'll be a database whizz(ard)...

You won't be asked to produce a really complicated report in the exam, but it's well worth knowing your way around the basic techniques. Oh, and remember to use a suitable title. And that's about it for databases.

Warm-Up and Worked Exam Questions

Warm-up Questions

1) What is a relational database?
2) Why should a database form be linked to a table?
3) What's the difference between what the "Sort ascending" and "Sort descending" buttons do?
4) What is the main function of a database report?

Worked Exam Question

The question below is the sort of thing you might get asked in your computer-based assessment.
Have a go at it before you read the answers — any files you need are on the CD at the back of this book.

Task One: Database

Mike Davies delivers milk to people in the villages of Fornkirk and Burncrumb.
Mike uses a database to record his customers' names, addresses and order details.

Recall the file **ORDERS** and open **TABLE**.

Two customers want to change their existing order with Mike.

a) Amend the following details in the database.

- Mr Peter Ropefellow would like 3 pints to be delivered on Monday and Thursday.
- Ms Louise Coatler would like 1 pint of skimmed milk to be delivered.

Sort the database into ascending order of surname.

Save a copy of the table as **TABLE1**.

(6 marks)

Recall the file **ORDERS**.

Mike wants to make his Tuesday deliveries in Fornkirk more efficient by planning his route.

b) Search **TABLE1** to find the addresses in Fornkirk that have a first delivery on Tuesday.

Save a copy of the query as **QUERY1**.

(6 marks)

a) Details amended accurately. ✔ [1 mark per detail]

Database sorted in ascending order. ✔ [1 mark]

Database sorted by surname. ✔ [1 mark]

Title	First_Name	Surname	Milk_Preference	Pints	Delivery_1	Delivery_2
Ms	Louise	Coatler	Skimmed	1	Monday	Thursday
Ms	Barbara	Dujour	Semi-skimmed	3	Monday	Friday
Mr	Richard	Faulkner	Skimmed	1	Tuesday	Friday
Mr	Donald	Fulcrum	Semi-skimmed	2	Tuesday	
Mrs	Kate	Harvey	Semi-skimmed	2	Thursday	
Mr	Terry	Hintow	Whole	2	Tuesday	Friday
Mrs	Julie	Knowles	Semi-skimmed	4	Wednesday	
Mrs	Patricia	Lofty	Whole	8	Monday	Friday
Mr	Robert	Moor	Whole	4	Friday	
Mr	John	Parlour	Whole	1	Monday	Friday
Mr	Tom	Richards	Skimmed	1	Tuesday	
Mr	Peter	Ropefellow	Whole	3	Monday	Thursday
Mrs	Anne	Tunsford	Skimmed	2	Tuesday	
Miss	Hannah	Turn	Semi-skimmed	3	Monday	Thursday
Mrs	Harriet	York	Semi-skimmed	4	Monday	Thursday
				0		

b) Query should be based on TABLE1. ✔ [1 mark]

Query searches the field Address_2 for "Fornkirk". ✔ [1 mark] ✔ [1 mark]

Query searches the field Delivery_1 for "Tuesday". ✔ [1 mark] ✔ [1 mark]

The field Address_1 should also be displayed in the results. ✔ [1 mark]

Field:	Address 1	Address 2	Delivery_1
Table:	TABLE1	TABLE1	TABLE1
Sort:			
Show:	☑	☑	☑
Criteria:		"Fornkirk"	"Tuesday"
or:			

Exam Questions

Computer-based assessment — you'll need a **computer** to answer this question.

Task One: More Databases

Bernard is a coin collector who has over 900 different coins. Bernard has asked you to set up a database that can store some information about each of his coins.

a) Create a database table for Bernard using the following instructions.

There should be five fields: ID, Date Found, Denomination, Mint Year, Condition.
Each field should have an appropriate data type.
The Date Found field should have an appropriate input mask.
The ID field is the primary key field.

Save the database and the table as **COINS**.

(12 marks)

Recall the file **COINS**.

b) Bernard uses four values to describe a coin's condition: Fine, Very Good, Good, Poor.

Make up a code for the values so each is a maximum of two characters.
Write the code in the Condition field's description.

Save the table as **COINS1**.

(3 marks)

c) Open your word processor. Write Bernard a note that explains **one** advantage of input masks and **one** advantage of coding data values.

Save the file as **NOTE**.

(4 marks)

Written assessment — you'll need a **pen** to answer this question.

1 Derek uses a flat-file database to record information about his customers.

a) What is a flat-file database?

....

....

(1 mark)

Derek's database contains some queries and a form.

b) i) Describe **one** function of a database query.

....

....

(2 marks)

ii) Describe **one** function of a database form.

....

....

(2 marks)

Graphics: Creating Images

Graphics. Images. Pictures. Call them what you like — you need to know how to make and use them.

Images — Either **Bitmaps** or **Vector Drawings**

These two basic types of graphic are stored and edited in different ways.

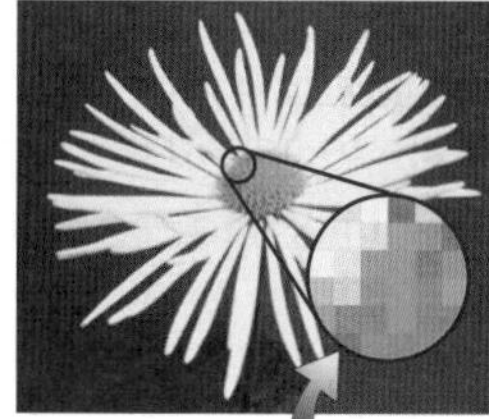

Bitmaps are made up of thousands or millions of these coloured dots — if you zoom right in, you can see them.

BITMAPS — these can be made and edited with 'Painting' software.
Digital photographs and scanned images are often stored as bitmaps.

1) A bitmap image is made up of a grid of coloured dots (pixels). Bitmap files take up a lot of memory because data is stored for every individual pixel.
2) To edit the image, you have to alter the individual dots (although bitmap-editing software has lots of different tools to make this easier).

VECTOR GRAPHICS — these are made with 'Drawing' software.

1) A vector image is stored as coordinates and equations — making file sizes a lot smaller. (But when you're making or editing a vector image, you never have to use equations — the software takes care of all that. You only ever have to use the software's drawing tools.)
2) You create or edit images by manipulating various lines and geometric shapes (simple shapes like squares and circles, or very complicated ones). You can stretch them, twist them, colour them, and so on.

Graphics Packages Help You **Create** and **Edit** Images

Here's a few things you can do with a vector-based graphics package...

Straight lines and freehand lines can be drawn with different properties — thickness or colour can be changed.

Vector software has tools to draw simple shapes like squares, rectangles, circles, triangles, and so on. You can then edit these basic shapes to make arrows, speech bubbles and other more complex designs.

Fill and shading tools let you change the colours and backgrounds of objects. You can have faded or patterned fills as well as single colours.

You can change the size of any object by dragging one of the handles (around the outside of the image) outwards or inwards. But if you don't keep the proportions the same, you can end up with very stretched or squashed images.

Because most vector graphics (except basic shapes) consist of separate objects, it's easy to change the colour of certain parts of the graphic, like this jacket and trousers, by recolouring individual objects.

It's also possible to construct an image using different objects — the seal originally balanced a ball but that part of the graphic can be removed and replaced with pretty much anything.

Picture this — being tested while sat at a computer...

The best thing to do is get yourself sat down in front of a computer and make sure you can do all the things on this page. Yep, every last one. If you're not sure about any of them, ask someone.

Graphics: Manipulating Images

There's still a bit more about graphics you need to know. And here it is.

Cropping Removes **Unwanted** Bits of Pictures

See the animated tutorial too.

Cropping is dead useful when you need to make a picture fill a hole in your document perfectly.

1) Cropping removes parts of the image you don't want — e.g. someone on the edge of the shot you want to get rid of. Cropping can reduce the size of the image by removing blocks from the edges.
2) It's quick and easy, although it can only remove whole edges — you can't use it to remove something in the middle of the graphic. (There's usually a separate tool for this.)

For example, suppose you've written a newsletter article, but your picture just doesn't fit...

3) Cropping is often a better way to make a picture fit a hole, rather than stretching or squashing it.

Looks a bit too much like road kill.

Paste Or **Insert** Graphics Into Other Documents

So you've made a beautiful graphic. But maybe you made it in a graphics program, and now need to get it into a document on your word processor. You have options...

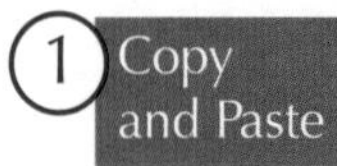

- Select the picture in your piece of graphics software.
- Copy it to the clipboard (Ctrl C).
- Paste (Ctrl V) it into your document.

- Save your picture.
- Insert the picture file.

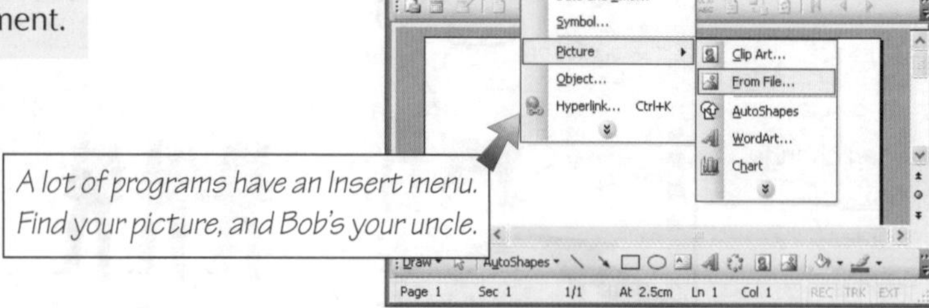

A lot of programs have an Insert menu. Find your picture, and Bob's your uncle.

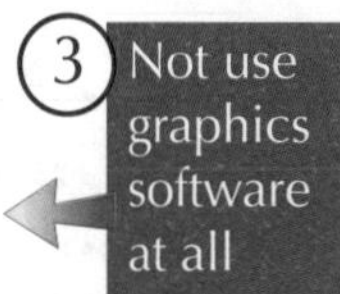

- A lot of software (e.g. some word processors, spreadsheets etc.) lets you make basic pictures without using special graphics software (see p93).
- This is best for quite simple graphics. For anything fancy, you're probably better off using a proper painting or drawing program.

So that's why newspaper pictures always fit the gaps...

You'd have quite a time trying to make a newspaper without the crop tool — it's dead handy, and a lot of word processors will have one. Give it a go. No I mean it, give it a go and make sure you can do it.

Presentation Software

Presentations are used for giving oral and visual information (i.e. speech and pictures) to an audience.

Presentations Combine **Oral** and **Visual** Communication

1) Presentations are used to communicate information to an audience, or to persuade them of something. Usually there's a speaker, and they might have some equipment or props to help them. For example...

Flipcharts

These are big pieces of paper on a pad — the speaker can flip from page to page. They're okay for a small room, but harder for a large audience to see.

Overhead transparencies (OHTs)

These are clear plastic sheets — the contents can be projected onto a screen. The size of the image can be adjusted, so they're better for large audiences. You can print transparencies from a computer or write them by hand.

Slideshows

These are usually made using presentation software — an LCD projector can be used to display a series of slides while the speaker gives their talk.

2) The idea is that the visual material (slides, OHTs, or whatever) help to support the spoken information.

Presentations made on a computer can look more professional than hand-written materials.

Presentation Software Uses **Tools** Like a **Word Processor**

Presentation software creates a series of slides in a single document. You can design your slides from scratch, or you can use a template. Either way, you can edit the layout with a range of tools and objects.

Text is Typed in Text Boxes...

...no surprises there. You can use all the usual text formatting options in a text box.

Bullet points are especially handy in presentations, since they split text into bite-size chunks of info. Plus, you can make bullet points appear on a slide one at a time.

You Can Add Notes to Slides

Notes aren't displayed on the slide, but they can be printed and used to remind the speaker about key points during the presentation.

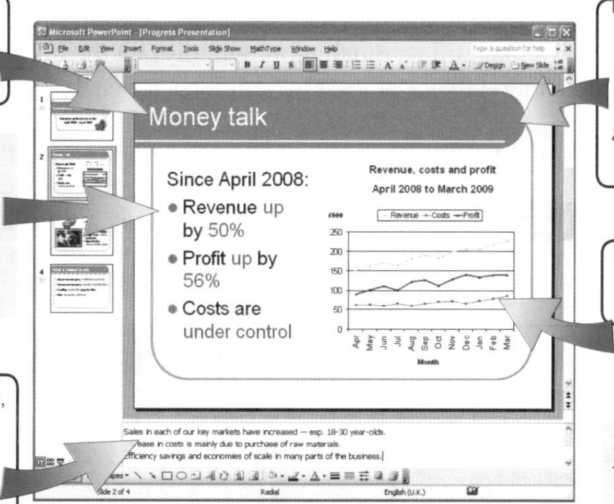

Use Colour Effectively

You can set the background colour for your slides, and use coloured shapes, boxes, lines and borders to draw attention to parts of the slide.

Insert Pictures Wisely

You can put pictures, charts or tables into slides.

Sometimes you can make these in the presentation software.

You can also insert pictures from clip art, or another source (e.g. a graphics package).

Use **Effects** to Add **Movement** to Your Slides

See the animated tutorial too.

1) **TIMINGS** Presentation software lets you decide when objects will appear on the slide. For example, each bullet point in a list can appear at just the right moment, or when you click the mouse.

2) **ANIMATION EFFECTS** can be used to make objects move on the screen in eye-catching ways.
   - For example, a line of text can appear one word at a time, or the size and style of the font can change.
   - A picture can grow, shrink, rotate, or move around along a set path.

3) **TRANSITIONS** are effects that come in when you change from one slide to the next. For example, new slides can fly in from one side of the screen, or the slides can 'open and close' like shutters or curtains.

Software can make presentations look more professional...

Presentation software is a useful tool, but it's best to keep things simple. Don't get carried away with jazzy effects — a lot of them can end up looking a bit... silly. There's more about all this on the next page.

Presentations

So, presentation software can do all kinds of exciting stuff. But it's <u>not always</u> the best option — you need to choose the <u>most appropriate method</u> to give an effective presentation.

Remember the **Rules** for Giving a **Good Presentation**

1) **CHOOSE THE BEST EQUIPMENT** — it's not always best to use fancy hi-tech presentation software.
    - Presentation software is great for making slides look <u>professional</u> — it's usually the best choice for <u>large companies</u> with a strong <u>corporate image</u>.
    - It's also good for making <u>attention-grabbing</u> presentations — animations and clever timings can help to keep an audience interested (and you can't use these on paper or OHTs).
    - But electronic <u>hardware</u> (e.g. computers and projectors) and <u>software</u> can be <u>pricey</u> — a flipchart/OHT approach might be more cost-effective for small firms.
    - <u>Technical issues</u> can also cause problems — it's important to <u>test</u> electronic presentations using the hardware that will be used in the <u>presentation</u>. E.g. large movie clips might run very slowly on some systems — it's <u>embarrassing</u> for the speaker if things don't go as planned.

2) **REMEMBER YOUR AUDIENCE** — the wrong choice of presentation technique can put people off.
    - A large company giving a presentation to important <u>stakeholders</u> would probably use an electronic slideshow with charts and diagrams. (Handwritten slides would look a bit shoddy in this situation.)
    - For a <u>small</u>, <u>informal</u> presentation, a flipchart might be better — especially since you can <u>add extra ideas</u> from the audience to a flipchart as you go along.

3) **DON'T OVERLOAD YOUR SLIDES** with <u>too much information</u>. A good slide should only contain a few <u>short points</u> and possibly a diagram — much more will <u>distract</u> the audience from the <u>talk</u>. As a general rule, you should aim to talk for at least <u>two minutes</u> for each of your slides.

4) **USE CONSISTENT SLIDES** — using a similar <u>style</u> and <u>layout</u> on each slide often looks more <u>professional</u>.

5) **USE PICTURES AND DIAGRAMS** if they'll help. A picture can speak a thousand words, after all. And remember that <u>charts</u> are really good for showing patterns and trends in a set of figures.

Handouts are **Paper Copies** of Presentation Materials

Print Your Slides as <u>Handouts</u>

Presentation software allows speakers to print their slides and give them to the audience as <u>handouts</u> so they can <u>make notes</u> on them during the presentation and refer to them <u>afterwards</u>.

You can set the print options to display <u>several slides</u> on one page — this <u>saves paper</u>, and the text should be large enough to read if the slides are well designed.

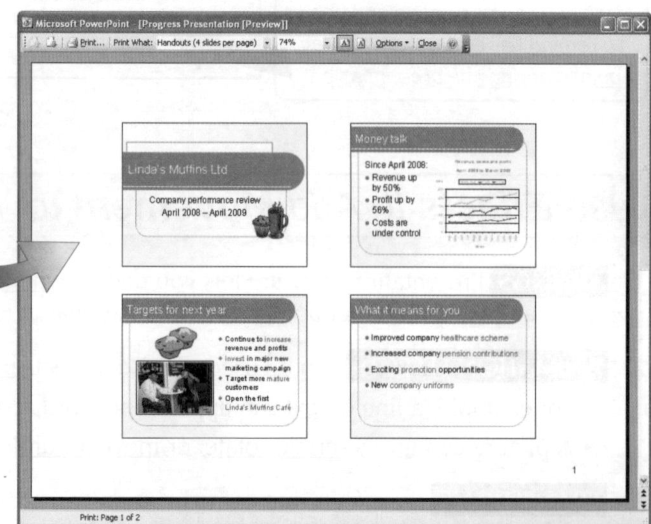

1) Handouts <u>don't</u> have to be made using presentation software.
2) They could be <u>photocopies</u> of OHTs, or <u>extra information</u> that might be useful.

Hold your handout — I've got a present(ation) for you...

There are lots of factors to keep in mind when planning a presentation. The best method to use depends on the <u>situation</u> and the <u>audience</u> — there's no point making things <u>more complicated</u> than they need to be.

Web-Authoring Software

You can create simple web pages using a word processor.
But web-authoring software can make it easier to put a complex web site together.

Web-Authoring Software is a Bit Like a Word Processor...

For the most part, using web-authoring software is similar to using a word processor.
You can add text, pictures and so on in much the same way.

See the animated tutorial too.

It's a good idea to use a similar 'look' on every page of a website...

Keep menus in the same place on each page to make it easier to navigate.

Make the page headings match the menu options.

Use a similar colour scheme on each page (you could always vary the colour scheme between different sections of the site).

Text should be easy to read on-screen.

The look of a business website should suit the business's image — see p76.

Borders and lines can help break up the page.

You can animate things to make them more eye-catching.

...With Some Important Differences

1) Any object on a webpage can be turned into a 'clickable' hyperlink to take you to a different page.
2) You can even make several links on the same image using 'hotspots'.
   For example, clicking on each town on this map might take you to a page about that town.

Think of the users when you're choosing graphics...

...high-resolution images look better on screen but they can take ages to download.

...low-resolution images download quicker, but can become pixelated (blocky).

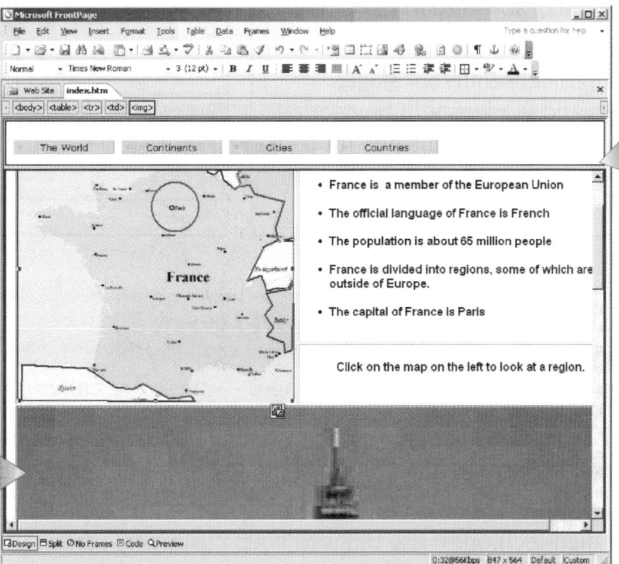

Frames allow different parts of the webpage to work independently. Here, when the user scrolls down the main part of the page, the top frame remains visible.

Frames allow you to keep useful buttons and menus on the screen at all times. But on small screens (e.g. PDAs and Smartphones), there's often not enough space for frames to work properly.

Write yourself a few words about web-authoring software...

Frames are a bit 'last year' really — not a lot of sites use them these days. But they're mentioned on the AQA specification, so make sure you know how to use them in whatever software you're using. It's adding hyperlinks between pages that you might need to practise — try it in a word processor if you need to.

Other Software Applications

The world is full to the brim with software. Here are some more packages that businesses often use.

DTP is Like a Frame-Based Word Processor

1) Desktop publishing (DTP) software has a lot in common with a word processor — you can use it to combine text and graphics on a page, and most of the tools and options are very similar.
2) The main difference is that DTP software is frame-based. Each object on the page is contained in its own frame (or box), which can be moved freely around the page without affecting other frames.

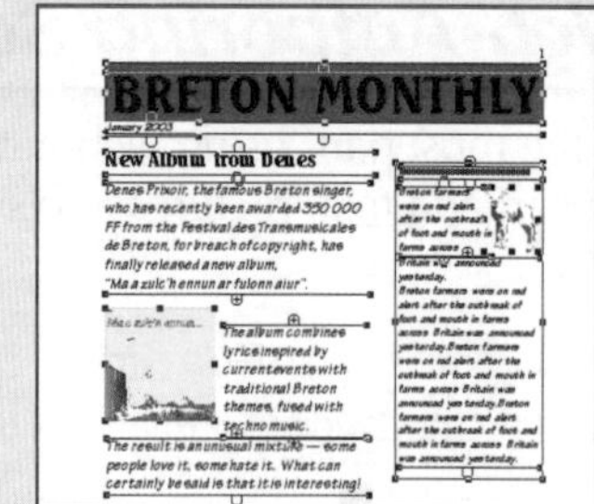

Software for Emailing, Organising and Planning

EMAIL SYSTEMS

These are used (obviously) for writing, sending and receiving emails, and creating address books.

1) **CLIENT-BASED SYSTEMS** use software stored on the user's computer.
2) **WEB-BASED SYSTEMS** are similar, but you need to be connected to the internet to use the service.

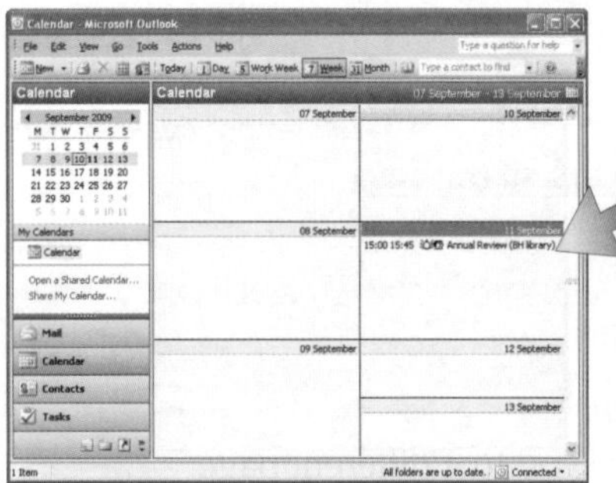

DIARY-MANAGEMENT SOFTWARE

1) This can be used to schedule meetings, appointments, and bookings — and remind you when they're coming up.
2) In a business, managers may have access to the diaries of their whole team — it can be easier to organise staff if you know what their schedules are.

Diary-management software is often included with client-based email.

PROJECT-PLANNING SOFTWARE

1) Some businesses use this type of software to help them plan projects efficiently (see p28).
2) It's possible to timetable a project's different stages, and decide when materials and workers will be needed, and what the costs will be. Charts (like this one for a building project) can provide a visual summary of what should happen when.

Weeks/Tasks	1	2	3	4	5	6	7	8	9	10
Prepare site	■	■								
Dig and lay foundations			■							
Build walls			■	■	■	■				
Fit roof joists							■			
Tile roof								■		
Plumbing									■	■

Web 2.0 Websites Can be Edited by Users

Some websites allow users to add and edit content on the pages — these are called Web 2.0 sites.

1) **WIKIS** are pages where individual users can add or edit existing content (some online encyclopaedias are put together this way). But it's hard to guarantee the quality of a wiki's content.
2) **BLOGS** are online diaries (web-logs), but the content of blog posts can be pretty much anything. Some businesses (especially high-tech ones) use blogs to keep customers up-to-date about new product developments (and to collect feedback from readers).

Get in the right frame of mind to learn about DTP...

Right, that just about concludes our run-down of software packages. I'm a big fan of DTP, myself — it makes it easy to do crazy things like *this*. You know the drill — make sure you know all about all of this.

Evaluating Software

Software packages have made many parts of businesses much more efficient. But as with everything else, it's important to use the best tools for the job. It's not always obvious which package to use for a task.

Choose the **Best** Type of **Package** for the **Task**

1) **WORD PROCESSORS** (p91-95) are designed specifically for editing text (words). You'd use a word processor to produce text-heavy documents like letters, memos and reports.

> Word processors can combine text with pictures to produce more complex documents. But it's not always the best option...

2) **DESK-TOP PUBLISHING** software (p116) is sometimes easier to use when you're making documents with more complex layouts — e.g. newsletters, flyers and brochures.

> This is because DTP software is frame based — if you move the contents of one frame it won't change the position of the other frames. With a word processor, moving one object can make everything else on the page move as well.

3) **SPREADSHEETS** (p98-102) are ideal for most things involving numbers — e.g. doing calculations, and producing graphs and charts. Many businesses use them to keep track of financial data.

> Spreadsheets can also be used to organise other types of data (e.g. text) into tables. But databases give you more options...

4) **DATABASES** (p105-108) are great for storing and processing large amounts of data — text, numbers, dates... you name it. You can search a database to pick out exactly the information you want, so businesses often use them to store things like customer details and product information.

> The main problem is that databases can be complicated to set up and use, especially relational databases.

Weigh Up Your Software **Options**

For modern businesses, there's usually a wide choice of software available from different sources. These are some of the things that might affect a business's decision about what to go for.

1) **PROPRIETARY and OPEN-SOURCE SOFTWARE**
   - PROPRIETARY software is sold to customers by the manufacturer — e.g. Microsoft® Office. It can be expensive for a firm to buy licences for all its staff, but the manufacturer will often offer customer support (e.g. downloadable upgrades).
   - OPEN-SOURCE software is free to use, so it can save money for a business. But there's no customer service department (though there is often a lot of advice available on the internet). Open-source code can be altered by anyone, so some people worry about security problems.

2) **LOCATION OF SOFTWARE** Until recently, software had to be installed on a computer or server. But some modern software is designed to be used over the internet.
   - Internet-based programs tend to be cheaper than installed software (or even free), and they leave more storage space free on your computer for other uses.
   - On the downside, sending and receiving data over the internet may be slower than working from a hard drive. And if there's a problem with the connection, you're stuck.

3) **COLLABORATIVE WORKING** means working as a team — some software makes it easier to do this.
   - Storing files on a local network allows different team members to access and edit the same files. Some software even labels people's changes with their name, so others can see who's added what.
   - People collaborating on a project might be in different places (and different time-zones even) — so things such as email, teleconferencing (p43), wikis, and diary management software can help too.

Basically, choose the best software for the job...

Not surprisingly, different software packages are designed to do different tasks. It's worth remembering that you can often make different packages work together by importing objects from one package into another.

Warm-Up and Worked Exam Questions

Warm-up Questions

1) Give one benefit of cropping an image.
2) Give three different media that can be used to give a presentation.
3) Why are hyperlinks used on websites?
4) Describe the main features of diary-management software?

Worked Exam Question

You'll be glad to hear that there's only a few pages left in this section. As usual, if you want to do this worked example yourself, you'll find all the files you need on the CD at the back of this book.

Task One: Creating Images

Paul is making a poster about healthy eating. He has asked you to make a picture similar to the one shown below using suitable graphics software. Paul has given you some instructions.

Use similar colours to the ones in the picture.
Align everything down the middle of the sign.

a) Use your graphics editor to create a suitable image.
   Make your image around 45 mm × 30 mm in size.
   Save your file as **IMAGE**.

(8 marks)

Recall the file **POSTER**. This is Paul's unfinished poster.

b) Insert your image into the centre of Paul's poster.
   Increase the size of your image by 50%.
   Save a copy of the poster as **POSTER1**.

(3 marks)

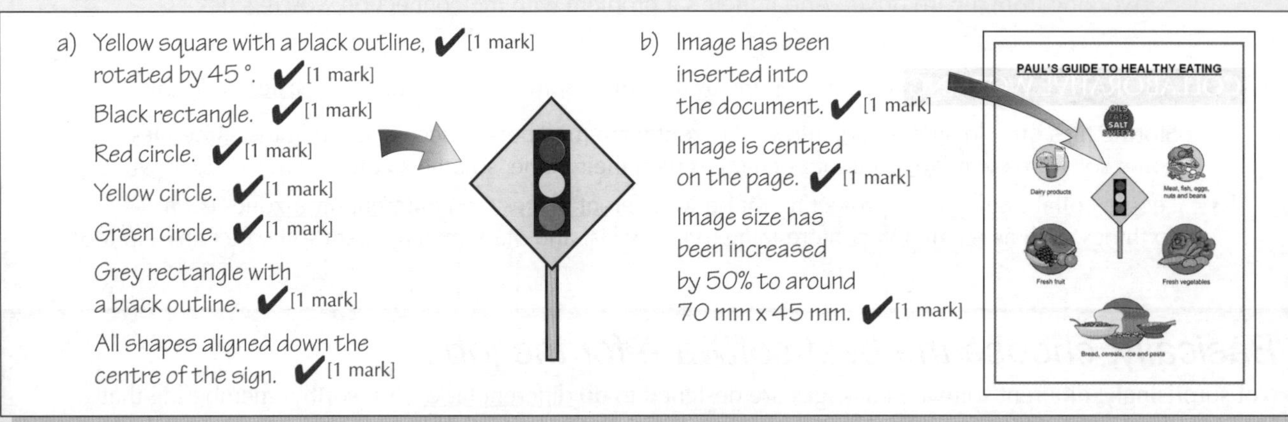

a) Yellow square with a black outline, ✔[1 mark]
rotated by 45°. ✔[1 mark]
Black rectangle. ✔[1 mark]
Red circle. ✔[1 mark]
Yellow circle. ✔[1 mark]
Green circle. ✔[1 mark]
Grey rectangle with a black outline. ✔[1 mark]
All shapes aligned down the centre of the sign. ✔[1 mark]
b) Image has been inserted into the document. ✔[1 mark]
Image is centred on the page. ✔[1 mark]
Image size has been increased by 50% to around 70 mm x 45 mm. ✔[1 mark]
PAUL'S GUIDE TO HEALTHY EATING

Exam Questions

Computer-based assessment — you'll need a **computer** to answer this question.

Task One: Presentation

Miranda works for Partition's, an ice cream manufacturer in Ritterton. She is due to present the annual sales figures to her manager. Miranda has asked you to make the presentation.

Recall the file **PRESENTATION**.

a) Miranda wants a new slide at the end of the presentation.

- Create a new slide and add the page title 'Final Thoughts'.
- Copy and paste the text from the file **TEXT** into the new slide as a bulleted list.

Save your file as **PRESENTATION1**.

(4 marks)

Recall the file **PRESENTATION1**.

b) Miranda would like you to make the following changes to the presentation.

- Insert slides 2 and 3 from the file **HISTORICAL** after slide 2.
- Choose one animation effect and apply it to all three graphs in the presentation.
- Choose one page transition and apply it to every slide in the presentation.

Print one copy of the presentation as a single page with all six slides on.

Save your file as **PRESENTATION2**.

(8 marks)

Written assessment — you'll need a **pen** to answer this question.

1 Read **Item A** and then answer the questions that follow.

Item A

David has been looking at new database applications to replace the software currently used in his company. David must choose between DataBayCE, which is proprietary software, and Base-A-Date, which is open-source software.

a) Describe **two** functions a database can perform.

....

....

(2 marks)

b) Describe **one** advantage to a business of each of the following.

(i) Proprietary software ....

....

(ii) Open-source software ....

....

(4 marks)

Revision Summary for Section Eight

I know — this page looks horrible. But this has been a long section. And long sections mean lots of questions. Grab yourself a pen, a computer, and a selection of software. For the last time in this book, have a crack at the questions below. As ever, if you struggle with any, revise that page again and have another crack.

1) Describe five different types of text formatting. Suggest a situation where each one might be used.
2) Use a word processor to create a flyer for a shop that sells fruit and vegetables.
   Use text boxes, clip art, WordArt and borders, and overlay some text on a graphic.
3) Business letters use 'fully-blocked style' and 'open punctuation'. What do these terms mean?
4) Use a word processor template to write a short business letter confirming a customer order.
5) Explain briefly how mail-merged letters are made. Why might a business want to use mail merge?
6) In a spreadsheet, what's the difference between an absolute cell reference and a relative cell reference?
7) a) Copy the table on the right into a spreadsheet.
   b) Use a formula and relative cell references to fill in the profits for 2006 to 2009 in column D (profit = revenue – costs).
   c) Use functions and relative cell references to fill in the totals and averages for columns B, C and D.

	A	B	C	D
1		Revenue (£000s)	Costs (£000s)	Profit (£000s)
2	2006	120	80	
3	2007	135	82	
4	2008	129	82	
5	2009	140	76	
6	Total			
7	Average			

8) a) Use the data from Q7 to produce a line graph showing how revenue, costs and profits changed between 2006 and 2009.
   b) Add a title, labels and a legend, and adjust the colours.
   c) Insert your chart into a blank word processor document.
9) In a database, what's the difference between a field and a record?
10) What is an input mask, and why might you use one?
11) Explain the reasons for using a form to input data into a table.
12) What's a wildcard search? How would you type a search for words starting with 'be'?
13) a) Create a database table containing these fields: first name, surname, gender, date of birth.
    b) Design a form for inputting data into this table. Include an input mask for the 'date of birth' field.
    c) Use the form to enter your details. Then enter details for five people who are older than you, and five people who are younger (you can make them up).
    d) Design a query to display all the people who were born after your birthday, so that the results are sorted in ascending alphabetical order by surname.
    e) Design a report to display the results of this query in a stylish way. Print it out.
14) Explain the main differences between bitmap and vector graphics.
15) Use a graphics package for this question and the next one.
    a) Put these shapes into a new file: a circle, a triangle, a rectangle, and a freehand star.
    b) Shade each shape a different colour. Give the rectangle a blue dashed outline.
    c) Find some vector clip art of a penguin, and put it on the page.
    d) Resize your circle so that it's a bit taller than the penguin (but still a circle, not an oval).
    e) Put the circle behind the penguin. Use the text tool to add a humorous speech bubble.
16) a) Find a bitmap photo of a building with lots of sky in the background. Crop out most of the sky.
    b) Save your cropped picture as 'building' and insert it into a new word processor file.
17) Discuss the pros and cons that using presentation software might have for a business.
18) Give three features of a good presentation slide.
19) Explain five things that can have an impact on the look and feel of a website.
20) What's the purpose of using frames on a website? Give a disadvantage of using frames.
21) Explain a major difference between a word processor and a desktop publishing package.
22) What is meant by a 'Web 2.0' webpage? Give two examples of this type of page.
23) Describe the differences between proprietary and open-source software.
24) Give one advantage and one disadvantage of using software over the internet.

Answers to Q7 b) and c)

	Revenue (£000s)	Costs (£000s)	Profit (£000s)
2006	120	80	40
2007	135	82	53
2008	129	82	47
2009	140	76	64
Total	524	320	204
Average	131	80	51

Assessment

Assessment — a whole shedload of things to do, and only a certain amount of time to do them in.

*You **Won't** Need to Learn **All** the Pages in This Book*

Okay... there's a lot to learn in this subject, but there is a little bit of good news.
You won't be tested on the whole book. Not quite, anyway.

AQA

- You won't be directly tested on pages 3 and 10 in Section 1 of this book.
  You also won't be directly tested on pages 17, 18 and 19 in Section 2.
  But you will need to know about the rest of Section 1 and Section 2.
- However, all the pages are useful background material — they contain some key ideas about business.

OCR

- You won't be directly tested on pages 34, 35, 36, 40, 41 and 42 in Section 4 of this book.
  But you will need to know about the rest of Section 4 (pages 37, 43, 44).
- However, all the pages are useful background material — they contain some key ideas about business.

Edexcel

- You won't be directly tested on pages 25, 28 and 30 in Section 3 of this book.
  But you will need to know about the rest of Section 3 (pages 23, 24, 29).
- However, all the pages are useful background material — they contain some key ideas about business.

*Make Sure You Know About **Your Assessment***

The different exam boards all set slightly different exam papers, worth slightly different numbers of marks.
Here's what you can expect...

AQA:

- A 1-hour Written Paper on Unit 8 — ICT Systems in Business. Worth 40% of your GCSE.
- A 1½-hour Computer-Based Examination on Unit 9 — Using ICT in Business. Worth 35% of your GCSE.
- A Controlled Assessment on Unit 10 — Investigating ICT in Business. Worth 25% of your GCSE.

OCR:

- A 1½-hour Written Paper on Unit A265
  — Businesses and Their Communication Systems. Worth 50% of your GCSE.
- A Controlled Assessment on Unit A266 — Developing Business Communication Systems.
  Worth 25% of your GCSE.
- A 1-hour Computer-Based Examination on Unit A267 —
  ICT Skills for Business Communication Systems. Worth 25% of your GCSE.

Edexcel:

- A 45-minute Written Paper on Unit 1 — Introduction to Small Business. Worth 25% of your GCSE.
  Mainly multiple-choice questions (no long-answer questions). Includes a question on balance sheets.
- A Controlled Assessment on Unit 2 — Investigating Small Business. Worth 25% of your GCSE.
- A 1½-hour Written Paper on Unit 4 — Business Communications. Worth 50% of your GCSE.
  Pretty varied — a mix of multiple-choice, written-answer, and scenario-based questions.

Nothing too taxing on that page, then...

An easy page, for a change — you're only going to need to pay attention to about a third of it.
There's even some good news at the top where it tells you which pages you don't need to learn. Lovely.

Controlled Assessment

Controlled assessment — it's an exam, but it could take a few weeks to finish. Weird.

Know What Your Controlled Assessment Will Involve

AQA: Unit 10 — Investigating ICT in Business

- You'll be given a business scenario. You'll then need to carry out some kind of task.
- The task will probably be quite open (e.g. "design a web page for a local business").

OCR: Unit A266 — Developing business communication systems

- You'll need to choose one of two possible scenarios. There will be a number of tasks for each scenario.
- There are 60 marks available — which is worth 25% of your GCSE.
- You'll probably need to investigate a local company and present your findings in a report for one of the tasks.
- You'll also probably have to produce a professional business document for one of the tasks, like a letter or a leaflet.

Edexcel: Unit 2 — Investigating Small Business

- You'll have to choose one of five possible tasks. The tasks will look like normal essay-style questions about business, but you'll have to apply your knowledge to a real business.
- You will need to research a real business (your teacher can help you choose one).

Controlled Assessment Tasks are Quite "Open"

1) Although there will be loads of ways to approach the task, that doesn't mean you can do what you like. In some ways, controlled assessment tasks are quite specific. For example, you might have to:
   - Plan a new business website.
   - Recommend how a business could improve its communications.
   - Research the methods a business uses to compete in its market, and decide which is the most important.

Ten people could answer the same question in ten completely different ways, but all get full marks.

2) So even though you'll have a bit of freedom to decide how you want to tackle the task, make sure you remember what it is you're supposed to be doing.

First You'll Do Research, Then You'll Produce a Report

All the boards give you time to do some research.

For AQA you get 5-8 hours.
Edexcel give you up to 6.
For OCR you get up to 10 hours.
Your teacher will be able to tell you more.

- You can ask your teacher for help during research time. (But your teacher can't help you with some things — like analysing your research.)
- You can work in a group while you're doing research. But... make sure you get the information you need.

You'll then be given more time to produce your actual written-up (or typed-up) piece of work.

AQA give you 4 hours, Edexcel allows 3 hours and for OCR you get 5 hours.

- You'll be supervised by your teacher, but you can't ask for help with this.
- And you can't work with friends. You're not even allowed to use other people's research.

Research task #1: find out which exam board you're doing...

Controlled assessment tasks can look daunting — the key is to keep your head and not panic.
It helps if you know what to expect. If you don't know already, find out which exam board you're studying.

Written Exams

So... your brain is stuffed with wholesome Business and Communications knowledge. Good.
This page gives you a few tips on what to expect in the written exam, and how to maximise your marks.

There Are **Different Types** of Question to Look Out For

WRITTEN-ANSWER QUESTIONS

1) These are the types of question you'll spend most of your time answering (except in Edexcel Unit 1).
2) For these questions, always look at the marks available and the amount of space you've been given. If a question's worth 10 marks, say, you'll have plenty of space for your answer — use it wisely.
3) Some short-answer questions will just ask you to remember and state a fact about Business Studies.
4) Other questions will give you a business scenario and ask you to apply your knowledge to that situation — but you won't be asked about anything you haven't been taught.
5) Data-response questions give you information (i.e. data) about a business — it might be a sales graph, a balance sheet, or even a newspaper article. You need to apply your knowledge to the data.

MULTIPLE CHOICE QUESTIONS (only Edexcel)

1) You might be asked to choose more than one answer — always tick the right number of boxes.
2) If you don't know the answer to a multiple choice question, it's worth guessing. Before you guess, try to rule out any options you know are wrong — that'll improve your chances of hitting the right ones.

Make Sure You Understand These **Command Words**

All exam questions have a key "command" word that tells you what to do. For example...

Define or What is Meant By — E.g. "What is meant by the term E-Commerce?" These questions are easy marks if you've learned all the definitions. You just have to know what the term means.

Describe — These need a bit more than "Define..." questions — e.g. "Describe the role of branding in a business." You'll have to make several points to answer this.

These test what
you know.

State or Identify — These words ask for a statement — you don't need to back it up with evidence.

Explain — These questions involve giving reasons. You need to show you understand the link between things that happen in the world and the effects they have on businesses.

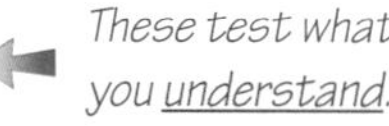

These test what
you understand.

Analyse — This means "Talk about in detail." Make sure you look at the main features of the thing you're analysing. Then explain how or why these features work together to lead to the end result.

These test your ability to make judgements.

Recommend   Discuss   Assess   Which is Most Likely/Appropriate   Evaluate

For these, you should always back up your points using your Business and Communications knowledge.

- Before you get started on your answer, make sure you've read the whole question carefully and you've understood what you're being asked to do. You'll lose marks if you take the wrong approach.
- In business situations, there are usually advantages and disadvantages to think about — to get all the marks, you'll need to give both sides of the argument before coming to a conclusion.
- Link your ideas together to build a structured argument.

All your questions about questions answered...

Each exam board sets its exams in a different way, but they're basically all testing you on the same skills. But different questions require different types of answers. My advice... read the question and think.

Computer-Based Assessment

If you're taking the AQA or OCR exam, you'll do a computer-based assessment too.
It's a mixture of practical computer-based tasks and Business and Communications theory.

You'll Need to Complete **Various Tasks** on a **Computer**

1) Computer-based assessments are taken under test conditions — you have to work on your own.
2) But you'll be working on a computer — not writing on paper.
3) The exam paper will give you all the instructions you need to complete the various tasks.
4) You'll have to use some ready-made computer files — your teacher will tell you where these are stored.
5) You'll need to print your work for each question and hand it in at the end of the exam.

The Tasks are All **Business-Related**

The exam will test your practical software skills, and your understanding of the use of software in business.

1) Each of the tasks will be based on a business scenario.
2) You could be asked to produce a business document. Possible examples include:
   - Text-based documents — e.g. a note, memo or business letter.
   - Documents with text and graphics — e.g. a flyer, leaflet or advert.
   - Slides for a business presentation.

   You might be given text and pictures to use — or you might need to write or make them yourself.

3) You could be asked to carry out some kind of process. For example:
   - Work with records in a database and produce a report.
   - Do calculations with numbers, and produce charts in a spreadsheet.
   - Set up a mail-merge for a set of business letters.

   You'll probably be given some data to work with.

4) Some questions will ask you to explain and discuss software issues. For example:
   - Explain why you've used particular formatting on a page.
   - Discuss the pros and cons of a type of software for a business (e.g. mail-merge, or presentation software).

   In these questions, you're normally giving advice to a business — you might need to do this in a letter or a memo.

Don't Lose Easy Marks

In the exam, don't forget to do the easy things well.

1) READ THE INSTRUCTIONS CAREFULLY — both the general instructions at the start of the paper, and the instructions for each task. There are some easy marks on these papers — don't throw them away.
2) DO EXACTLY AS YOU'RE TOLD — some questions will ask you to use a particular format (e.g. landscape). Or you might need to save your work using a particular filename. Follow the instructions to the letter. And make sure you include your name and candidate number when told.
3) TAKE CARE WHEN SAVING — don't save over the top of files you might need to use again or hand in.
4) CHECK YOUR PRINTOUTS — it's surprisingly easy to miss mistakes on screen — so check your printouts carefully before you hand them in.

Time to face some hard questions about software...

Computer-based assessments test how well you know your way around software, so make sure you know how to use all the tools and features in Section 8. But you might also have to explain how software can be useful in business — so make sure you revise that side of things too. Be careful — that's all I'm saying.

Practice Controlled Assessment

All being well, you now know all the facts about Business and Communications that you'll need for your assessment. But this is a real-world subject, and so you need to be able to use your knowledge in the real world. That's what the Controlled Assessment is all about — applying your knowledge to real businesses.

Controlled Assessment Practice — just like the ones your Exam Board will set...

The Controlled Assessment tasks for AQA, Edexcel and OCR are all similar, but all slightly different too (see page 122). Over the next few pages, we've provided three sets of tasks that are just like the real thing.

Controlled Assessment: Set A — these are just like the AQA tasks
— we've provided three tasks, but you only need to do **one**

Controlled Assessment: Set B — these are just like the Edexcel tasks
— we've provided three tasks, but you only need to do **one**

We've provided some spares — in case you want some extra practice.

Controlled Assessment: Set C — these are just like the OCR tasks
— you need to do **both** tasks, but we've provided different scenarios to choose from

How you should use these Practice Controlled Assessment tasks

- In the real Controlled Assessment, you might have to go and visit real businesses to collect your data. But we realise that while you're revising, you might not have time to do that, so we've tried to write tasks that you can either research over the Internet, or that you might be able to find out about easily.
- That **doesn't** mean you **shouldn't** go and visit local businesses — if you can, then great. But if you can't, that shouldn't stop you doing one (or more) of the tasks for practice.

And remember...

There are no right or wrong answers in a Controlled Assessment... only answers backed up by evidence, and answers that aren't. (See page 146 to see what answers we came up with for one of the tasks.)

General Certificate of Secondary Education

GCSE Practice Paper **CGP**

AQA / OCR: *Business and Communication Systems*
Edexcel: *Business Communications*

Controlled Assessment

Time allowed	Set A (per task)	Set B (per task)	Set C (per scenario)
Research/data collection:	8 hours	6 hours	10 hours
Writing your report:	4 hours	3 hours	5 hours

- Depending on the nature of the task, you may use either suitable computer software to create your submission, or you may write a report by hand.
- All submissions should be clearly structured.
- You are required to submit a record of your research. You may present this as a table, or a list of the resources (both electronic and paper-based) that you have used.

Controlled Assessment: Set A (AQA)

A government-funded organisation wants to attract more young people to come to your local area. It wants students to stay for **holidays/weekend breaks**, for **study trips** and to get **work experience** in local firms. They have asked you to perform the following **two** activities:

(i) Complete **one** of the three tasks below,

and (ii) Design a logo to represent your local area.

List of tasks

1. Make a simple web site that you could use to explain the benefits of a stay in your area.

The web site should be aimed at young people, and should explain why a holiday or a study trip to your area might appeal to them.

2. Make a PowerPoint presentation that a local business could use to appeal to young people.

The presentation should focus on the benefits of gaining work experience there.

3. Make a leaflet that would appeal to young people in different parts of the country.

The leaflet should describe local attractions, and explain why young people from other parts of the country might enjoy or benefit from a holiday or study trip there.

Whichever task you choose, you will need to **research** and **plan** the task carefully.

- You should look at existing publications *(including **printed** materials such as brochures and leaflets and **electronic** materials such as websites)* designed to appeal to the target age range.
- You should examine their **content**, **layout** and **design**, and identify features that you think are particularly effective (or ineffective).
- Your final work should include an **annotated printout** of your web page / presentation / leaflet (which should include your **new logo**) explaining your ideas and describing the research that informed them.

Controlled Assessment: Set B (Edexcel)

Choose any **one** task from the list below.

You should then:

- choose a business that you will be able to research:
  - **either** – a local business (ideally a small business),
  - **or** – a business that you can research on the internet
- collect and analyse useful data
- evaluate your findings, and present your conclusions in the form of a report

List of tasks

1. To what extent has a business you are familiar with been affected by recent changes in economic conditions?

2. How would you explain the choice of marketing mix for a company you have researched?

3. How does a business you have researched manage to compete successfully with rivals?

Controlled Assessment: Set C (OCR)

For this investigation, you are acting as a consultant to **one** of the companies described below.

Local-Lec — a local retail electrical store that would like you to investigate its communications with **suppliers**

MegaMegaBowl — a large city-centre leisure centre that would like you to investigate its communications with **customers** (existing customers *and* potential customers)

See page 128 for information about **Local-Lec** and **MegaMegaBowl**.

a **retailer** in your local area — whose communications with *either* their **suppliers** *or* their **customers** you can investigate

a **leisure venue** in your local area — whose communications with their **customers** you can investigate

- For the company you have chosen, write a **formal business report** recommending how to improve the communications you have been asked to look into.
- To write your report, you will need to carry out **both** of the tasks below.
- You should **explain the reasoning** behind any recommendations that you make.

Task 1

Your report should contain details of:

- the *communications systems* currently used
- the *types of messages* that are currently sent
- the *media* that are currently used
- the *advantages and disadvantages* of the current system
- the *opinions of the suppliers or of the customers* (depending on the firm you are researching) on the current systems of communication
- your *recommendations* of how communications could be improved
- the *impact* you expect your changes to have

Task 2

Create a **leaflet** that the managing director of the firm you are investigating can use to convince its *suppliers or customers* to accept your proposed changes.

Your leaflet should:

- be of a *professional quality*
- show clearly the *advantages* of adopting the new communication system

Local-Lec Ltd.

- **Local-Lec Ltd.** is a small, family run electrical retail business.
- The business owns **three** town-centre stores, all within 15 miles of each other.
- They have a **range of suppliers**.
  - **Most electrical items** on sale come from a **wholesaler**. This wholesaler is a **large** company that **imports** goods from various countries and **sells them on** to (smaller) retail businesses.
  - **Some electrical items** on sale come **directly** from the manufacturers. These are all manufacturers with factories in the area **close to Local-Lec**, and with whom the family running Local-Lec have a **good relationship**.
  - Goods that are **not for resale** (i.e. those goods that Local-Lec needs in order to run the business, such as stationary, vehicles, office furniture etc.) are bought **locally**. Local-Lec has negotiated **preferable terms** with some of these suppliers, meaning it gets a **discount** on their normal retail prices.
  - The business also uses **local providers of services** (such as banks and accountants).
- Most communication is currently done via **email** or over the **phone** (particularly if Local-Lec has a good relationship with the business). Local-Lec also uses the post quite a lot for sending out **invoices** if it has supplied goods to local businesses.

MegaMegaBowl

- **MegaMegaBowl** is a large **city-centre leisure centre**, offering a **variety** of entertainment facilities, including ten-pin bowling, swimming pool, gym, a sports hall that can be used for various sports, as well as a café.
- MegaMegaBowl **opened very recently**, and is part of **MegaMegaEnts**, a large international leisure group based in the USA.

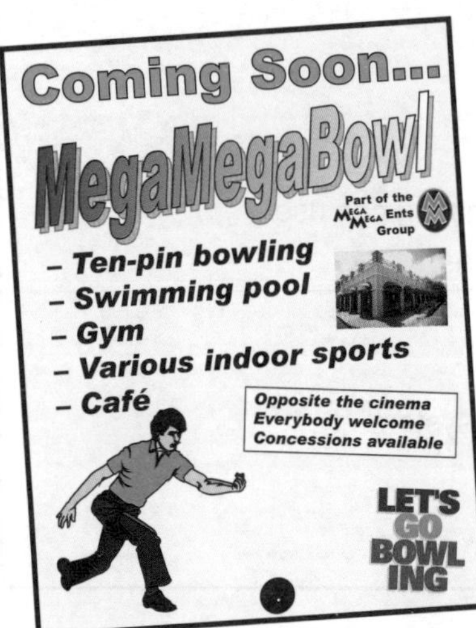

- MegaMegaBowl aims to attract people **of all ages**. It also wants to attract people from **all income brackets**, and currently offers **discounts** to various groups, such as **pensioners**, **students** and the **unemployed**.
- The only advertisements that MegaMegaBowl currently uses are posters (as shown on the left) displayed on **billboards** around the town. They were put up a month before MegaMegaBowl opened to give information about the **types of facilities** that would be available.
- The **website of MegaMegaEnts** has a page dedicated to facilities that are **'Opening Soon'**. This includes details of MegaMegaBowl, as well as of other facilities in different **European countries** and the **USA**.

Practice Written Papers

Once you've been through all the questions in this book, you should feel pretty confident about the written exam. As final preparation, here are **two mock papers** to really get you set for the real thing.

(Note for students doing the Edexcel course: We didn't include multiple-choice questions, but if you can answer the questions on this paper, you'll be able to answer any multiple-choice question you might eventually be faced with.)

- There are four questions in each of these papers — your real exam paper might be slightly different.
- Give yourself 70 minutes per paper — then you'll have to work at about the same speed as in the real exam.
- Marks aren't deducted for wrong answers.
- In calculations show clearly how you work out your answers.
- Remember... you're assessed on "your ability to present information clearly and logically, using specialist vocabulary where appropriate. Your spelling, punctuation and grammar are also taken into account."

Paper 1

Leave blank

1. Numeris plc is a computer supplier. Numeris has received a letter from another company placing an order for a new computer. The letter states that the order is urgent, but some of the details in the letter are unclear. An employee from Numeris is about to contact the company to clarify the details of the order. She intends to use an urgent, formal channel of communication.

(a) What is meant by each of the following phrases?

(i) "formal channel of communication"

....

....

(2 marks)

(ii) "urgent channel of communication"

....

....

(2 marks)

(b) Recommend a suitable medium for the Numeris employee to use. Explain your answer.

....

....

....

(4 marks)

(c) Once the information has been clarified, a senior manager in Numeris wants to tell the Production department supervisor to process this order as quickly as possible.

Recommend a suitable medium for the manager to use. Explain your answer.

....

....

....

(4 marks)

Turn over

Leave blank

2. Aamil has just applied for a job at a local quarry. The job advert said that the position involved flexitime, good training and fringe benefits.

(a) What is meant by the term "flexitime"?

....

....

(3 marks)

(b) Explain the benefits of training to an employee.

....

....

....

(4 marks)

(c) (i) What is meant by the term "fringe benefit"?

....

....

(2 marks)

(ii) Describe two examples of fringe benefits.

....

....

....

....

(4 marks)

(d) The starting wage for this job is £9.80 per hour. After six months, this increases by 15%. Calculate the hourly rate after six months.

....

....

(2 marks)

(e) This is a dangerous job, and Aamil is worried about Health and Safety issues. Explain to Aamil the responsibilities of employers and employees regarding Health and Safety.

....

....

....

....

....

(6 marks)

Leave blank

3. Flora is a director of a large company, whose organisation chart is shown on the right.

Directors
Managers
Operatives

(a) The chart shows layers of directors, managers and operatives.

Explain what is meant by the following terms:

(i) directors

....

.... *(2 marks)*

(ii) operatives

....

.... *(2 marks)*

(b) Flora is concerned that the firm's internal communication is inefficient.

Explain why poor internal communication is a problem for a business.

....

....

.... *(4 marks)*

(c) Flora wants to encourage managers to send more memos in order to improve communication.

(i) What is a memo?

.... *(2 marks)*

(ii) Describe one advantage and one disadvantage of using memos.

....

.... *(4 marks)*

(d) Discuss **two** other ways in which Flora could change her firm's internal communication to try to improve it.

Which **one** of these ways would you recommend? Give reasons for your answer.

....

....

....

.... *(6 marks)*

Leave blank

4. Adam is the IT Systems Manager for a large engineering company. He is replacing the equipment the company sales representatives use when they visit other businesses. Adam is going to give each sales representative a laptop.

(a) Adam is unsure whether the capacity of the laptops' internal hard disks will be sufficient. He is considering whether each representative will also need an external hard disk.

What is meant by "internal hard disk" and "external hard disk"?

....

....

....

(4 marks)

(b) The sales representatives can use the laptops to log in to their company email accounts. All the email accounts, as well as the laptops themselves, are password protected.

(i) Explain the importance of password protection in this situation.

....

....

(3 marks)

(ii) Explain why the sales representatives should change their email passwords regularly.

....

....

(2 marks)

(c) The sales representatives will need to use their laptops for:

- carrying out complex price calculations based on their customers' requirements
- writing letters to customers

What software would you recommend for each of these tasks? Explain your answers.

(i) carrying out price calculations

....

(2 marks)

(ii) writing letters

....

....

(2 marks)

(d) The sales representatives are regularly reminded of the need for clear communication when dealing with customers.

Describe **two** potential barriers to communication that should be avoided.

....

....

....

(4 marks)

Paper 2

Leave blank

1. Read **Source A** and then answer the questions that follow.

> **Source A**
>
> Connor runs a chain of skateboard shops with branches in six cities. He makes a small profit each year, but is contemplating using e-commerce as an alternative to advertising and selling on the high street, as he believes it may be more profitable. However, he is reluctant to take risks with his business, because he has worked very hard to build it into a success.

(a) What is meant by "e-commerce"?

....

(1 mark)

(b) Suggest **two** ways in which Connor could use the Internet to promote his business.

....

....

....

(4 marks)

(c) Explain one advantage and one disadvantage for Connor's customers of a switch to e-commerce.

....

....

....

....

(4 marks)

(d) Would you advise Connor to change from a high-street business to an e-commerce business? Give reasons for your answer.

....

....

....

....

....

....

....

....

(9 marks)

2. Darren runs a successful small restaurant. Recently, a large chain restaurant opened up nearby. The chain restaurant offers similar food to Darren's restaurant. Darren is worried that the new restaurant will take away some of his customers.

(a) Darren is planning on carrying out some market research to help him decide how to respond to the threat of the new restaurant.

(i) What is meant by "market research"?

....

....

....

(3 marks)

(ii) Explain two suitable methods of market research that Darren could use.

....

....

....

....

(5 marks)

(b) The marketing mix consists of four different factors: Product, Price, Promotion and Place. Recommend how Darren could change **one** of these factors to respond to the competition from the large chain restaurant. Give reasons for your answer.

....

....

....

(3 marks)

(c) Darren has decided that however he responds to the competition, he will need extra finance in order to avoid cash flow problems.

(i) What is meant by the term "cash flow"?

....

....

(2 marks)

(ii) Discuss **two** possible sources of extra finance for Darren.

....

....

....

....

(4 marks)

Leave blank

3. Eve wants to set up her own business, and has asked various people for advice.

(a) Dave says that the key to business success is to spot a gap in the market.

What is meant by a "gap in the market"?

....

....

(2 marks)

(b) Anna believes that the most important thing is to make sure a new business is located in the most suitable position.

Explain **two** factors that might influence where a new business decides to locate.

....

....

....

....

(4 marks)

(c) Sabeena says that the most important factor is luck.

Do you think that luck can play an important role in the success or failure of a business?

Explain your answer.

....

....

....

(3 marks)

(d) Discuss what you think is the most important factor in the success or failure of a business.

Give reasons for your answer.

....

....

....

....

....

....

....

....

....

(8 marks)

Lea
blar

4. Read the description below, and then answer the questions that follow.

> Joe owns a business, and wants to do something worthwhile while raising his company's profile. He plans to ask people in town to suggest a charity the business could help. He wants to gather as many responses as he can, analyse the results using a computer, and then provide the town's residents with some feedback.

(a) In communication, what is meant by the term "feedback"?

....

....

(2 marks)

(b) Suggest **two** ways that Joe could collect suggestions from the people in the town.

....

....

....

....

....

....

(5 marks)

(c) Explain one input device and one output device that Joe's computer system will need.

Input device ....

....

Output device ....

....

(4 marks)

(d) Discuss possible methods Joe could use to communicate his eventual decision to the town's residents.

....

....

....

....

....

....

(7 marks)

Practice Computer-Based Assessment

Over the next four pages are two mock computer-based assessments for you to have a go at. *(Note for students doing the Edexcel course: you won't have a computer-based assessment, so you can safely ignore these pages.)*

- Each assessment should take you about 90 minutes.
- You should try all the tasks in each of the assessments.
- Part of the assessment is to present your work clearly.
  Your spelling, punctuation and grammar are also taken into account on certain questions.
- Put **your name** and the **number/name of the task** at the top of each page **before printing**.
- Do not use the Internet while working on these tasks.

Computer-Based Assessment 1

Scenario

You have recently been employed in the Product Development Department of Addentes Ltd.
Addentes Ltd. is a small computer equipment manufacturer which is looking to expand.
You have been asked to look into areas of the computer market the firm could potentially exploit.
You have also been asked to find any of the company's factories not being used efficiently.
You will then have to make a recommendation to the company's board.

Task One: Using a Spreadsheet to Analyse Production Figures

Recall the file **FACTORIES**.
This file shows to what extent Addentes' four factories are currently being used.

a) There are two wrong entries in the spreadsheet.
   - The current annual production in the North Factory is 16 000 units.
   - The annual capacity of the East Factory is 36 800 units.

   Change the relevant entries to show the correct figures. *(4 marks)*

b) The board are interested in two figures for each factory.

   (i) The "spare capacity" in each factory, which is found by subtracting the current production from the annual capacity.
   Insert formulas in column D to find the spare capacity of each factory.

   (ii) The "percentage utilisation" of each factory, which is found by dividing the current production by the annual capacity.
   Insert formulas in column E to find the percentage utilisation of each factory.
   Format these cells as percentages to one decimal place. *(6 marks)*

c) Change the fill colour of the row showing the factory used least efficiently to yellow. *(2 marks)*

d) Make **three** other improvements to the appearance of the table. *(3 marks)*

e) Add a suitable title to the spreadsheet's header, and change the page orientation to "landscape".
   Save the spreadsheet as **FACTORIES1**.
   Print out one copy on a single sheet of paper to use as a handout during a presentation. *(3 marks)*

Task Two: Making a Database Report

Recall the file **PRODUCTS**, and open the table **MARKET DATA**.
This database shows the total sales of products from different market sectors, as well as the number of potential customers for each of those products.

a) Make a query to show goods that:
   - are in the "PC" sector
   - have "Not currently" in the "Already manufactured by Addentes" field

   The entries in the query should be sorted so that the figures for Number of Potential Customers are shown in descending order.

   All the table's fields should be displayed.

   Save your query as **QUERY1**. *(8 marks)*

b) Make a report based on your **QUERY1** that can be shown to the board.

   Your report should be suitably laid out, with a title, and all pieces of information clearly labelled.

   Save your report as **MARKET REPORT**. Print one copy of your report.

   You are going to suggest that Addentes manufacture the product at the top of your list. *(6 marks)*

Task Three: Making a Presentation

Recall the file **PRESENTATION**.

a) The presentation needs a more professional look. Make the following changes to the slides.
   - Add a background colour to each of the slides.
   - Add bullet points to the lists on slides 2 and 3.
   - Animate the bullet points on slides 2 and 3 so they appear one at a time, as the mouse button is clicked. *(8 marks)*

b) Complete the final bullet points on slides 2 and 3, using your results from Task One and Task Two. *(2 marks)*

c) Add some "presenter's notes" to slide 1, explaining **two** important features of a good presentation.

   Save your presentation as **PRESENTATION1**.

   Print one copy of slide 1, showing both your slide and your presenter's notes.
   Then print out all three slides on a single piece of paper. *(5 marks)*

Task Four: Making a Web Page *(AQA only)*

The board would like you to make a simple website for the managers of the firm's factories to access.

The website should contain the same information as on your slides, spread over three pages.

Create a simple set of three webpages.

- The first page should be a "Home" page.
  You should add links to the other two pages under the bottom line of text on the Home page.
- The other two pages should contain the information from the final two slides in your presentation.
  You should add a link on each of these pages to return to the Home page.

Save your webpages with suitable filenames.

Open a new word processing document, and paste a screen dump (print screen) of each of your pages onto a single page of your document. Print this page. *(13 marks)*

End of Computer-Based Assessment 1

Computer-Based Assessment 2

Scenario

Electrerum Ltd. is a small manufacturer of electronic components. Among its customers is LeutenAuto, a German car manufacturer. Electrerum has recently received a complaint from LeutenAuto saying that a batch of Electrerum components seems to be malfunctioning.

Each of the Electrerum components contains a small microprocessor. Data can be downloaded from these microprocessors to help diagnose the fault. This data is stored in a spreadsheet.

Task One: Analysing Data Using a Spreadsheet

Recall the file **COMPONENT DATA**.
This spreadsheet shows 100 readings from a component's microprocessor.

The following information is taken from Electrerum's Quality Control Manual.

Faults are shown by:

- a **minimum** reading **below 0.05**.
- a **maximum** reading **above 3**.
- an **average** value **below 1 or above 3**.
- **more than 5** readings out of 100 **below 0.1**.
- **more than 10** readings out of 100 **above 2.5**.

a) Use functions to calculate the following information:

- the minimum reading
- the maximum reading
- the average reading

Enter your results in cells **B105:B107**. *(6 marks)*

b) Enter an IF() function in cell **C2** whose outputs are:

- 1, if the reading in cell B2 is **less than 0.1**.
- 0, otherwise

Copy your function into cells **C3:C101**.
Each cell in Column C should now contain:

- 1, if the reading in the same row is less than 0.1
- 0, otherwise *(4 marks)*

c) Enter an IF() function in cell **D2** whose outputs are:

- 1, if the reading in cell B2 is **above 2.5**.
- 0, otherwise

Copy your function into cells **D3:D101**.
Each cell in Column D should now contain:

- 1, if the reading in the same row is above 2.5
- 0, otherwise *(4 marks)*

d) Use functions to find:

- the total number of readings below 0.1 by finding the sum of the entries in column C
- the total number of readings above 2.5 by finding the sum of the entries in column D.

Enter your functions in cells **C102:D102**.

Save a copy of your spreadsheet as **DATA1**.

Print out cells A77:D107 on a single page. *(3 marks)*

Turn over

Task Two: Using a Database to Analyse Sales Figures

Recall the file **SOLD**, and open the table **SALES**.

This database contains Electrerum's sales data for January 1st to March 1st 2010.
It shows how many of this type of component were sold to firms, the date each order was placed, and a batch number showing which batch the purchased components came from.

The faulty consignment was purchased by LeutenAuto on 15th January 2010.

a) Write a query to show details of the purchase made by LeutenAuto on 15th January 2010.
Save your query as **BATCH**. *(7 marks)*

b) Write another query to show the names of all the customers who bought components with the same batch number as the LeutenAuto purchase above, and the dates of their purchases.
Save your query as **CUSTOMER**. *(5 marks)*

Task Three: Creating Graphics *(AQA only)*

The faulty component is malfunctioning because a label has been attached the wrong way up.

A label showing "This way up" should have been attached to the other end of the component, as shown in the sketch below.

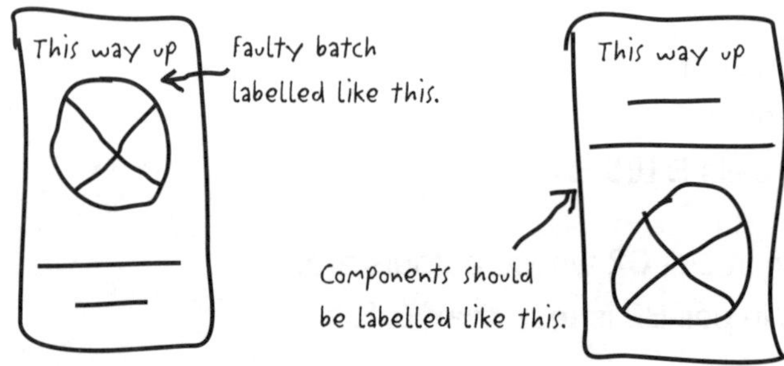

Using a suitable graphics package, create a neat version of this sketch.

Your diagram should be approximately 2 cm tall by 5 cm wide, and should look professional enough that it can be sent to customers.

Save your graphic as **LABEL**. *(12 marks)*

Task Four: Writing a Memo

Write a memo to Tom Mee, the Sales Manager of Electrerum, informing him of what has happened. Include the following information:

- some components purchased from Electrerum have been mislabelled (you should include your diagram from Task Three)
- the batch number of the faulty components
- the dates the components were purchased, and who purchased them

*(If you are studying with OCR and did not make the graphic in Task Three, then use the file called **OCRLABEL** instead.)*

Your memo should also reply to the following questions, which were sent to you in an earlier email:

> *Should we contact the customers affected? If we do contact them, how should we do it?*

Save your file as **MEMO**. Print one copy of your memo. *(19 marks)*

End of Computer-Based Assessment 2

Answers

Note about "Judgement" Questions

In Business and Communications Systems, you're expected to show that you can "**analyse** and **evaluate evidence** to make **reasoned judgements**".
(These kinds of questions often say "What do you think...", "Recommend...", "Discuss whether you think...", and so on.)

In the answers to this type of question below, we've tried to show the kind of answer you *could* give in an exam — so we've made a judgement about a situation and tried to back up that judgement using ideas about Business and Communications Systems. But there's often no 'right' answer to judgement questions. So if you disagree with our conclusion and have written something different, then that's fine... **as long as you've explained how you arrived at your conclusion**.

Section One — Business Essentials

Page 4 (Warm-Up Questions)

1) E.g. they might start a business to make money; they might enjoy the freedom of being their own boss; they might enjoy the challenge; they might want their business to benefit others.
2) To make a profit in order to survive.
3) It is easy to set up as a sole trader. Sole traders have the freedom to decide for themselves how to run the business and spend the profit.
4) A business that is owned and controlled by its workforce (producer cooperative) or customers (retail cooperative).
5) Private limited company; public limited company

Page 5 (Exam Questions)

1 a) A business or other institution owned by the government ***(1 mark)***.

b) A business that has bought the right to sell another firm's products ***(1 mark)*** or use their trademarks ***(1 mark)***.

c) Running a business as a franchise is less risky ***(1 mark)***, since Anna is selling established products that have already shown themselves to be popular ***(1 mark)***. However, she will probably not have complete freedom to run the business as she wishes ***(1 mark)***, since the franchisor will want their products/trademarks used in a way they approve of ***(1 mark)***.

2 a) For example:
1. initiative ***(1 mark)*** — to seek out opportunities and be willing to take advantage of them ***(1 mark)***
2. networking skills ***(1 mark)*** — these allow an entrepreneur to identify people who will be willing and able to help in the enterprise activity ***(1 mark)***

b) A calculated risk is one where the probability and benefits of success ***(1 mark)*** have been weighed up against the probability and consequences of failure ***(1 mark)***, and the risk is believed to be worth taking ***(1 mark)***. Planning is necessary to understand the risks associated with a venture ***(1 mark)***. Only then can you decide if the possible losses or gains seem like a good bet ***(1 mark)***.

Page 12 (Warm-Up Questions)

1) A market-driven firm starts by investigating the market and finding out what product(s) customers would like but which aren't currently available — it then makes these products. A product-driven firm designs a new product and then tries to sell it.
2) A product trial is when a customer first buys a new product to try it out. A repeat purchase is when customers buy a product again because they know they like it. Repeat purchases are important because they mean that customers like the firm's product and its price. Repeat purchases also mean that the firm sells many items to a single customer — this is important as otherwise the firm would have to constantly spend money to try and attract new customers.
3) *Internal*: e.g. owners, employees; *External*: e.g. customers, suppliers, the government, trade unions, pressure groups
4) Survival; profitability; growth; market share; customer satisfaction; ethical considerations; environmental sustainability
5) An invention is just a new idea, but an innovation is when a new idea is successfully introduced onto the market.
6) The WEEE (Waste Electrical and Electronic Equipment) Regulations say that firms making or selling electrical goods are responsible for collecting and recycling/disposing of old electrical products.

Page 13 (Exam Questions)

1 a) 1. Goods must be fit for purpose (do what they're designed for) ***(1 mark)***.
2. Goods must match their description ***(1 mark)***.
3. Goods must be of satisfactory quality ***(1 mark)***.

b) For example:
1. If Karen will need to employ people to work in her shop ***(1 mark)***, she should consider the likely labour supply in a location ***(1 mark)***.
2. Karen should consider whether people from her target market will be present in a location ***(1 mark)***. This will be important since she will want her shop to attract as many customers as possible ***(1 mark)***.

c) Because the picture was created by someone else, they will own the copyright ***(1 mark)***. This means that Karen should seek permission ***(1 mark)*** before using the image, otherwise she could find herself in legal trouble.

d) Karen needs to provide 'added value' in some way — she needs to offer her customers something that competing shops do not offer ***(1 mark)***. Karen could offer lower prices ***(1 mark)*** in order to attract customers, but it might be better if she can find or create some kind of unique selling point ***(1 mark)*** that will make customers want to buy from her shop without eating into her profits. For example, she could offer better customer service ***(1 mark)*** than her competitors (e.g. knowledgeable sales staff who can help customers choose the right equipment) ***(1 mark)***. Or perhaps she could make buying from her shop more convenient ***(1 mark)*** (e.g. by offering free delivery on large items or locating her shop in a particularly convenient location, such as near a car park) ***(1 mark)***.
(Plus 2 marks for a well-written and well-structured answer.)

e) Sometimes businesses fail for reasons that are beyond their control ***(1 mark)***. For example, the overall health of the economy affects the chance of business success ***(1 mark)***. Similarly, there might be a change in the market (e.g. competitors might launch a product that wildly changes customer demand) ***(1 mark)***. If a business cannot respond to this change, it may fail ***(1 mark)***.

Section Two — Marketing and Finance

Page 20 (Warm-Up Questions)

1) Primary research is when a business carries out its own research. Secondary research is research that has already been carried out by another organisation.
2) This would be quantitative data, since it can be expressed as a number.
3) Fixed costs do not change, even if the company's output changes. Variable costs increase or decrease as the company's output rises or falls.
4) A credit period is the time between a customer receiving a product and having to pay for it.
5) Destocking is when a company sells stocks of goods that have already been made (instead of making new goods). It improves cash flow because the company still receives income from sales, but doesn't incur production costs.
6) A recession is a period when a country's GDP decreases ("its economy shrinks"). During a recession, demand for goods and services falls, so firms can struggle to sell their products.

Page 21 (Exam Questions)

1 a) A market map is a summary of the key features about the market ***(1 mark)*** such as the number and type of customers in a market, and competitors and products that are popular or unpopular ***(1 mark)***.

b) It is important to identify any unfulfilled customer wants or needs ***(1 mark)***. This might involve looking at weaknesses of competitors and competing products to see if there are any market gaps that can be exploited ***(1 mark)***, and how best to do this ***(1 mark)*** (e.g. whether to try and produce a better product than is currently available, or just aim to produce a product that is cheaper). Insufficient market research could lead to a product failing ***(1 mark)***, which could cause financial difficulties for a firm ***(1 mark)***.

c) If the value of the pound goes up then this could make the cost of the Smoothies to European customers higher ***(1 mark)***, meaning fewer sales there for Brit Smoothies (or if Brit Smoothies don't increase prices, profits from European sales will be lower) ***(1 mark)***. Raw materials from Europe will become cheaper, though ***(1 mark)***. However, this may not affect Brit Smoothies greatly since it uses British fruit ***(1 mark)***. If the value of the pound against the Euro falls, the opposite would happen ***(1 mark)***.

2 a) It is an estimate ***(1 mark)*** of the future flow of cash into the business as it makes sales, and out of the business as it makes payments ***(1 mark)***.

b) A business needs to know how much cash it will have at particular points in the future ***(1 mark)***, so that it can plan for any future cash flow problems, e.g. arrange a short term loan ***(1 mark)***. Otherwise it may not be able to pay its bills when they are due ***(1 mark)***.

c) If interest rates increased, then Electronorum's interest payments would rise ***(1 mark)***, meaning more cash flowing out of the business ***(1 mark)***. It could also mean that its customers would spend less ***(1 mark)***, meaning less money flowing into the business ***(1 mark)***.

Section Three — Organisation and Administration

Page 26 (Warm-Up Questions)

1) A matrix structure allows groups of operatives to work under more than one manager (e.g. a department manager and a project manager).
2) Storing; processing; retrieving; disseminating
3) E.g. VAT; income tax; corporation tax
4) E.g. filing, inputting data.
5) Non-routine tasks are often unpredictable and can mean a person making important decisions based on his/her judgement (and then taking responsibility for that judgement).

Page 27 (Exam Questions)

1 a) To calculate the VAT owed to the government, it needs records of the amount paid to suppliers ***(1 mark)*** and the income from the sales of goods to customers ***(1 mark)***.

b) Good administration helps a business run smoothly and efficiently ***(1 mark)***. For example, managers will have access to up-to-date, reliable information ***(1 mark)***, which will help them make sound business decisions for the benefit of the company ***(1 mark)***. Accurate financial records can help a company work out areas where spending can be reduced ***(1 mark)***, so that costs can be reduced and profits potentially increased ***(1 mark)***. Poor administration can lead to incorrect information being passed on to customers ***(1 mark)***, which is an example of poor service ***(1 mark)***.

2 a) A routine task is one that is carried out regularly ***(1 mark)*** and is basically the same each time ***(1 mark)***.

b) They are decisions that involve a lot of judgement, since no two people are the same ***(1 mark)***. If a business employs an unsuitable member of staff, it can be very disruptive (and expensive) for the business, and very awkward for the employee ***(1 mark)***. This means they are very important and responsible decisions ***(1 mark)***.

c) For example:
I would recommend that the manager makes these decisions himself ***(1 mark)***. This is because deciding which products are put on special offer may depend on a range of factors ***(1 mark)*** that only senior members of staff would be in a position to know ***(1 mark)***. For example, the decision may depend on current stock levels, or the level of competition from other supermarkets (who might also have products on special offer) ***(1 mark)***. Although more junior members of staff may know individual pieces of information ***(1 mark)***, it is unlikely that they would be as aware as the manager of the complete picture ***(1 mark)***.

Page 31 (Warm-Up Questions)

1) Deciding that a task is more important than other tasks, and so dealing with it sooner or devoting more time/resources to it.
2) A firm that reduces its spending on a task, but does not carry out the task successfully as a result, has not been efficient. And a firm that spends lots of money on equipment to save a very small amount of time is probably also not being very efficient, since that money may have been better spent elsewhere.
3) Effective planning can lead to greater efficiency, since the time and other resources that need to be allocated to tasks is then decided in advance. Otherwise the wrong amount of time or staff may be allocated to tasks, e.g. more staff may be allocated to a task than are actually needed or deadlines may be too short for the number of staff allotted, resulting in corners being cut.
4) If a business is operating efficiently, it will use as few natural resources and create as little waste as possible. This will reduce unnecessary depletion of the Earth's natural resources, and pollution levels will be kept relatively low.
5) Cellular offices, since solicitors will probably need to talk to their clients in private.

Page 32 (Exam Questions)

1 a) Efficiency means achieving your aims ***(1 mark)*** while using as few resources (e.g. money, energy) as possible ***(1 mark)***.

b) A building that's too large will be expensive to buy/rent ***(1 mark)***, and also expensive to heat ***(1 mark)***.

c) Good planning will allow Sue to use her resources (e.g. time, money) ***(1 mark)*** as efficiently as possible ***(1 mark)***. She will be able to carry out tasks in a logical order, prioritising those parts of her task that are more important ***(1 mark)***.

d) I would recommend that Sue first identifies her objectives ***(1 mark)***. For example, she will want to consider the likely savings of different buildings for the company as it is now, but she might also want to consider what would happen if the firm continued to grow ***(1 mark)***. She should then break the investigation down into separate tasks ***(1 mark)*** (e.g. she might want to consider buildings in the nearby area first, and only then consider places further away) ***(1 mark)***. She should then estimate the time required to complete each part of her investigation ***(1 mark)***, and the resources she will need (e.g. she may need help at times) ***(1 mark)***. Finally, she may need to consider how circumstances beyond her control will affect her project ***(1 mark)*** (e.g. if more properties are available at certain times of year, prices may be lower due to excess supply) ***(1 mark)***.

e) I would not recommend that the firm move into the building ***(1 mark)***. The building is old and inefficient ***(1 mark)***, so the savings on rent and heating will not be as great as they could achieve in a different building perhaps ***(1 mark)***. Sue's company is also growing rapidly ***(1 mark)***, so they may need space for the firm to grow into ***(1 mark)***. If they move into a building that is a suitable size for the company as it is now, it may soon be too small ***(1 mark)***, and moving again into a larger building will incur lots of relocation costs again ***(1 mark)***.
(Plus 2 marks for a well-written and well-structured answer.)

Section Four — Human Resources

Page 38 (Warm-Up Questions)

1) Part-time work means working "less than a full working week" (where a full working week is typically 35-40 hours).
2) There is no end date on the contract. So the person stays at the firm unless they choose to leave, are made redundant, or are dismissed.
3) More people will probably see the advert, which should mean there will be more applicants for a firm to choose from. But it can be quite expensive (especially if the advert is to be seen nationally).
4) Letters of application can be hard to compare, because different applicants could have given very different information about themselves — some of this information could even be of no interest to the firm.
5) Incompetence and misconduct (though it would have to be serious incompetence or misconduct — a firm can't just sack someone for making a very minor mistake).
6) They can take the company to an employment tribunal. If the tribunal finds that the employee has been unfairly dismissed, it can order the firm to reinstate the employee, or pay compensation.

Page 39 (Exam Questions)

1 a) CV stands for Curriculum Vitae ***(1 mark)***. A CV is a written summary ***(1 mark)*** of a person's qualifications, skills, experience, and personal details ***(1 mark)***.

b) A skill is something that a person has learnt how to do ***(1 mark)***, whereas an attitude is a personal quality that they have not needed to learn ***(1 mark)***.

c) Interviews are useful for assessing a candidate's confidence, social and verbal skills ***(1 mark)*** and whether they will fit in with the other workers in the department ***(1 mark)***. Candidates can all be asked the same questions and their answers compared ***(1 mark)***.

d) Candidates may not act naturally during an interview (so they may come across either better or worse than they might expect) ***(1 mark)***. For a lot of jobs, the skills needed to perform well in an interview may be very different from those needed to do the job ***(1 mark)***.

e) For example:
I think the relative importance of skills and attitudes depends on the nature of the job ***(1 mark)***. Although a skilled person may need little technical training in order to be able to do a job ***(1 mark)***, they may not be suitable if they have a poor attitude (for example, they may not work well as part of a team) ***(1 mark)***. It may also be difficult to change a person's attitude ***(1 mark)***, whereas for some jobs, a person with a good attitude can be taught the skills they will need ***(1 mark)***. For these jobs, I therefore think a good attitude is more important. However, if it is *not* possible to teach the skills needed (if a person will require many years of training, for example), then it may be more important to consider a person's skills than their attitudes ***(1 mark)***.

Page 45 (Warm-Up Questions)

1) Induction training is initial training done when an employee starts working for a firm.
2) Total wage = pay rate × amount of work done
(e.g. total wage = wage per hour × number of hours worked
or total wage = wage per item produced × number of items produced)
3) A benefit that's given to staff in addition to their pay.
4) Hot-desking means that employees don't have their own special desk but must sit at any free desk. This can mean that firms need less office space, saving them money. But it can be more stressful for employees, as they don't know where they're going to working from one day to the next.
5) Both the employer and employees are responsible for health and safety at work.

Page 46 (Exam Questions)

1 a) Better trained employees will be able to do their jobs better ***(1 mark)***, which should mean they become more efficient ***(1 mark)***. They are also more likely to be happy in their job, and so less likely to leave the firm ***(1 mark)***. This will reduce the company's recruitment costs ***(1 mark)***.

b) Teleworking involves people working away from the normal workplace ***(1 mark)***, probably from home. This would mean that Heath Insurance Services could use less office space ***(1 mark)***, which would save money and hopefully increase profits ***(1 mark)***.

c) Teleworking can make it harder to keep information secret ***(1 mark)***, since information will need to be transferred between sites more often ***(1 mark)***. It could also lead to the employees becoming lonely ***(1 mark)***, as they will have less contact with their colleagues ***(1 mark)***.

d) For example: (But see the notes on p141 about 'Judgement' questions)
I think the firm should introduce a bonus scheme, as long as they do the kind of work where targets could be set ***(1 mark)***. If workers knew that they could receive a bonus for meeting their targets ***(1 mark)***, they would be motivated to work harder to meet those targets ***(1 mark)*** — increasing productivity. Increasing wages could cost the company a lot of money, with no guarantee that productivity would increase ***(1 mark)***. It could also even lead to demotivation of the hardest working employees ***(1 mark)***, who may feel that they are not being rewarded for working harder than other employees ***(1 mark)***.
(Plus 2 marks for a well-written and well-structured answer.)

Section Five — Businesses and Data

Page 53 (Warm-Up Questions)

1) Hardware means physical devices that you can actually touch.
Software refers to the programs used on the computer (such as an operating system or an application like a word processor).
2) For example, you'd need to think about *where* you'd use the computer (if you're moving around a lot, then a laptop might be best, but if you're going to be working in an office, then a desktop could be more convenient). You should also consider *what tasks* you'll be doing (if you need a really large monitor, then a laptop might not be ideal, for example).
3) A concept keyboard has symbols marked on the buttons which represent quite complex pieces of data, rather than single letters and numbers. They can make inputting the same piece of data over and over again very quick.
4) Optical Character Recognition — it's a piece of software that can turn scanned text into something that can be edited in a word processor.
5) Internal storage devices are built into a computer, while external devices are separate from a computer, and so can usually be removed.

Page 54 (Exam Questions)

1 a) Primary data is data collected first-hand by the business that's going to use it ***(1 mark)***. Secondary data is data that's already been collected by someone else ***(1 mark)***.

b) Primary data will probably be more directly relevant to Clare's business than secondary data ***(1 mark)*** but it could be more expensive to collect ***(1 mark)***. Secondary data will be more easily available than primary data ***(1 mark)*** but might not be as up to date ***(1 mark)***.

2 a) EPOS stands for electronic point of sale ***(1 mark)***. An EPOS device can read barcodes on items and automatically add up the prices of all items bought ***(1 mark)***, so it would reduce the time spent by customers at the till ***(1 mark)***. It can also be connected to a store's computer system to keep track of how many of each item are currently held in stock ***(1 mark)***, so this should make stock control easier and more accurate ***(1 mark)***.

b) For example:
1. Clare will probably need a keyboard, which she could use for entering text or numerical data ***(1 mark)***.
2. She should also get a mouse, which can be used with many different types of software to select things on screen ***(1 mark)***.

3 a) All data is vulnerable to being damaged or lost ***(1 mark)***. For example, Clare's data could be stolen/damaged by viruses, or the building where the data is stored could be burnt down ***(1 mark)***. Backing up data is essential so that it can be recovered if it is damaged or lost ***(1 mark)***.

b) Clare could easily lose the memory stick ***(1 mark)***, so other people could access Clare's data ***(1 mark)***.

Page 59 (Warm-Up Questions)

1) It means a document that has been printed out on paper.
2) a) Laser printers are fast, good quality and quiet, but can be expensive to buy or repair.
b) Ink-jet printers are often cheaper and smaller, but slower and more expensive to run (the ink cartridges are quite expensive).
3) If someone's away from their desk, it means that no one else can see what's on their screen (apart from the screensaver) if they don't know the person's password.
4) Malware ("malicious software") is any software that's been designed to damage a computer system or its data.
5) A data subject is a person who has data about them held by someone else.

Page 60 (Exam Questions)

1 a) For example:
1. The data should be protected against loss or corruption. ***(1 mark)***
2. Data should not be kept for longer than is necessary. ***(1 mark)***
3. The data stored must be accurate and kept up to date. ***(1 mark)***

b) 1. Terry should ensure the data is password-protected ***(1 mark)*** to prevent unauthorised users gaining access to it ***(1 mark)***.
2. Terry should regularly check ***(1 mark)*** whether it is still necessary for him to keep the data he has stored ***(1 mark)***.
3. Terry should tell his employees what data about them he is going to be storing ***(1 mark)***, so that they can tell him if any details change ***(1 mark)***.

c) The Data Protection Act says that people whose data is stored ***(1 mark)*** have the right to view data held about them ***(1 mark)***, so Terry should allow his employee to see the data held about her (but only the data about her) ***(1 mark)***.

2 A projector would be useful for Sarah. It would be fairly small and light ***(1 mark)***, and so easy for her to carry around ***(1 mark)***. It will allow her to project the output from her computer onto a suitable screen or wall ***(1 mark)***, which will make it much easier for large audiences to view ***(1 mark)***. However, to work well, these projectors need a dimly lit room ***(1 mark)***, which might not always be convenient ***(1 mark)***. They can also be damaged quite easily ***(1 mark)***.
(Plus 2 marks for a well-written and well-structured answer.)

Section Six — Communication

Page 65 (Warm-Up Questions)

1) Transmitting information from a sender to a receiver.
2) A confidential channel, definitely.
3) It may result in inefficient working and mistakes being made. Staff may also feel that their opinions are misunderstood or ignored. This isn't good for staff morale or productivity, which may affect profits.

4) E.g. businesses communicate with their suppliers to agree the size, cost and delivery dates of orders.
5) A business that sends out documents containing errors will look unprofessional. Any errors could also cause confusion, or more serious problems. (It's a good idea for *everyone* to check documents for errors before sending them really — but for a business it's particularly important.)

Page 66 (Exam Questions)

1 a) Internal communication is the passing of messages ***(1 mark)*** inside a company ***(1 mark)***.

b) E.g. one benefit is that staff may be better informed about what's going on in the company ***(1 mark)***. This may improve the staff's motivation ***(1 mark)***. Another benefit is that staff should be able to see where they can improve customer satisfaction ***(1 mark)*** — this could lead to improved customer service (and increased profits) ***(1 mark)***.

c) i) E.g. making people aware of this project could improve the image of Stallion Sneakers ***(1 mark)*** which may help generate extra sales for the company ***(1 mark)***.

ii) E.g. an email could be automatically removed by a spam filter ***(1 mark)***, so an email may not be the best medium to use ***(1 mark)***. There could be cultural/language differences ***(1 mark)***. Stallion Sneakers could either translate the documents itself, or allow the customers to translate them, but either way there's a risk of mistakes ***(1 mark)***. The article about the racecourse regeneration project may contain jargon ***(1 mark)***, which may not be understood by customers reading the report ***(1 mark)***.

Page 72 (Warm-Up Questions)

1) The most important thing for most business letters is that they get their message across clearly. This means they tend to have a simple layout and use a plain font that is easy to read, rather than have lots of fancy pictures and interesting-but-weird fonts.
2) Memos can sometimes seem more serious, so they might be useful for certain types of message.
3) E.g. good spelling, punctuation and grammar; clear sections of information.
4) They can be fiddly to type and they're often too short to say things in a formal way (words are often abbreviated, for example).
5) A satnav system can be used in vehicles to give directions. It uses signals from satellites to determine its location, and it can then use data stored in its memory to tell a driver which roads to take to get to a particular location.
6) E.g. they can be expensive to buy; they're often very complex, so staff may need extra training to use them.

Page 73 (Exam Questions)

1 a) E.g. a website can be accessed by anyone with an internet connection ***(1 mark)*** so messages can reach a large and global audience ***(1 mark)***.

b) For example:
Details of the customer, e.g. their name ***(1 mark)***.
Details of what the customer has bought ***(1 mark)***.

c) <u>For example:</u>
Method of communication: send a business letter ***(1 mark)***.
Reason 1: Sending a letter means Terry will have a record of the complaint stored on his computer ***(1 mark)***, which may help if he needs to follow up his initial communication ***(1 mark)***.
Reason 2: If Terry sends the letter using recorded delivery ***(1 mark)***, he will be able to check that Lacquer Luster has received his letter ***(1 mark)***.
(Email would also be a suitable way for Terry to send his complaint, since that would also allow him to keep a record, which is probably the most important thing here. It would also have the advantage of being much quicker than sending a letter.)

d) i) E.g. a memo could be sent to each staff member ***(1 mark)***.

ii) For example:
Advantage: staff receive a hard copy of the procedure ***(1 mark)***, which they can refer back to later ***(1 mark)***.
Disadvantage: the memo needs to be printed on paper ***(1 mark)***, which means it will cost Lacquer Luster money to produce ***(1 mark)***.

Page 78 (Warm-Up Questions)

1) It's when people gather in the same place to discuss business.
2) It makes it easier to raise personal issues.
3) E.g. it allows oral messages to be delivered at any time, but the sender doesn't receive instant feedback.
4) It's an audio or video file that's downloaded from a website and played on a computer or a portable device. A business might use a podcast to promote new products.
5) E.g. if the celebrity is involved in a scandal, the company they're endorsing may look bad.
6) A slogan is a catchy phrase that businesses sometimes use to sum up something about their company.

Page 79 (Exam Questions)

1 a) i) Teleconferencing is when ICT technology is used to allow people in different locations ***(1 mark)*** to communicate as if they're in a face-to-face meeting ***(1 mark)***.

ii) For example:
Advantage: people in the meeting can see the people they're talking to ***(1 mark)***, which makes the meeting more personal ***(1 mark)***.
Disadvantage: there's a risk of technical failure ***(1 mark)***, which would end any meetings in progress ***(1 mark)***.

b) <u>For example:</u>
One suitable protocol for the meeting may be to have a chairperson ***(1 mark)***. A chairperson is someone who controls the discussion in a meeting ***(1 mark)***, so this could reduce the rowdiness of the weekly meeting at Blut Bank plc ***(1 mark)***. Another protocol that could be introduced is the use of an agenda ***(1 mark)***. This allows people to know what will be discussed at the meeting in advance and so to prepare ***(1 mark)***. Following an agenda should also mean that the meeting stays focussed ***(1 mark)***. The taking of minutes could also be a suitable protocol to introduce ***(1 mark)***. Minutes are a written record of what is discussed in the meetings ***(1 mark)***, and they could be sent to the branch managers who didn't take notes ***(1 mark)***.

Section Seven — Businesses and the Web

Page 87 (Warm-Up Questions)

1) E.g. through surveys; through guestbooks.
2) E.g. companies can put adverts on their own websites or pay to put them on other websites.
3) E.g. customers may sue the company if their information or money is stolen.
4) An intranet is an internal network — but which uses the same technology as websites on the internet.
5) E.g. businesses that rely on face-to-face contact may feel that they don't need a website — it might not be something that their customers would use.

Page 88 (Exam Questions)

1 a) i) It's a human-friendly name ***(1 mark)*** linked to a particular IP address ***(1 mark)***.

ii) E.g. Dynamo Dynamics Ltd. won't be allowed the domain name ***(1 mark)*** because the 'ac.uk' part of the domain name is reserved for academic institutions like universities ***(1 mark)***.

b) E.g. because it's less expensive than buying web servers ***(1 mark)***.

c) E.g. the purpose of a website should be considered ***(1 mark)***. This decides how the content of the website will be presented ***(1 mark)***. The budget for a website should also be considered ***(1 mark)***. This decides how ambitious the website can be, e.g. features like secure e-commerce facilities may be too expensive ***(1 mark)***.

d) <u>For example:</u>
Dynamo Dynamics could measure whether its brand awareness had increased ***(1 mark)***. Surveys could be used to see if more people had heard about Dynamo Dynamics Ltd. after the launch of its website than before ***(1 mark)***. Another measure that could be used is the company's overall sales ***(1 mark)***. If overall sales are higher after the launch of the website, then this could be a sign that the website has been successful ***(1 mark)*** (though there may be other reasons for increased sales too). The website will also have been successful if it reduces costs for the company ***(1 mark)***. This could be because the website can provide information where previously the company would have relied on printed brochures or catalogues ***(1 mark)***.
(Plus 2 marks for a well-written and well-structured answer.)

Section Eight — Business Applications

Page 96 (Warm-Up Questions)

1) E.g. the sender's name; the receiver's name; the date; the subject of the message; the message itself.
2) Callouts are used to label things on a page / make speech bubbles.
3) E.g. the sender's address; the date; a reference; a greeting line; a closing line.
4) E.g. a spreadsheet; a database.

Page 97 (Exam Questions)

Computer-based assessment

For example:

a) **Maximum of 3 marks** available for font formatting, e.g.:
   - change in font ***(1 mark)***
   - use of bold/italics/underline ***(1 mark)***
   - font size ***(1 mark)***
   - font colour ***(1 mark)***.

   Maximum of 3 marks available for paragraph formatting, e.g.:
   - increase in line spacing ***(1 mark)***
   - use of bullet points ***(1 mark)***
   - aligning text to the centre of the page ***(1 mark)***.

   Maximum of 1 mark available for the use of one appropriate clipart image, e.g. a sale sign / a picture of one of the ranges in the sale ***(1 mark)***.
   Maximum of 2 marks available for emphasising in some way suitable key points, e.g.:
   - the company name ***(1 mark)***
   - the type of sale ***(1 mark)***
   - the start and end days ***(1 mark)***.

b) For example:

   Tim,
   I decided to use the font type 'Lucida' to make it stand out from a more standard font type ***(1 mark)***. I also increased the font size and added some colour to make the advertisement more eye-catching ***(1 mark)***. I changed the list of ranges in the sale into a bulleted list to draw people's attention to them ***(1 mark)***, and centre-aligned the first three lines of the advertisement to make them stand out ***(1 mark)***. The clipart image that I chose is appropriate for a sale advertisement, and makes a visual impact so the advertisement is more eye-catching ***(1 mark)***. Finally, I emboldened the key points of the advertisement so people would be more likely to remember them ***(1 mark)***.

Written assessment

1) a) One advantage of using templates is that they're already set up with the right fonts and formatting applied ***(1 mark)***. This means people don't have to start from scratch every time, saving time ***(1 mark)*** and reducing the number of formatting mistakes made ***(1 mark)***. This consistent look also helps to create a kind of visual identity for the firm (e.g. perhaps they always use a particular, distinctive header or footer) ***(1 mark)***.

   b) It's important to check for spelling and grammatical errors because they make written communication look unprofessional ***(1 mark)***, which could lead to them not being taken seriously ***(1 mark)***. It's also important to check for these errors because they could affect the clarity of the message ***(1 mark)***, by making it unreadable or ambiguous ***(1 mark)***.

Page 103 (Warm-Up Questions)

1) The selected cells join together to become one big cell.
2) It's an absolute cell reference. It's used in formulae that are to be copied but that need a cell reference within them to remain fixed.
3) Yes. *The condition is true (i.e. 6 is greater than 4), so the output is the text after the first comma.*
4) E.g. bar chart; pie chart; line graph.

Page 104 (Exam Questions)

Computer-based assessment

a) For example:
   The chart is a line chart / bar chart ***(1 mark)*** made from data in the range A5:E17 ***(1 mark)***. The chart has an appropriate title, e.g. "Where did customers hear about Sundials 'R' Us?" ***(1 mark)***, and a legend/key ***(1 mark)*** that displays the different media ***(1 mark)***. The horizontal axis has a suitable label, e.g. 'Month' ***(1 mark)***, and the vertical axis has a suitable label, e.g. 'Number of people' ***(1 mark)***. The data has been used correctly when creating the chart (i.e. all the bars are the correct height) ***(1 mark)***.

   For example:

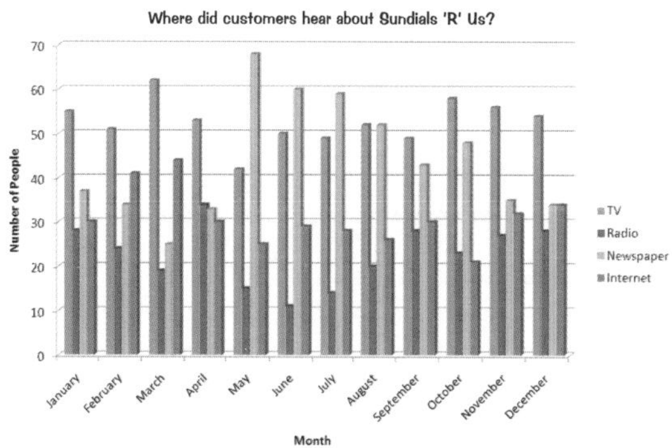

b) Correct effect described (i.e. the increase in newspaper responses in May) ***(1 mark)***. Label is correctly positioned ***(1 mark)***.

   For example:

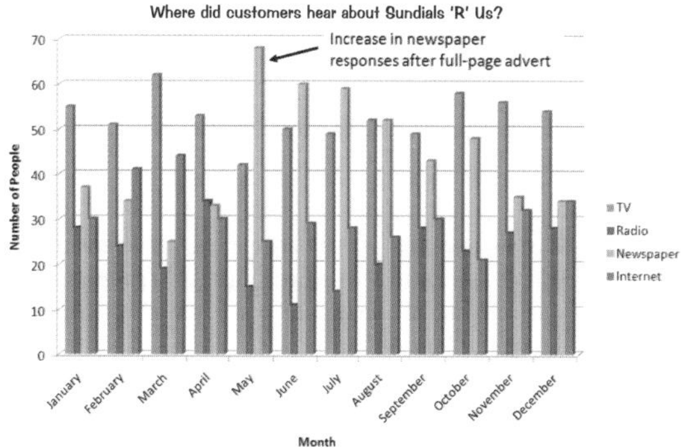

c) Chart has been printed on one sheet ***(1 mark)***, with nothing else on the page ***(1 mark)***.

Written assessment

1) a) For example:

   Software application — spreadsheet ***(1 mark)***.

   Reasons — a spreadsheet is like a large table, and perfect for recording data like the results from Philip's experiments ***(1 mark)***. This would mean that Philip could save time as he would not have to draw tables by hand ***(1 mark)***. Spreadsheets can do calculations, and they have functions for mathematical analysis ***(1 mark)***, so Philip wouldn't have to use a calculator to analyse it ***(1 mark)***. Spreadsheets can also make graphs and charts of the data ***(1 mark)***, which Philip could use to help people to understand it ***(1 mark)***.

Page 109 (Warm-Up Questions)

1) It's a database that contains several tables, each containing a different type of information. The tables are linked to each other by certain common fields.
2) It's so the data is stored in the correct place.
3) The "Sort ascending" button puts text in alphabetical order, numbers in order starting with the smallest, and dates in order starting with the earliest. The "Sort descending" button puts text in reverse alphabetical order, numbers in order starting with the biggest, and dates in order starting with the most recent.
4) A database report is used to present certain information from the database, in an attractive way that's clear and easy to understand.

Page 110 (Exam Questions)

Computer-based assessment

a) ID field present *(1 mark)* with appropriate data type, e.g. Autonumber *(1 mark)*. ID field has been set as the primary key field *(1 mark)*.
Date Found field present *(1 mark)* with appropriate data type, e.g. date/time *(1 mark)*. The Date Found field has an appropriate input mask, e.g. 99/99/00;0;_ for DD/MM/YY *(1 mark)*.
Denomination field present *(1 mark)* with appropriate data type, e.g. text *(1 mark)*. Mint Year field present *(1 mark)* with appropriate data type, e.g. number *(1 mark)*. Condition field present *(1 mark)* with appropriate data type, e.g. text *(1 mark)*.

For example:

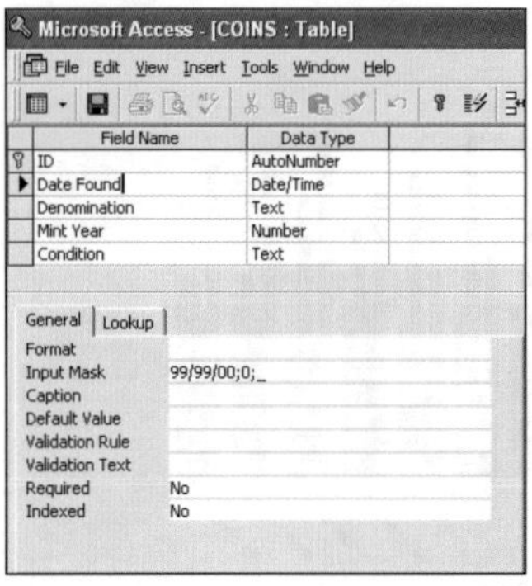

b) An appropriate code has been used:
e.g. Fine (F), Very Good (VG), Good (G), Poor (P) *(1 mark)*, and no value has more than two characters *(1 mark)*.
The code has been entered in the Condition field's description *(1 mark)*.

For example:

Field Name	Data Type	
ID	AutoNumber	
Date Found	Date/Time	
Denomination	Text	
Mint Year	Number	
Condition	Text	Fine (F), Very Good (VG), Good (G), Poor (P)

c) For example:

Bernard,
One advantage of input masks is that data can only be entered in a particular format *(1 mark)*, which reduces mistakes *(1 mark)*. Encoding makes data values shorter *(1 mark)*, which saves time when entering values into a database *(1 mark)*.

Written assessment

1) a) A flat-file database is a database that contains only one table *(1 mark)*.
b) (i) A query is used to filter data from a database *(1 mark)* that meet certain criteria *(1 mark)*.
(ii) A form is used to enter data into a database table *(1 mark)* using a simple, user-friendly interface *(1 mark)*.

Page 118 (Warm-Up Questions)

1) You can make an image fit a gap without stretching or squashing it.
2) E.g. slides; overhead transparencies (OHTs); flipcharts.
3) They allow people to easily move around and between webpages.
4) E.g. they can schedule meetings / appointments / bookings, and remind you of when they are happening.

Page 119 (Exam Questions)

Computer-based assessment

a) New slide added to the end of the presentation *(1 mark)*. Slide title is 'Final Thoughts' *(1 mark)*. Text from the file TEXT has been pasted in the body of the new slide *(1 mark)* as a bulleted list *(1 mark)*.

For example:

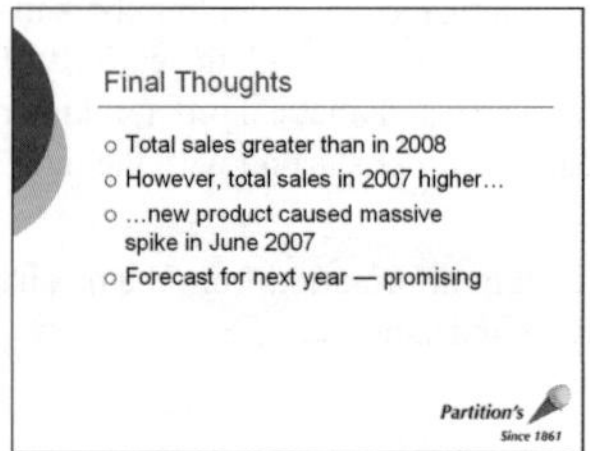

b) Slides 2 and 3 from the file HISTORICAL have been inserted *(1 mark)* after slide 2 *(1 mark)*. One type of animation effect *(1 mark)* has been applied to all three graphs *(1 mark)*. One type of page transition *(1 mark)* has been applied to every slide *(1 mark)*. A handout has been printed *(1 mark)* with all six handouts on a single page *(1 mark)*.

For example:

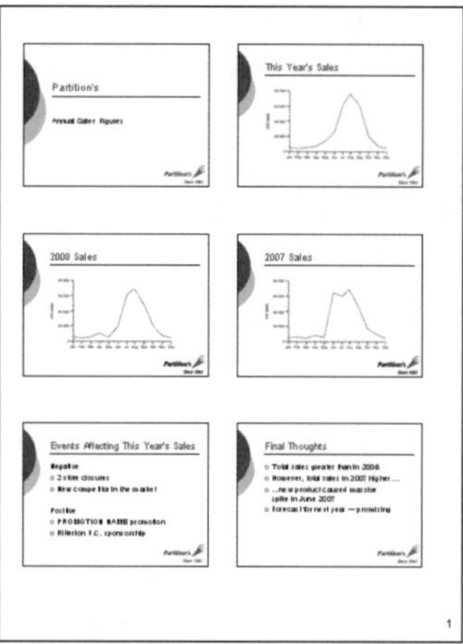

Written assessment

1) a) E.g. databases are used to store large amounts of data organised in a structured way *(1 mark)*. Databases can perform queries to find data stored in them that meet certain criteria *(1 mark)*.
b) For example:
(i) Proprietary software — the manufacturer will often offer customer support *(1 mark)*, so users can get help if they have any problems *(1 mark)*.
(ii) Open-source software — the software is free to use *(1 mark)* so this can save money for a business *(1 mark)*.

Controlled Assessment

Here are our thoughts on how we went about tackling one of the Controlled Assessment tasks (we tackled Task 1 of the Set A (AQA) Investigations).

Remember... there's no single correct way to do a Controlled Assessment task. But we wanted to give you a feel for some of the thought processes we went through while we were trying to complete the task.

We've only included our sample answer for the first AQA investigation — but if you're doing OCR or Edexcel, the approach for your Controlled Assessment will be very similar. You'll still need to come up with ideas, make a plan, do some research, analyse your findings, and produce a final document.

And if you've done the same AQA investigation and come up with a completely different kind of answer, then that doesn't mean you should worry. There are loads of possible answers — it's how you justify your decisions using findings from your research that counts.

Set A (AQA) Task 1

Initial thoughts...

First, I need to gather my thoughts a bit and plan the research I need to do...

- I need to be very clear about who my site is aimed at, and what it's trying to achieve. As I see it at the moment, this is what I'm trying to do:
  1) I'm trying to make a website that will appeal to young people.
  2) When they first see my web page, I must make them *want* to carry on reading — so my page must be **visually attractive** to look at.
  3) If people want to read what's on my website, I then need to make it easy for them to do that. To do this, my website must be **clearly laid out**.
  4) Once they've read what's on my website, I need them to realise that coming to Cumbria either on holiday, a study trip or work experience, would be a good idea. So I need to make my page **persuasive and informative**.
- If I can achieve those four things, then I think I'll have succeeded.
- I need to look at existing websites, so I need to find a couple of sites that are trying to achieve a similar kind of aim. The above points will be useful when it comes to judging other people's sites.
- I need to look at the features other websites use to achieve their aims, and I need to evaluate how well those features work. I can then use the best ideas when it comes to designing my own site.

Review of other websites

- I found a couple of sites with a similar(ish) aim to mine.
  I've added a few notes to each of them, pointing out what I think are important features.

  i) www.golakes.co.uk

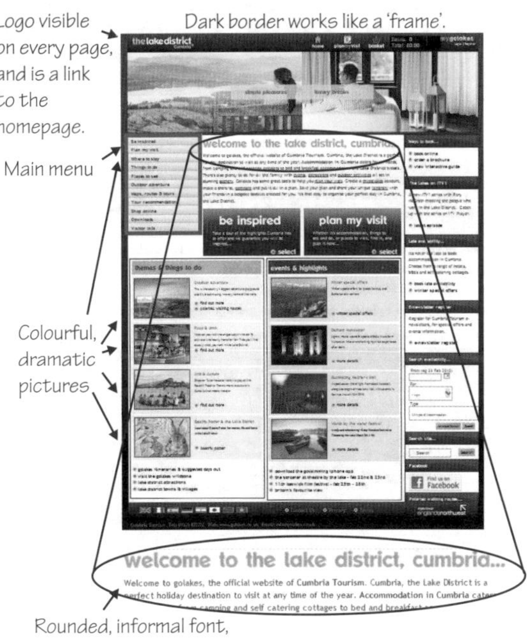

  ii) www.cumbriavision.co.uk

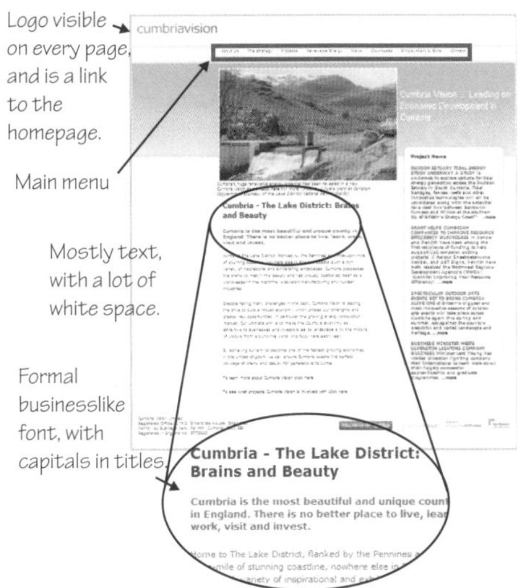

- I made the following notes as I was looking at these websites...
  - *My first impression was of how different the sites are. They use very different colour schemes, and while the golakes site uses lots of pictures, the Cumbria Vision site has just one photo, and is a lot less 'busy' overall.*
  - *A lot of the pictures on the golakes site are really colourful and dramatic, which really helped to catch my eye and get me interested in looking further. That might be useful for my website.*
  - *I think the Cumbria Vision site had a more businesslike look. As well as having fewer pictures, there was more text and fewer menus — as though they wanted as few 'distractions' from their message as possible.*
  - *Actually, this is quite an important difference — the golakes site generally has more links on each page, whereas the Cumbria Vision pages are a lot simpler, with more white space. But both designs are clear, and easy to find your way round, which is the most important thing.*
  - *One of the things that makes them easy to navigate is that they both have a really prominent main menu that you notice as soon as you look at the home page. And both sites keep the menu visible as you navigate about the site (the full golakes menu appears when you hover over a hotspot).*
  - *Both sites use a consistent look. The Cumbria Vision site uses the exact same colour scheme on all pages. The golakes site, on the other hand, uses a consistent layout and look on all the pages, but with different sections colour-coded in different ways. However I decide to do it, this consistent look is something I'll definitely need on my site.*
  - *The font used on the golakes site is quite 'rounded' and unusual, and has quite a 'relaxed' feel (the rounded corners actually made me think of cushions). The lack of capitals in titles also adds to this informal feel.*
  - *By contrast, the Cumbria Vision site uses a more formal font, and uses capital letters in titles — giving a more traditional, businesslike look.*
  - *I think all these differences are because the aims of the two websites are different — the Cumbria Vision site is mainly trying to <u>inform</u> people about business-related projects, whereas the golakes site is trying more to <u>persuade</u> people to visit the area for a relaxing leisure break.*

Initial planning

I reckon I'm ready to start thinking about my own website now.

- The first thing is probably to work out how many pages I need to include, and what information each page will need to contain. I'm going to start by keeping it simple (I can always add more links later on). This is my first idea for a suitable site structure:

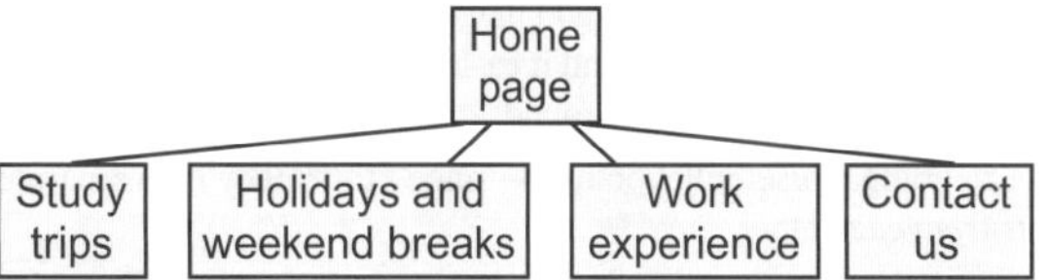

- I need to think about how to grab people's attention on the home page (if the home page is dull, they might not bother with the other pages). So I'm going to use some photos of the local area (the more colourful and exciting, the better). And I need to emphasise the benefits of study trips and work experience on this page too (but not in detail — that'll be on other pages).
- I've seen that the font used can be really important, and really helps to set the tone for the entire site. I want my web site to be fun and lively, but I also need it to have a serious side. I'll try and find a font to match.
- It's a good idea to have the menu visible on every page to make navigation easy. I like the idea of having a bar going across the top of the page.
- I need to include contact details or an enquiry form for the organisation. In fact, the 'Contact Us' page is maybe one of the most important things on the site, so I'm going to put that link on the main menu.
- I noticed on the golakes and Cumbria Vision websites that there are lots of links to external web pages (i.e. pages that are part of different websites altogether). That might be handy for my pages too, then I'll be able to concentrate on explaining why this new scheme is so good, and leave it to other people to explain things that I don't know quite so much about.
- For my consistent look, I'm going to try a dark background, a horizontal menu, and colourful pictures. I need to design a logo later too, so I'm going to leave a space for that for now.

Initial page design

It's taken me a few goes, but this is what I've come up with:

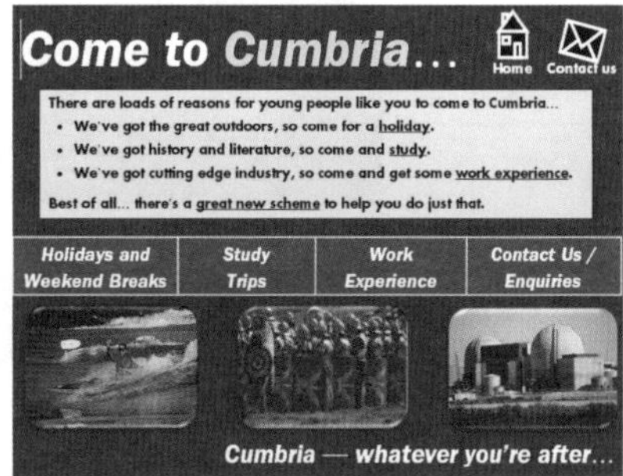

My logo's going to go where that "Come to Cumbria" heading currently is. And here's one of the other pages:

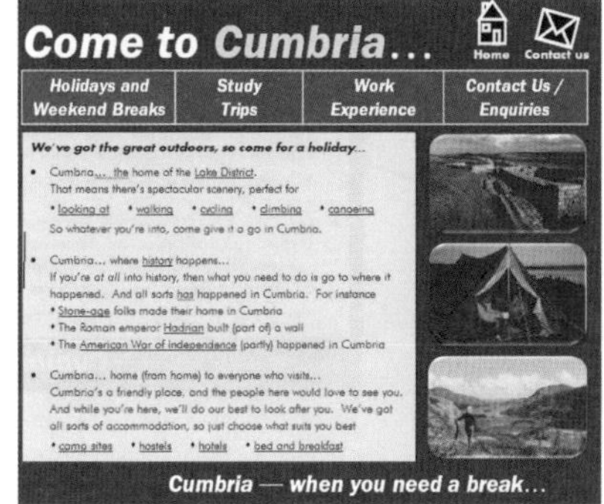

Here's a 'template' I made for all the pages on my website — to speed up the process of creating more pages.

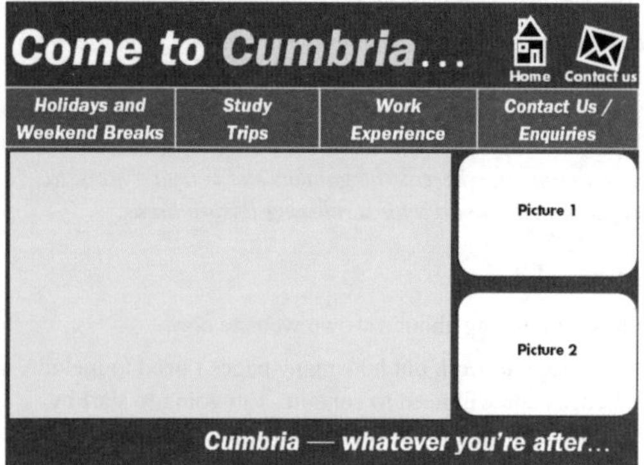

- Having the text on a light area (and the rest of the page fairly dark) helps draw the eye to it, I think. Plus I found it easier to read dark text on a light background than the other way round.
- And I'm going to use bullet points — since I think they help separate different points from each other.

Designing a logo

I quite like simple logos. And I quite like the phrase "Come to Cumbria" — it has a nice "tum-ti-tum-da-da" rhythm about it. Its message is also very clear.

I tried to gather all my ideas together for what could be on my logo:

- *I decided that a map would be useful — the coastline of Cumbria is in the shape of a "C", which is also the first letter of "Come", so I thought the letter could sit inside the map.*
- *I wanted to show "motion towards" Cumbria as well, since that's what the name "Come to Cumbria" suggests.*
- *And I wanted to show "happy" and "relaxed" in some way.*

My final designs

I ended up with something very simple indeed for my logo.
(The curved arrow is supposed to look hand-drawn, which I thought gave it a bit of a relaxed, casual feel.)

So one of my final pages looks like this (and the others are broadly similar):

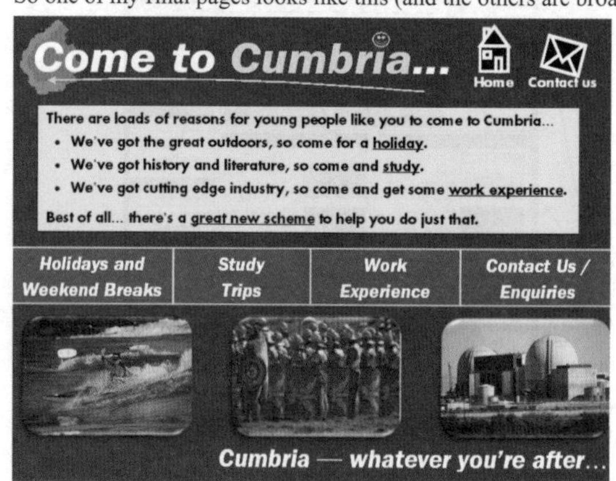

My final document

I annotated a couple of pages below to show the kind of thing that I'd need to do if this was my real exam (though I'd do all the pages — not just two of them).
I'd also make sure that I referred to the sources I'd used in my research and talked about any improvements I could make to my website.

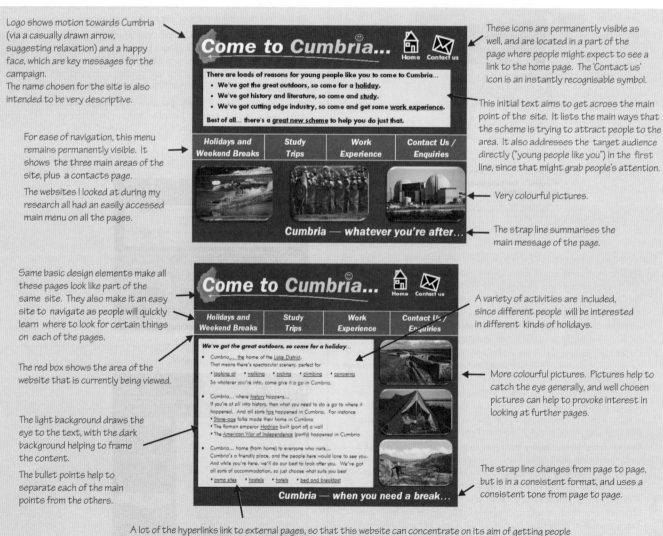

Logo shows motion towards Cumbria (via a casually drawn arrow, suggesting relaxation) and a happy face, which are key messages for the campaign.
The name chosen for the site is also intended to be very descriptive.

These icons are permanently visible as well, and are located in a part of the page where people might expect to see a link to the home page. The 'Contact us' icon is an instantly recognisable symbol.

This initial text aims to get across the main point of the site. It lists the main ways that the scheme is trying to attract people to the area. It also addresses the target audience directly ("young people like you") in the first line, since that might grab people's attention.

For ease of navigation, this menu remains permanently visible. It shows the three main areas of the site, plus a contacts page.

The websites I looked at during my research all had an easily accessed main menu on all the pages.

Very colourful pictures.

The strap line summarises the main message of the page.

Same basic design elements make all these pages look like part of the same site. They also make it an easy site to navigate as people will quickly learn where to look for certain things on each of the pages.

A variety of activities are included, since different people will be interested in different kinds of holidays.

The red box shows the area of the website that is currently being viewed.

More colourful pictures. Pictures help to catch the eye generally, and well chosen pictures can help to provoke interest in looking at further pages.

The light background draws the eye to the text, with the dark background helping to frame the content.

The bullet points help to separate each of the main points from the others.

The strap line changes from page to page, but is in a consistent format, and uses a consistent tone from page to page.

A lot of the hyperlinks link to external pages, so that this website can concentrate on its aim of getting people to consider coming to Cumbria. Other web sites will provide more detailed information on particular subjects.

Practice Exams

Paper 1

1 (a) (i) A formal channel of communication is one that is used for official business ***(1 mark)***. Things said using a formal channel can be taken as a view/promise of the company (and not just the views of an individual employee, for example) ***(1 mark)***.

(ii) An urgent channel of communication is one that can deliver a message quickly ***(1 mark)*** and reliably ***(1 mark)***.

(b) E.g. I would recommend that she use email ***(1 mark)***. With email, she can quickly contact the business no matter where it happens to be ***(1 mark)***. Also, any reply she receives will probably also be written ***(1 mark)***, which is important since computer equipment can be complex, making it important to have a record of what has been ordered ***(1 mark)***.

(c) E.g. Again, I would use email ***(1 mark)***, since it will arrive almost instantly ***(1 mark)***. And because it is a written medium, it can be re-read ***(1 mark)*** and so should reduce the kind of misunderstandings that can happen on the telephone ***(1 mark)***.
(Using the phone would also be a good way to do this — it would be quick; the manager can be sure the message has arrived if he or she has actually spoken to the Production manager; and the Production manager can ask questions, which should help avoid any misunderstandings.)

2 (a) Flexitime means that employees can vary when they work ***(1 mark)***. Usually, they have to work during certain core times ***(1 mark)***, but can then work when they want until they have worked the total weekly/monthly number of hours specified in their contract ***(1 mark)***.

(b) Training allows an employee to keep their skills up to date ***(1 mark)***, which should allow them to do their job efficiently with the minimum of frustration ***(1 mark)***. It may also mean they can be promoted within a company and earn higher wages or take on more responsibility ***(1 mark)***, or find a job more easily in a different company if they prefer ***(1 mark)***.

(c) (i) A fringe benefit is a reward given to employees ***(1 mark)*** in addition to their normal wages ***(1 mark)***.

(ii) Examples of fringe benefits are staff discounts ***(1 mark)***, where employees can buy goods from their company at reduced prices ***(1 mark)***, and medical insurance ***(1 mark)***, meaning employees can claim back money if they have private medical treatment ***(1 mark)***.

(d) 1% of £9.80 = £9.80 ÷ 100 = 9.8p.
So 15% of £9.80 = 15 × 9.8p = 147p = £1.47 ***(1 mark)***.
So the new hourly rate is £9.80 + £1.47 = £11.27 ***(1 mark)***.

(e) Both employers and employees have Health and Safety responsibilities. Employers must provide basic facilities such as toilets and first-aid facilities ***(1 mark)***. Employers must also assess and then minimise the risks involved ***(1 mark)***, by providing all the necessary safety equipment and training ***(1 mark)***. Employees must use the safety equipment provided ***(1 mark)*** and carry out tasks as they've been trained to do ***(1 mark)***. If any accidents do happen, the employer must make sure that they are recorded in the firm's accident book ***(1 mark)***.

3 (a) (i) A limited company's directors are appointed by the owners (i.e. the shareholders) to decide on the firm's strategy ***(1 mark)***, and are responsible for the overall performance of the company ***(1 mark)***.

(ii) Operatives are employees ***(1 mark)*** who are not responsible for other members of staff ***(1 mark)***.

(b) Poor internal communication could result in general ineffectiveness ***(1 mark)***, e.g. poor business decisions and mistakes being made ***(1 mark)***. This can then lead to low morale among staff ***(1 mark)***, and reduced profits ***(1 mark)***.

(c) (i) A memo is a formal, written message ***(1 mark)*** sent to a person, or people, within an organisation ***(1 mark)***.

(ii) Using a memo means that a hard copy exists of the message ***(1 mark)***, which can be useful if the message needs to be re-read at a later date ***(1 mark)***. However, memos do not arrive as quickly as some other forms of communication (e.g. emails) ***(1 mark)***, and so it is not possible to have a "conversation" using memos (i.e. communication is one way) ***(1 mark)***.

(d) Flora could remove some of the layers in her firm's hierarchy ***(1 mark)***. This would mean that some messages have fewer layers of the hierarchy to travel through ***(1 mark)***. Flora could also encourage emails instead of memos ***(1 mark)***, because memos only go "one way" ***(1 mark)***, whereas people can quickly respond to emails, which could lead to more effective, two-way internal communication ***(1 mark)***. I would recommend encouraging emails because that is something that could be done relatively quickly and easily ***(1 mark)***.

4 (a) An internal hard disk is built into the computer ***(1 mark)*** and cannot easily be removed ***(1 mark)***. An external hard disk is a separate piece of equipment ***(1 mark)*** that plugs into a computer and can be easily removed if necessary ***(1 mark)***.

(b) (i) Password-protection can help keep data secure ***(1 mark)***, because only those who know the correct password can gain access to the data ***(1 mark)***. Using a password on the laptops themselves is especially important here, since the laptops are small and will be taken to different sites, meaning it would be relatively easy to steal or lose one ***(1 mark)***.

(ii) Changing a password regularly means that if someone does manage to find out a password ***(1 mark)***, they will only be able to access the emails for a short time ***(1 mark)***.

(c) (i) A spreadsheet program ***(1 mark)***, since they have lots of built-in functions for manipulating numbers and performing numerical calculations ***(1 mark)***.

(ii) A word processor ***(1 mark)***, since a word processor has many features to make text-editing and formatting easier ***(1 mark)***.

(d) The sales representatives should avoid using unnecessary jargon ***(1 mark)*** that might not be understood by the customers ***(1 mark)***. They should also avoid using an unsuitable medium for any communication ***(1 mark)***. For example, they should not use a mobile phone to call a customer if they are in a noisy environment, or somewhere where the mobile phone signal could be weak ***(1 mark)***.

Paper 2

1 (a) E-commerce is the buying and selling of goods over the Internet ***(1 mark)***.

(b) Connor could create a website for his own business ***(1 mark)*** and promote his products on that ***(1 mark)***. Alternatively, he could place adverts for his products ***(1 mark)*** on other websites ***(1 mark)***.

(c) Connor's customers would be able to place orders at any time and from any place ***(1 mark)***, which can be more convenient than having to get to a shop during its opening hours ***(1 mark)***. However, they cannot look closely at goods on a website, or try them out ***(1 mark)***, so they will not be certain that what they are buying is suitable ***(1 mark)***.

(d) E.g. I think Connor should move his business away from high-street sales and towards e-commerce ***(1 mark)***, but gradually, with the change from one type of business to the other taking place over a long time ***(1 mark)***, and with no (or few) stores closing before the website is proving to be a success ***(1 mark)***. This means that in the long term, Connor's costs should fall ***(1 mark)***, since eventually most or all of his sales will be done over the Internet ***(1 mark)***. However, in the short term, he will need to maintain his high street stores so that he can still sell his goods and avoid cash-flow problems ***(1 mark)***. When the website is proving successful, I would recommend he then close down his shops one at a time, starting with the least profitable ***(1 mark)***.
(Plus 2 marks for a well-written and well-structured answer.)

2 (a) (i) Market research means finding out about what potential customers want from a business ***(1 mark)***, how much they would be prepared to pay for it ***(1 mark)***, and what other companies currently provide ***(1 mark)***. This all helps a company make decisions.

(ii) Darren's business is small, so his research methods will need to be low-budget ***(1 mark)*** and not take up too much time ***(1 mark)***. He could ask his customers to fill in a questionnaire after their meal ***(1 mark)***. He could also run a focus group of relevant people to discuss the topics he is interested in ***(1 mark)***. He might get more information from a discussion, and it would be cheap to organise ***(1 mark)***.

(b) E.g. Darren could concentrate on making sure his product is better than that of the large chain restaurant, since this is where Darren's more limited finances will be less of a problem ***(1 mark)***. Darren should concentrate on making sure his food is of a very high quality ***(1 mark)*** and on offering excellent customer service ***(1 mark)***.

(c) (i) Cash flow is the movement of money into a business as customers pay for goods ***(1 mark)***, and the movement of money out as the business pays for materials it uses ***(1 mark)***.

(ii) Darren could apply for a bank loan ***(1 mark)***, as this should be relatively easy to obtain, given that the business has been successful up to now, but it would need to be repaid with interest ***(1 mark)***. Another possible source would be an overdraft ***(1 mark)***, as long as the money will only be needed for a short period of time ***(1 mark)*** (otherwise it could be an expensive source of finance).

3 (a) A gap in the market is a customer need/want ***(1 mark)*** that is not fulfilled by existing products ***(1 mark)***.

(b) Businesses need to locate in places that will help maximise their income ***(1 mark)*** or minimise their costs ***(1 mark)***. For example, if a business will need to employ staff, it should locate somewhere with a good supply of labour with suitable skills ***(1 mark)***. And if products need to be taken from one place to another, then a business should locate in a place with good transport links ***(1 mark)***.

(c) E.g. Some events are beyond the control of any business. For example, the state of a country's economy ***(1 mark)*** cannot be controlled by a business, but could be crucial to its success or failure ***(1 mark)***. Similarly, chance events can make life difficult for companies ***(1 mark)***, as the volcanic ash did for airlines.

(d) E.g. I think that good planning is the most important factor in the success or failure of a business. Although bad luck can have a disastrous effect on a company's fortunes, a lot of problems can be avoided if enough proper planning has been done ***(1 mark)***. For example, good market research ***(1 mark)***, which results in a company providing a product that customers genuinely want, can avoid a company launching a product that then flops ***(1 mark)***. Good planning can also help avoid cash-flow problems, since the need for extra finance can often be anticipated, meaning that the best source of finance can be found in good time ***(1 mark)***. Good planning also means that there should be fewer problems with making/providing a product (e.g. it should prevent a factory running out of essential component parts for a product) ***(1 mark)***. Good planning also means making arrangements for what to do when things *do* go wrong, which should mean that unfortunate events do as little damage to the business as possible ***(1 mark)***.
(Plus 2 marks for a well-written and well-structured answer.)

4 (a) Feedback is information given by the receiver of a message to the sender ***(1 mark)*** to show the effect of that communication (e.g. feedback might show that something has or hasn't been understood, or it might show approval or disapproval of an idea) ***(1 mark)***.

(b) E.g. Joe needs to involve as many people as possible, given that one of his aims is to raise his company's profile ***(1 mark)***. One way to do this might be to conduct a survey at a local shopping centre ***(1 mark)***, since even people who don't offer any opinion about what charity to help might still notice what Joe is doing ***(1 mark)***. He could also set up a website where people can make suggestions ***(1 mark)***. He could even advertise this website while he is carrying out his survey at the shopping centre ***(1 mark)***.

(c) Joe's computer will need a keyboard ***(1 mark)*** which he can use to input information into the software he uses to analyse his survey results ***(1 mark)***. Joe's computer will also need a monitor ***(1 mark)***, so that he can see the results ***(1 mark)***.

(d) If Joe uses a website to collect suggestions of charities, then he should use the same website to announce his decision about which one(s) he will help ***(1 mark)***. He could also place an advert in the local newspaper, and the paper might even write a story about his efforts, which would be good publicity ***(1 mark)***. He could also reply personally to anyone who made a suggestion to thank them for their help, either emailing them if they provided an email address ***(1 mark)***, or by writing a letter to those that didn't ***(1 mark)***. He could use mail merge for both emails and letters ***(1 mark)***.
(Plus 2 marks for a well-written and well-structured answer.)

Practice Computer-Based Assessment Tasks

Computer-Based Assessment 1

Task One: Using a Spreadsheet to Analyse Production Figures

(a) Remember to check the labels of all the columns — they're labelled "(thousands of units)", so 16 000 units is represented by just "16".

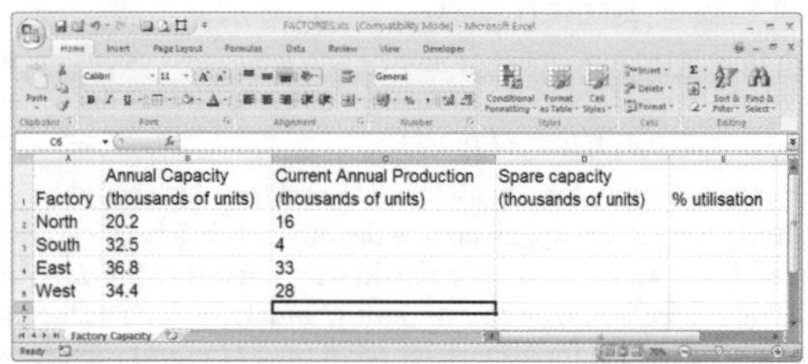

Factory	Annual Capacity (thousands of units)	Current Annual Production (thousands of units)	Spare capacity (thousands of units)	% utilisation
North	20.2	16		
South	32.5	4		
East	36.8	33		
West	34.4	28		

- *1 mark for "16" and 1 mark for putting this in cell C2.*
- *1 mark for "36.8" and 1 mark for putting this in cell B4.*

(b) (i) The formula in cell D2 should be: "=B2–C2".
You can then copy and paste this into cells D3:D5.

- *2 marks available for correct formula in every cell, otherwise 1 mark for correct formula in any cell.*

(ii) The formula in cell E2 should be: "=C2/B2".
It's best to format this cell before you copy and paste it — right-click on the cell and click **Format Cells...**, and then select **Percentage** from the box on the left-hand side, and set **Decimal places** to 1.
You can then copy and paste this into cells E3:E5.

- *2 marks available for correct formula in every cell, otherwise 1 mark for correct formula in any cell.*
- *2 marks available for correctly formatting every cell as percentages to one decimal place, otherwise 1 mark for correctly formatting any cell.*

(c) The most inefficiently used factory is the **South** factory.
It has the greatest spare capacity and the lowest percentage utilisation.

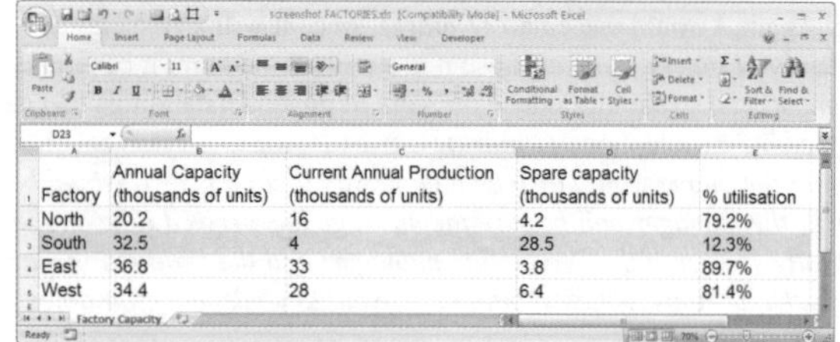

Factory	Annual Capacity (thousands of units)	Current Annual Production (thousands of units)	Spare capacity (thousands of units)	% utilisation
North	20.2	16	4.2	79.2%
South	32.5	4	28.5	12.3%
East	36.8	33	3.8	89.7%
West	34.4	28	6.4	81.4%

- *1 mark for highlighting row 3.*
- *1 mark for correctly applying a yellow background to the cells.*

(d) Possible improvements include:

- centrally aligning the labels and data to neaten them up
- adding borders to the cells
- making the background of the title row grey, so that it looks distinct from the rest of the text.

Factory	Annual Capacity (thousands of units)	Current Annual Production (thousands of units)	Spare capacity (thousands of units)	% utilisation
North	20.2	16	4.2	79.2%
South	32.5	4	28.5	12.3%
East	36.8	33	3.8	89.7%
West	34.4	28	6.4	81.4%

- *1 mark for each of three suitable changes to the appearance of the table.*

(e) In Microsoft® Excel®, the settings to change the header and page orientation, and to choose to print out the table on a single sheet of paper are in the **Page Setup** dialogue.

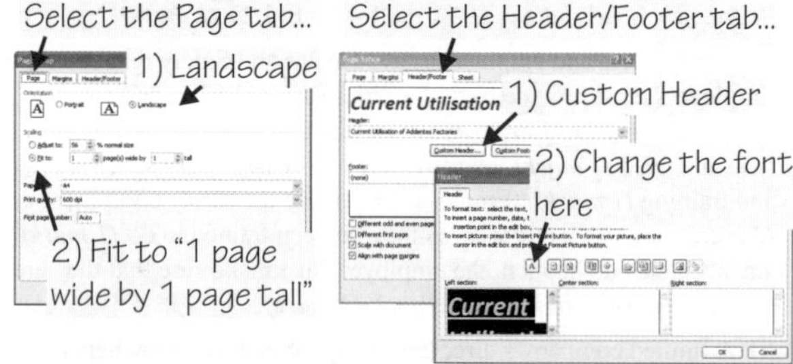

Before you print, you might need to **Set Print Area** to make sure you only print out the range of cells you're interested in.

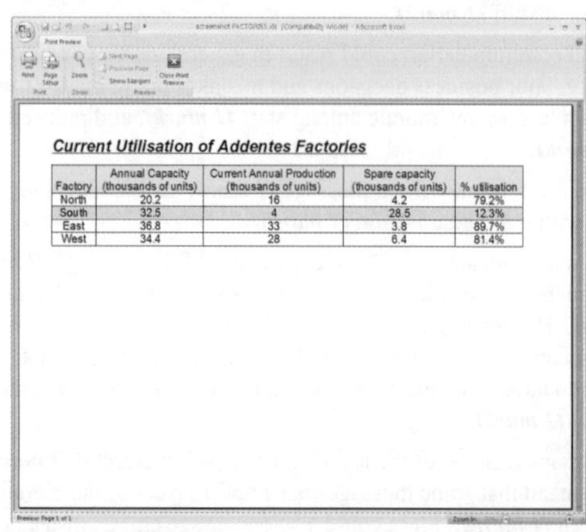

Current Utilisation of Addentes Factories

Factory	Annual Capacity (thousands of units)	Current Annual Production (thousands of units)	Spare capacity (thousands of units)	% utilisation
North	20.2	16	4.2	79.2%
South	32.5	4	28.5	12.3%
East	36.8	33	3.8	89.7%
West	34.4	28	6.4	81.4%

- *1 mark for including a suitable title, plus 1 mark if it is in a header.*
- *1 mark for changing the orientation of the paper to landscape.*

Task Two: Making a Database Report

(a) The first thing to do is to make sure you understand what the information in the table is telling you. You can always look at the design view of the table to see if there's any clues there (which there is in this case).
Here's what the design of your query should look like:

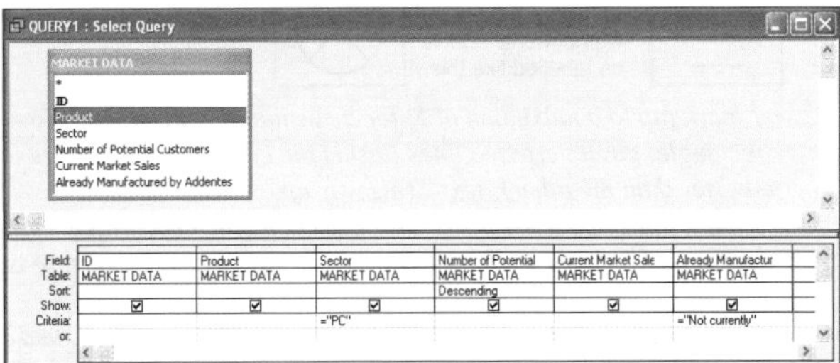

There's a bit of an awkward catch here — make sure that in the "Already Manufactured by Addentes" field, your query criteria is **"Not currently"** ("NOT CURRENTLY" and "not currently" will also work). The important thing is that "**Not**" is **inside** the quote marks, because using **Not "currently"** will give you **very** different results.

- *1 mark for the use of the table MARKET DATA in a query.*
- *1 mark for including all the table's fields in the query.*
- *1 mark for the correct search criteria entered in the Sector field.*
- *2 marks for the correct search criteria entered in the 'Already manufactured' field, but only 1 mark if you put 'Not' outside the quotes.*
- *1 mark for sorting the correct field, plus 1 mark for sorting it in descending order.*
- *1 mark if query functions correctly (13 records should be displayed).*

(b) I used the wizard to generate my report initially, and then tidied it up a bit at the end (since some of the longer field headings had had bits chopped off). Here's how my report ended up looking:

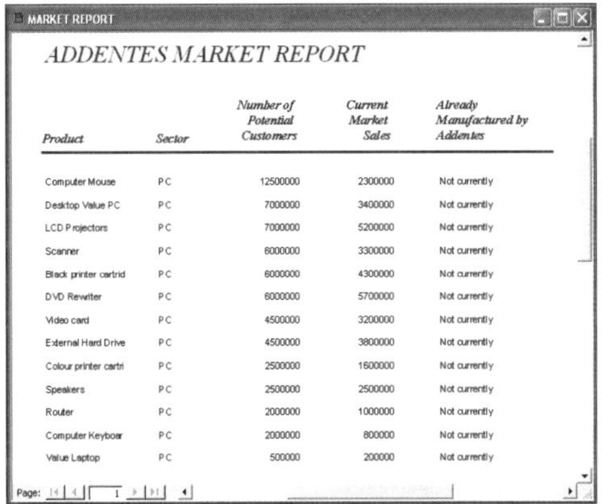

MARKET REPORT

ADDENTES MARKET REPORT

Product	Sector	Number of Potential Customers	Current Market Sales	Already Manufactured by Addentes
Computer Mouse	PC	12500000	2300000	Not currently
Desktop Value PC	PC	7000000	3400000	Not currently
LCD Projectors	PC	7000000	5200000	Not currently
Scanner	PC	6000000	3300000	Not currently
Black printer cartrid	PC	6000000	4300000	Not currently
DVD Rewriter	PC	6000000	5700000	Not currently
Video card	PC	4500000	3200000	Not currently
External Hard Drive	PC	4500000	3800000	Not currently
Colour printer cartri	PC	2500000	1600000	Not currently
Speakers	PC	2500000	2500000	Not currently
Router	PC	2000000	1000000	Not currently
Computer Keyboar	PC	2000000	800000	Not currently
Value Laptop	PC	500000	200000	Not currently

- *1 mark for creating a report based on QUERY1.*
- *1 mark if all the fields are displayed (but do not lose marks if the ID field is not included).*
- *Up to 2 marks for clearly labelled field names, but lose 1 mark if any field names are not clearly visible.*
- *1 mark for including a suitable report title.*
- *1 mark for displaying the report's results.*

Task Three: Making a Presentation

Here are my completed slides:

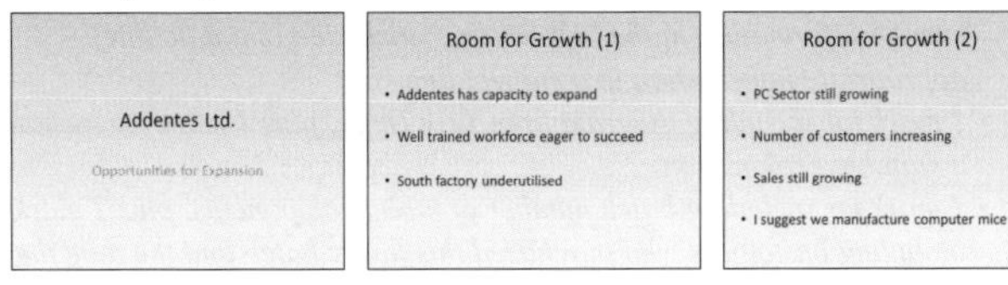

(a) • *2 marks if all three slides have a background colour, or 1 mark if only one slide has a background colour.*
- *2 marks if slides 2 and 3 have bullet points, or 1 mark if only one slide has bullet points.*
- *1 mark if bullet points are animated in some way.*
1 mark if bullet points on each slide appear one at a time.
1 mark if bullets appear as the mouse button is clicked.
1 mark if all the above is done consistently for both slides.

(b) • *1 mark if "South" filled in on slide 2.*
- *1 mark if "computer mice" filled in on slide 3.*

(c) Two important features of a good presentation:
1. Don't overload the slides with too much information, otherwise the audience will be distracted from the person speaking.
2. Use pictures and diagrams when they can clearly show things that will need many words to explain.
- *4 marks available — 1 mark for each point that has been stated, plus 1 mark for each explanation.*
- *1 mark if the points have been added as presenter's notes.*

Task Four: Making a Web Page (AQA only)

Here are my completed web pages.

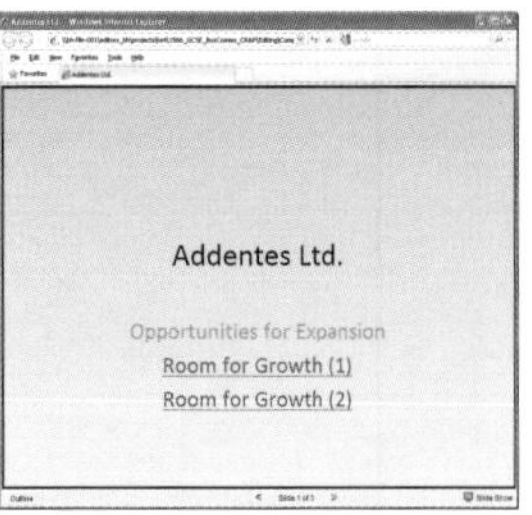

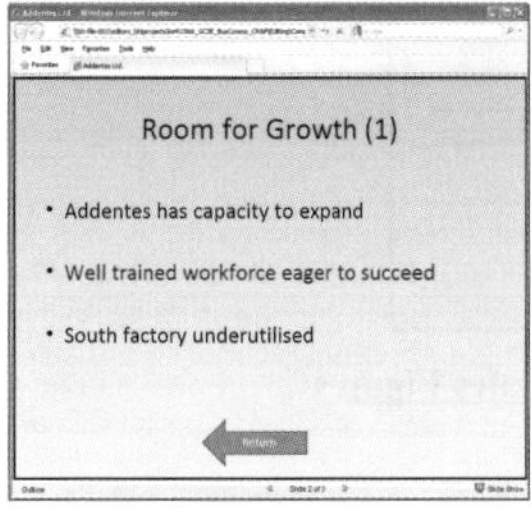

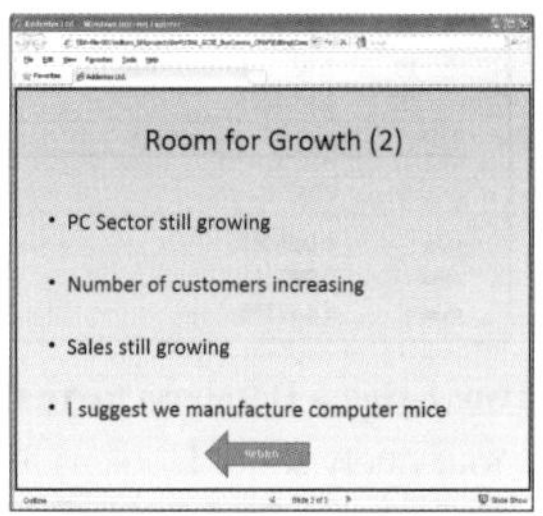

- *1 mark for each web page that is created containing the relevant text from Task Three (to a maximum of 3).*
- *2 marks available for each correctly functioning hyperlink, otherwise 1 mark for each link added that does not function correctly (making a maximum of 8 marks available for functioning hyperlinks).*
- *2 marks if all hyperlinks are clearly labelled with their 'targets', otherwise 1 mark if at least one link is correctly labelled.*

Computer-Based Assessment 2

Task One: Analysing Data Using a Spreadsheet

(a) Cell B105 should contain the entry "**=MIN(B2:B101)**"
Cell B106 should contain the entry "**=MAX(B2:B101)**"
Cell B107 should contain the entry "**=AVERAGE(B2:B101)**"
- *1 mark for the use of the =MIN() function, plus 1 mark for use of the range B2:B101.*
- *1 mark for the use of the =MAX() function, plus 1 mark for use of the range B2:B101.*
- *1 mark for the use of the =AVERAGE() function, plus 1 mark for use of the range B2:B101.*

(b) Cell C2 should contain the entry "**=IF(B2<0.1, 1, 0)**"
This should then be copied and pasted into cells C3:C101, so that cell C3 contains the entry "**=IF(B3<0.1, 1, 0)**", and so on.
- *3 marks for the correct formula in cell C2, otherwise 1 mark for an IF() function containing "B2<0.1", and 1 mark for including at least one correct output (either 1 or 0).*
- *1 mark if this is correctly copied and pasted into cells C3:C101.*

(c) Cell D2 should contain the entry "**=IF(B2>2.5, 1, 0)**"
This should then be copied and pasted into cells D3:D101, so that cell D3 contains the entry "**=IF(B3>2.5, 1, 0)**", and so on.
- *3 marks for the correct formula in cell D2, otherwise 1 mark for an IF() function containing "B2>2.5", and 1 mark for including at least one correct output (either 1 or 0).*
- *1 mark if this is correctly copied and pasted into cells D3:D101.*

(d) Cell C102 should contain the entry "**=SUM(C2:C101)**"
Cell D102 should contain the entry "**=SUM(D2:D101)**"

- *1 mark for the use of the =SUM() function.*
- *1 mark for use of the range C2:C101.*
- *1 mark for use of the range D2:D101.*

Your results should look like this:

76	2.674842	0	1
77	2.686481	0	1
78	1.533115	0	0
79	2.156325	0	0
80	0.148436	0	0
81	0.364781	0	0
82	2.627023	0	1
83	0.734154	0	0
84	2.111162	0	0
85	2.840625	0	1
86	0.668372	0	0
87	0.9647	0	0
88	1.187062	0	0
89	1.502895	0	0
90	0.524963	0	0
91	1.835123	0	0
92	1.883822	0	0
93	1.647896	0	0
94	0.248549	0	0
95	1.752365	0	0
96	2.172888	0	0
97	1.117869	0	0
98	1.971606	0	0
99	2.737241	0	1
100	0.534896	0	0
		3	27
min	0.053083		
max	2.997123		
mean	1.687576		

Task Two: Using a Database to Analyse Sales Figures

(a) Your query should look as follows:

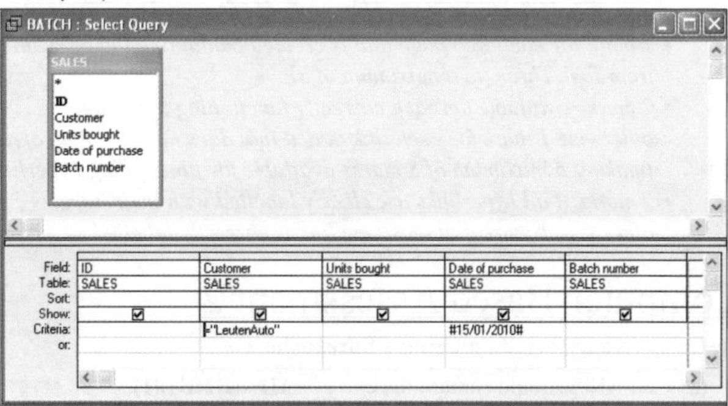

This gives one result, which has Batch number **SAK685L**.

- *1 mark for the use of the table SALES in a query.*
- *2 marks for including the 'Customer', 'Units Bought', 'Date of Purchase', and 'Batch number' fields in the query, or 1 mark for including <u>any two</u> of these.*
- *1 mark for the correct search criteria entered in the Customer field.*
- *2 marks for the correct search criteria entered in the Date of Purchase field, or 1 mark for using an incorrect date.*
- *1 mark if your query returns just one result, with correct batch number.*

(b) Your query, and its results, should look as follows:

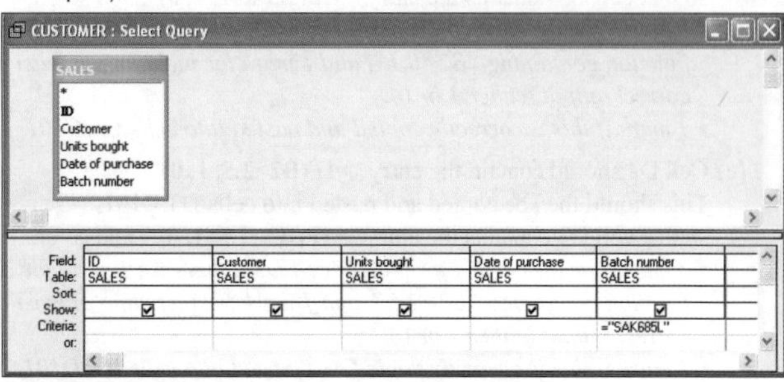

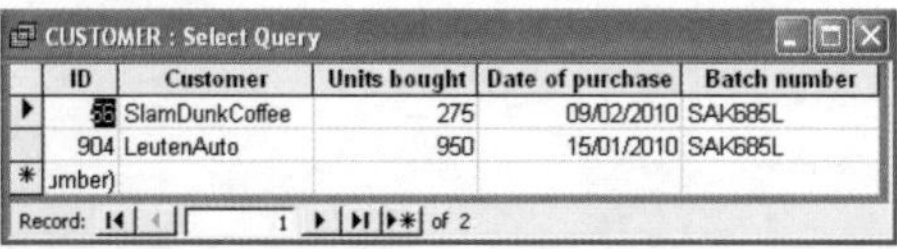

CUSTOMER : Select Query

ID	Customer	Units bought	Date of purchase	Batch number
3	SlamDunkCoffee	275	09/02/2010	SAK685L
904	LeutenAuto	950	15/01/2010	SAK685L
umber)				

Record: 1 of 2

- *1 mark for the use of the table SALES in a new query.*
- *2 marks for including the 'Customer', 'Batch number' and 'Date of purchase' fields in the query, or 1 mark for including <u>any two</u> of these.*
- *1 mark for the correct search criteria entered in the Batch Number field.*
- *1 mark if your query returns the correct two results.*

Task Three: Creating Graphics *(AQA only)*

Your diagram should look like this:

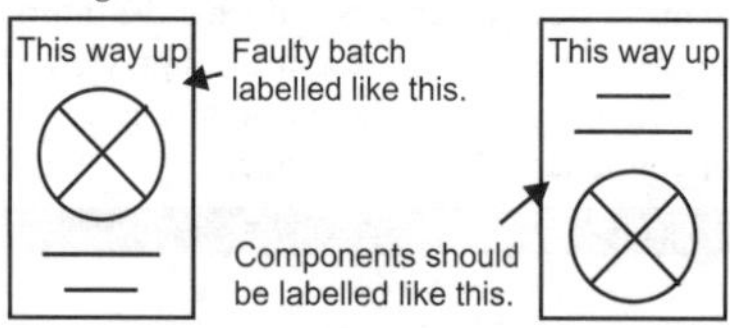

- *1 mark (up to a maximum of 5) for inclusion of each of the following: rectangle; circle; crossed lines (inside the circle); parallel lines (one shorter than the other); text "This way up".*
- *1 mark if the above elements have been combined accurately to make one complete label accurately, and 1 mark if the second picture is also produced accurately.*
- *Plus 1 mark for reproducing the text between the two labels, and 1 mark if at least one arrow is correctly drawn.*
- *1 mark if the graphic is approximately 5 cm wide.*
- *1 mark if the graphic is approximately 2 cm tall.*
- *1 mark if the correct dimensions have been achieved without distorting the image.*

Task Four: Writing a Memo

Your memo should look something like this:

Memorandum

To: Tom Mee
From: (your name)
Date: (today's date)
Re: Faulty components

Some of the components we have sold have been mislabelled. The diagram below shows how these components have been mislabelled.

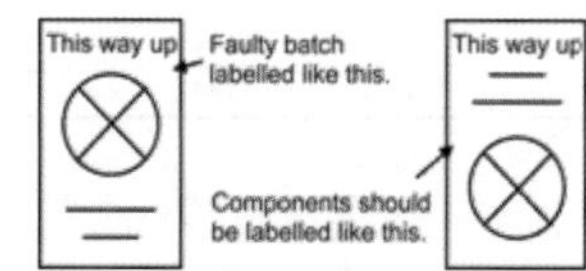

The batch number of the faulty components is SAK685L.

Two companies purchased these faulty components:

- LeutenAuto, who purchased them on 15th January 2010
- SlamDunkCoffee, who purchased them on 9th February 2010

I think we should contact the affected customers as soon as possible, since the goods we have sold do not work as intended and do not meet their description.

Since the companies may use these faulty components in their own goods, the best thing to do would be to contact them urgently. We could phone them first, because that will be quickest. However, we should then confirm all the relevant details in writing as soon as possible, possibly by email.

If we do not act responsibly, our reputation will suffer, and we may lose business in the future.

- *1 mark for each of the following (up to a maximum of 5): memo or Memorandum as heading; correct information in the "To" line; correct information in the "From" line; inclusion of a date line; appropriate information in a subject line.*
- *1 mark for including diagram from Task Three, plus 1 mark for including a suitable explanation.*
- *1 mark for including batch number of faulty components, plus 1 mark for including customers who purchased this faulty batch and the date they bought them.*
- *Up to 4 marks for an appropriate recommendation, with justification, using the context of the question.*
- *Up to 3 marks for recommending how to contact the companies, with justification, using the context of the question.*
- *Up to 3 marks for a well written and well structured memo.*

Index

A

accident books 44
adding value 9
administration 24
advertisements 69, 76, 92
after-sales support 6
agendas 74
animation effects (in a presentation) 113
annual general meetings (AGMs) 7, 74
adware 57
appraisals 74
Article of Association 3
assets 18
audio conferencing 43, 56, 75
authorised users 57, 70

B

back up (of data) 48, 51, 52
bankruptcy 1
bar codes 50
barriers to communication 64
bitmap graphics 111
blogs 116
body language 62, 74, 75
bonuses 41
brand 9, 85
brochures 69, 82, 85
budgets 86
bullet points 91, 113
business cycle 19
business letters 67, 94, 95
business plans 10
business strategy 23

C

call centres 30
callouts 92
cash flow 18
catalogues 69, 81, 82, 85
CDs 52
celebrity endorsements 76
cell references (in a spreadsheet) 98, 99
cellular offices 30
chairperson 74
channels of communication 62, 64
charities 1
charts and graphs 93, 101, 102
circular charts 23
clip art 92, 113
co-operatives 3
collaborative working 117
columns (of text) 93
command words (in exam questions) 123
commission 41
commodity markets 17
communication systems 62, 77
competition 7, 10, 16, 82
complaints 81
Computer-Based Assessment 124, 137
concept keyboards 49
confidential data 57, 70, 82
consumer protection laws 11, 84
contracts of employment 34, 37
Controlled Assessment 122, 125
copyright 10, 11, 84
core hours 43
corporation tax 24
corrupted files/data 57
costs 17, 77, 82, 85
credit terms 18
cropping images 112
curriculum vitae (CV) 36, 69
customer service 6, 63, 81, 82, 85

D

data capture forms 50, 106
Data Protection Act (1998) 11, 58, 84
data security 57
data storage 51, 52, 58
data types (in a database) 105
data-processing systems 48
databases 50, 105-108, 117
decision-making 25
deductions (from pay) 42
deed of partnership 3
demand 17, 19
designs 76
desktop computers 49
desktop publishing (DTP) 116, 117
destocking 18
diary-management software 116
digital cameras 50
directors 7, 23, 25, 74
disabilities 37, 49
discipline procedures 34, 37
discrimination laws 11, 37
dismissal 11, 34, 37
disseminating data 24
domain names 83
downloading 69, 81
DVDs 52

E

e-commerce 81, 82, 84, 86
economy 8, 10, 19
efficiency 24, 28, 29, 40, 71, 77
electronic communication 70, 71
emails 68, 69, 70, 116
employment laws 11, 34, 37
encryption 57, 70, 84
entrepreneurs 1, 2, 18
environmental issues 1, 7, 8, 29, 81
EPOS (Electronic Point-Of-Sale) 50
equilibrium 17
ergonomics 30
ethical considerations 8
evaluating software 117
exam boards/papers 121
exam questions 123
exchange rates 19
exports 19
external communication 63

F

failure (of a business) 2, 18
FAQs (frequently-asked questions) 81, 82
fax machines 67, 70
feedback 62, 63, 67, 74, 75, 81
fields (in a database) 105
finance 18
financial documents 24, 69
financial rewards 41, 42
firewalls 57
first-aid 44
flexible working 43
flexitime 43
flipcharts 113, 114
flyers 92, 69
fonts 91
forms (in a database) 106
formulas (in a spreadsheet) 99
four Ps (marketing mix) 15
frames (on a web page) 115
franchises 3
fraud 84
freedom of information 11
fringe benefits 42
full-time work 34
fully-blocked style 94
functions (in a spreadsheet) 100

G

gaps in the market 2, 16
gigabytes (GB) 51
government 1, 7, 8
graphics software 111–112
gross domestic product (GDP) 19
gross pay 42
growth 8, 19
guestbooks (on a website) 70, 81

H

hacking 11, 57
handheld computers 49
handouts 114
hard copies 48, 55
hard disks 51
headers and footers 94, 98
headphones 56
Health and Safety 11, 30, 44
hierarchies 23, 63
hot-desking 43, 77
hotspots 115
hyperlinks 115

Index

I

identity theft 57
image (of a business) 63, 76
importing objects (into a word processor) 93
imports 19
income tax 24
incorporated 3
inefficiency 29
innovations 9
input devices 49, 50
input masks (in a database) 105
inserting graphics 112
interest 18, 19
internal communication 63, 68
internet 69, 70, 75, 81, 83, 86
interviews 36
intranets 70, 83
investors 2
invoices 69
IP addresses 83

J

jargon 64
job advertisements 35
job descriptions 35, 36
joysticks 49
junk mail 57, 58

L

labour supply 10
laptops 49
leaflets 69
legal structures 3
letters 67, 94, 95
limited company 18
limited liability 3, 7, 74
line spacing 91
loans 2, 18, 19
local community 7
location 10
logos 76, 92
loyalty cards 71
Ltd 3

M

magnetic tape 52
mail merge 67, 94, 95
malware 57
managers 7, 23, 25, 63
market 10
- analysis 16
- niches 2
- research 6, 8, 15, 16, 63
- share 1, 8, 82, 85

marketing 15, 16, 82
matrix structure 23
medium (of communication) 62–64
meetings 74
megabytes (MB) 51
memos 68, 91
Memorandum of Association 3
memory cards/sticks 51
messages 62
methods of communication 62
microphones 50, 75
minimum wage 11, 37
minutes (from a meeting) 74
mission statements 81
mobile phones 71, 75
motivation 37, 40, 63, 68
mouse 49
multi-tasking 77

N

National Insurance 24
net pay 42
netbooks 49
networks 48, 49, 51, 57, 81, 83
newsletters 68, 93
not-for-profit 1
notices 68, 71

O

objectives 1, 8, 28, 77
office layout 30
open punctuation 94
open-plan offices 30
open-source software 117
operatives 23, 25, 63
Optical Character Recognition (OCR) 50
oral communication 62, 74, 75, 113
organisational structure 23
output devices 55, 56
overdrafts 18, 19
overhead transparencies (OHTs) 113, 114
overtime 41, 42, 82
ownership structures 3

P

packaging 29
paper documents 55, 69, 70
paper-based systems 48
part-time work 34, 43
partnerships 3
passwords 57, 70, 84
patents 10
pay methods 41, 42
pension schemes 34, 41, 42
performance targets 41
performance-related pay (PRP) 41
permanent records 55, 68, 67
person specifications 35, 36
Personal Digital Assistants (PDAs) 49
planning 2, 28
plc 3
podcasts 75
pollution 7, 29
pop-up advertisements 57
presentations (and presentation software) 113, 114
prices 15, 17
primary key (database) 105
primary research 15
printers 55
privacy regulations 11
private limited companies 3
processing data 24, 48
producers 17
product trials 6
productivity 40, 63, 68
products 15, 16
profit 1, 2, 7, 8, 17, 63
profit-sharing schemes 41
projectors 56, 113
project-planning software 116
promotion (of a product) 15
promotion (in a job) 28
proprietary software 117
protective equipment 44
protocols (in communication) 74, 75
public limited companies 3
public sector 1

Q

qualitative data 15
quality 84
quantitative data 15
queries (in a database) 107
QWERTY keyboards 49

R

raw materials 10
receivers (of messages) 62
recessions 19
records (in a database) 105
recruitment 35, 36, 40
recycling 11, 29
redundancies 34, 37, 77
remote storage 52
repetitive strain injury (RSI) 30, 44, 49
reports 68, 74, 122
reports (in a database) 108
research (for Controlled Assessment) 122
resolution 55, 56
resources 28, 29
retained profits 18
revenue 17
RFID (Radio Frequency IDentification) 71
risks 2, 10, 44
robots 49
routine tasks/decisions 25

Index

S

salaries 41, 42
Satnavs 71
scanners 50
screen-savers 57
secondary research 15
security 51, 57, 70, 84
selection process (for a job) 36
servers 49, 51, 83, 86
shareholders 3, 7, 8, 74
sickness pay 34
slides (in a presentation) 113
slogans 76
Smartphones 49
SMS 71
social enterprises 1
social policies 81
software updates 81
sole traders 3
spam emails 57
speakers 56, 75
spreadsheets 95, 98-102, 117
spyware 57
stakeholders 7, 8, 63
start-up finance 18
stock exchanges 3
stock levels 18
storage devices 51, 52
storing data 24, 48, 57
straplines 76
success (of a business) 8–10
supervisors 23, 63
suppliers 7, 63
supply 17
surveys 85

T

tables (in a database) 105
tables (in a word processor) 93
targeted marketing 71
tasks 28, 29
teleconferencing 43, 75
telephones 75
teleworking 43, 77
templates (for business documents) 94
text formatting 91
text boxes (in a word processor) 92
touch-sensitive screens 49
trade unions 7
trademarks 3
trading names 76
training 40, 44, 71, 77

U

unauthorised access 57, 82
unincorporated 3
unique selling point (USP) 9
unlimited liability 3
usernames 57, 84

V

validation checks 50
Value Added Tax (VAT) 24
vector graphics 111
venture capital 18
video cameras 75
video conferencing 56, 43, 75
viruses 57
visual communication 62, 75, 76, 113
voice-recognition systems 50

W

wages 41, 42
warranties 6
Waste Electrical and Electronic Equipment (WEEE) 11, 29
Web 2.0 116
web browsers 81, 86, 115
web hosts 83
web-authoring software 86, 115
web-based file storage 52
webcams 50
webcasts 75
webinars 75
websites 6, 70, 81-86
creating a website 86
wikis 116
WordArt 92
word processors 67, 91-95, 117
workstations 49
World Wide Web (www) 81, 83
written communication 62–64, 67–70
written-exam advice 123

Make sure you're not missing out on another superb CGP revision book that might just save your life...

...order your **free** catalogue today.

CGP customer service is second to none

We work very hard to despatch all orders the **same day** we receive them, and our success rate is currently 99.9%. We send all orders by **overnight courier** or **First Class** post.
If you ring us today you should get your catalogue or book tomorrow. Irresistible, surely?

- Phone: 0870 750 1252 (Mon-Fri, 8.30am to 5.30pm)
- Fax: 0870 750 1292
- e-mail: orders@cgpbooks.co.uk
- Post: CGP, Kirkby-in-Furness, Cumbria, LA17 7WZ
- Website: www.cgpbooks.co.uk

...or you can ask at any good bookshop.

BLJCS41